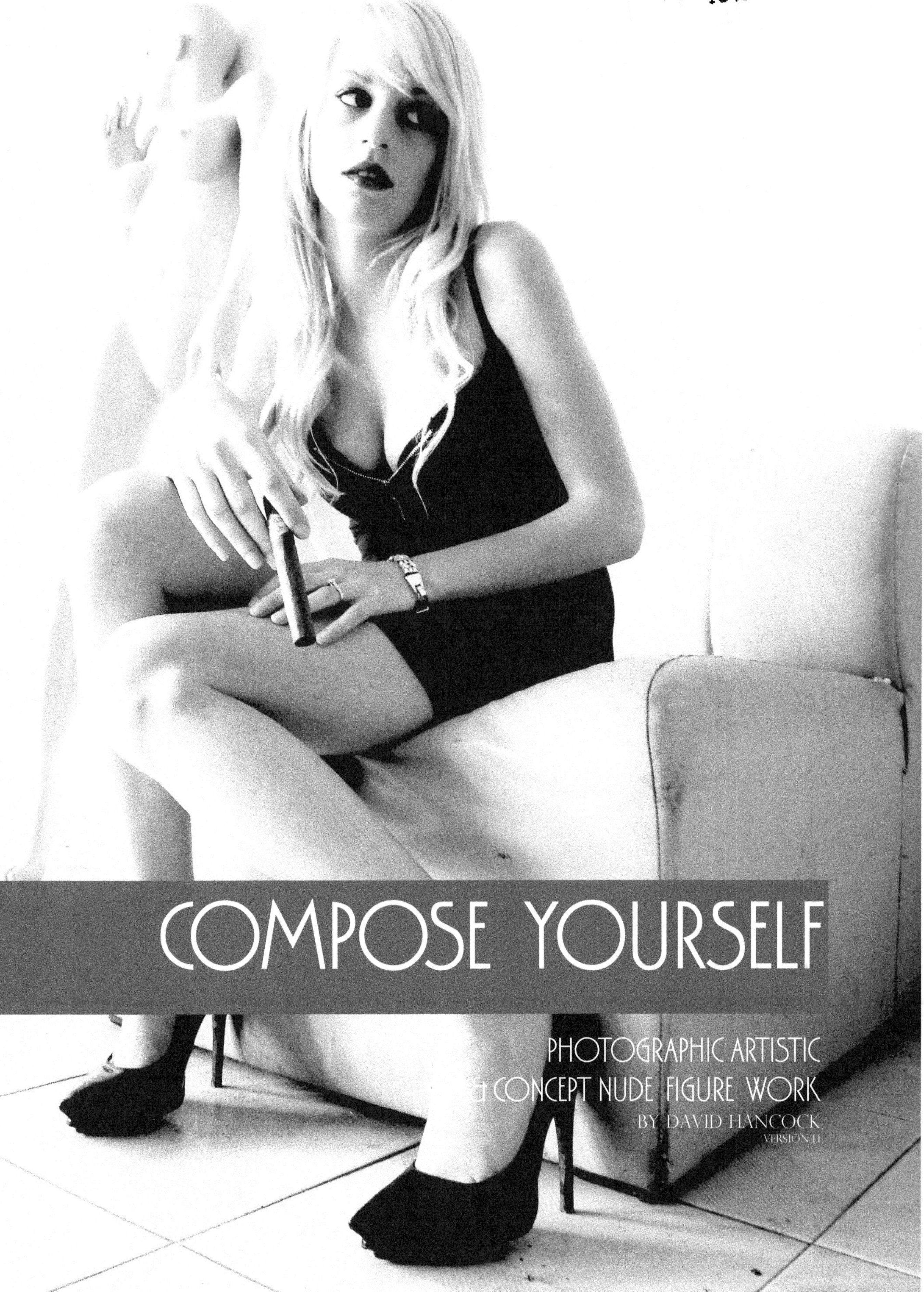

COMPOSE YOURSELF

PHOTOGRAPHIC ARTISTIC & CONCEPT NUDE FIGURE WORK

BY DAVID HANCOCK

VERSION II

Published by Australian Portraits
PO Box 111, Tailem Bend SA 5260
images@hypervision.com.au

Printed in the United States
Distributed in Australia

COMPOSE YOURSELF

ARTISTIC NUDE FIGURE WORK

BY DAVID HANCOCK

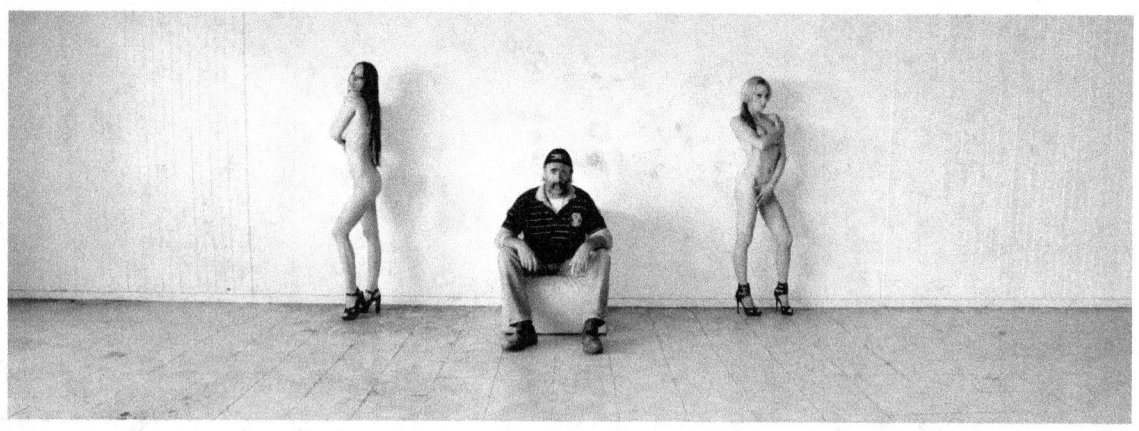

ABOUT DAVID

For over 30 years, David Hancock has been the Creative Director
of multi award winning multimedia production house, Hypervision.
Currently based in Adelaide, Australia.

David has been responsible for creating and producing hundreds of video productions,
television programs, cinema and television commercials, for some of the highest
profiled companies in the nation, including comprehensive work for most of
Australia's Tourism Commissions.

David has received over 22 National awards for creative work, including
2 nominations from the international Black & White Spider Awards and
"highest honours nationally" from the Australasian Video Producers Association.
and from the Australian Cinematographers Society

Starting his visual career as a freelance cameraman with Channel 9 in the early 80's,
he quickly moved into video editing and then onto directing and producing other projects
around the country including an award winning TV series on "Fishing & Boating"
and Children's TV series "The Fairies" now being broadcast internationally.

Turning 40 and now a father, was the time to put much of his working and
personal development into a passion that had beckoned him for years and where
his interest began... photography.   Rather than trying to capture 25 frames per second,
he wanted to come home with only one frame that told the story.

Of course, the digital realm was not new to him, as video chips and sensors had
been the staple diet of the video industry for many years, so to some extent,
it was familiar territory and digital stills was a long way behind.

Spending 80 - 100 hours per week, working with other peoples ideas,
budgets and deadlines, was starting to lose much of it's appeal and having
to constantly drive past great locations in pursuit of false client expectations
or pack up great locations just as the "magic hour of light" arrived because
of crazy timelines, made David feel that he had traded in the very reason
he had started in the industry... "to express, capture and create"

David's work is already appearing in magazines all around the world.

His artistic work has a refreshingly, raw style and is gaining enormous popularity
internationally, fast! His intentional snub toward software is food for thought in an
industry that has always prided itself on realism and credibility.

I believe that where ever you go, there is a shot to be had, some huge and
some humble, all are interesting and all require a different approach.

Everyone will see the same shot differently.

Choice! It's one of the few things left in this increasingly "same" world,
that each of us can interpret anyway we want.

Most of my concept photography stays away from the big shots often seen repeated
over and over and focuses more closely on creative themes and concepts and
a little bit of incidental Australia, the varying moods, character and experience of an area,
rather than that one big "hero" shot rarely seen by the visitor.

But above all else, I believe...
"you need to compose yourself, before you compose the shot"

David

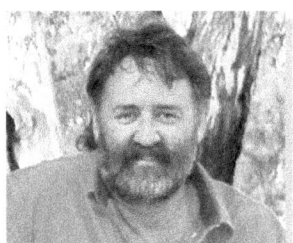

David Hancock
Photographic Concept Artist

David Hancock
Photographic Concept Artist

Concept
"a unique quality; since they exist in the mind only
they can transcend all language barriers,
an abstract or general idea inferred or derived from
specific instances "

Artist
"a person whose creative work shows sensitivity and imagination
the process or product of deliberately arranging elements
in a way that appeals to the senses or emotions.
It encompasses a diverse range of human activities,
creations, and modes of expression…"

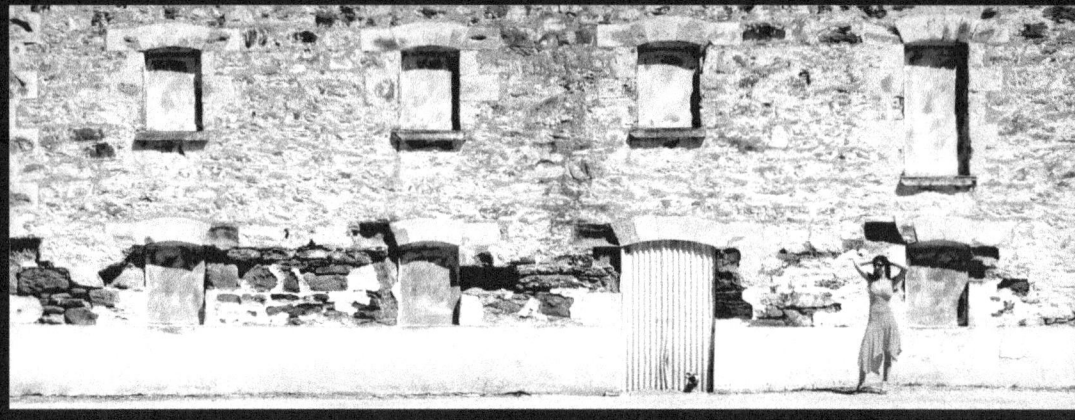

INTRODUCTION

"In my opinion,

the moment you manipulate

a photograph with software

it's no longer your photo…"

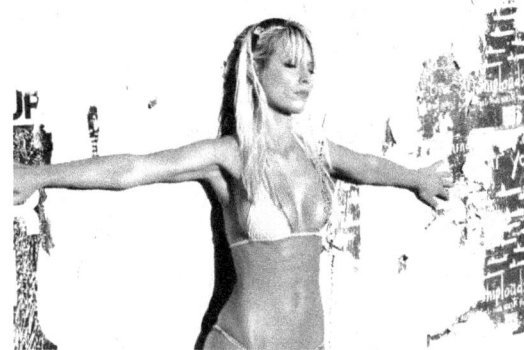

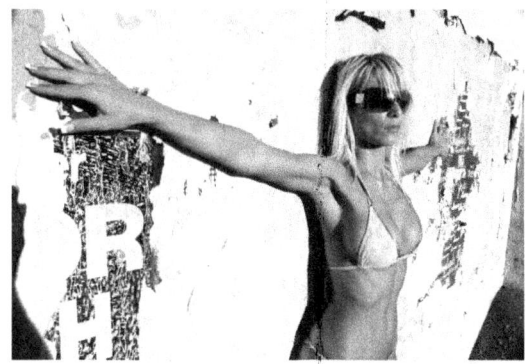

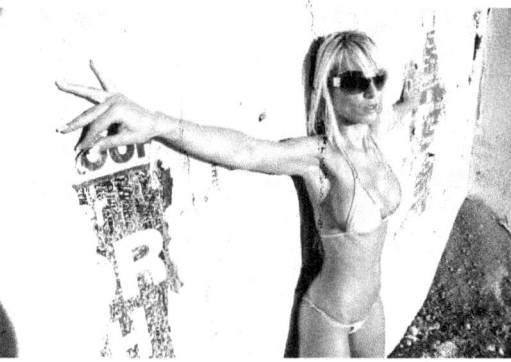

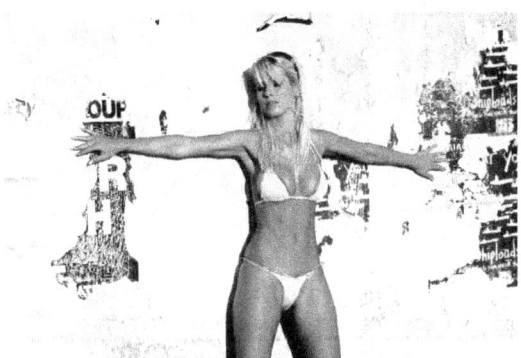

Let me start by saying, that I consider myself more of a photographic concept artist rather than a photographer. I am certainly not the world's greatest photographer, nor do I profess to be, in fact, for me, taking a photograph is only a way to capture or immortalise what I saw or created. I can't draw or paint, so the camera is my creative tool of trade.

I think the first part of being a good creative, is to understand what you are good at and stay away from the things you do not do well! That way, it's all good!

My interest, which helps make it my strength, is storytelling through composition, complimented by textures and interesting locations. The actual photo is only a canvas to paint the final thought process onto.

Consequently, I don't get too hung up on what brand of camera I use, how many megapixels it is, how amazing my lighting rig is or creating a software masterpiece from a photographic terd.

It's my camera, and I like to use it as a creative tool and make up my own rules. I like to be the artist that got there and changed their mind or intentionally chose the wrong end of the brush, it's all part of the fun, experimetation and experience.

There is no right or wrong, if you acheived what you set out to do.

I have dedicated my working life to designing and producing creative sales tools and campaigns for clients and my photography is about what "I" want to do... not them.

For the record, I do not call a photograph something that gets spat out of *photoshop* or the like. I do not own a copy of *photo shop*, nor do I use it. This is a purposeful decision of choice. I like taking photographs, good or bad, not polishing badly composed or exposed terds on a computer and creating "software art" or reproductions.

I am sick to death of the virtual world that is replacing ours.

Money somehow got in the way of our real lives and had replaced it with virtual replications and reproductions of what we love. Only the virtual world is so much more perfect, because it has been manufactured to be the "perfect experience" and fit in with our busy schedules and replace parts of our lives that we no longer have access to.

You can hear the entertainment manufacturers laughing accross the globe everytime a park is closed, a play ground shut down or some land sold off. They want us in our living rooms, replacing our social, sporting, shopping and recreational lives with manufactured replications of what we once did during the normal course of a week.

And so, it has spilled into our art...

Photos now seem to be manufactured reproductions of everything and anything. Crap exposure, don't worry! If the sky wasn't any good, insert one, a cloudy day, fix it!, Good location, but no people, insert some! It doesnt seem to matter what it is, it seems that photography has fallen into the money makers and manufacturing hands again and they tell us how a perfect photo should look and so it becomes all the same yet again.

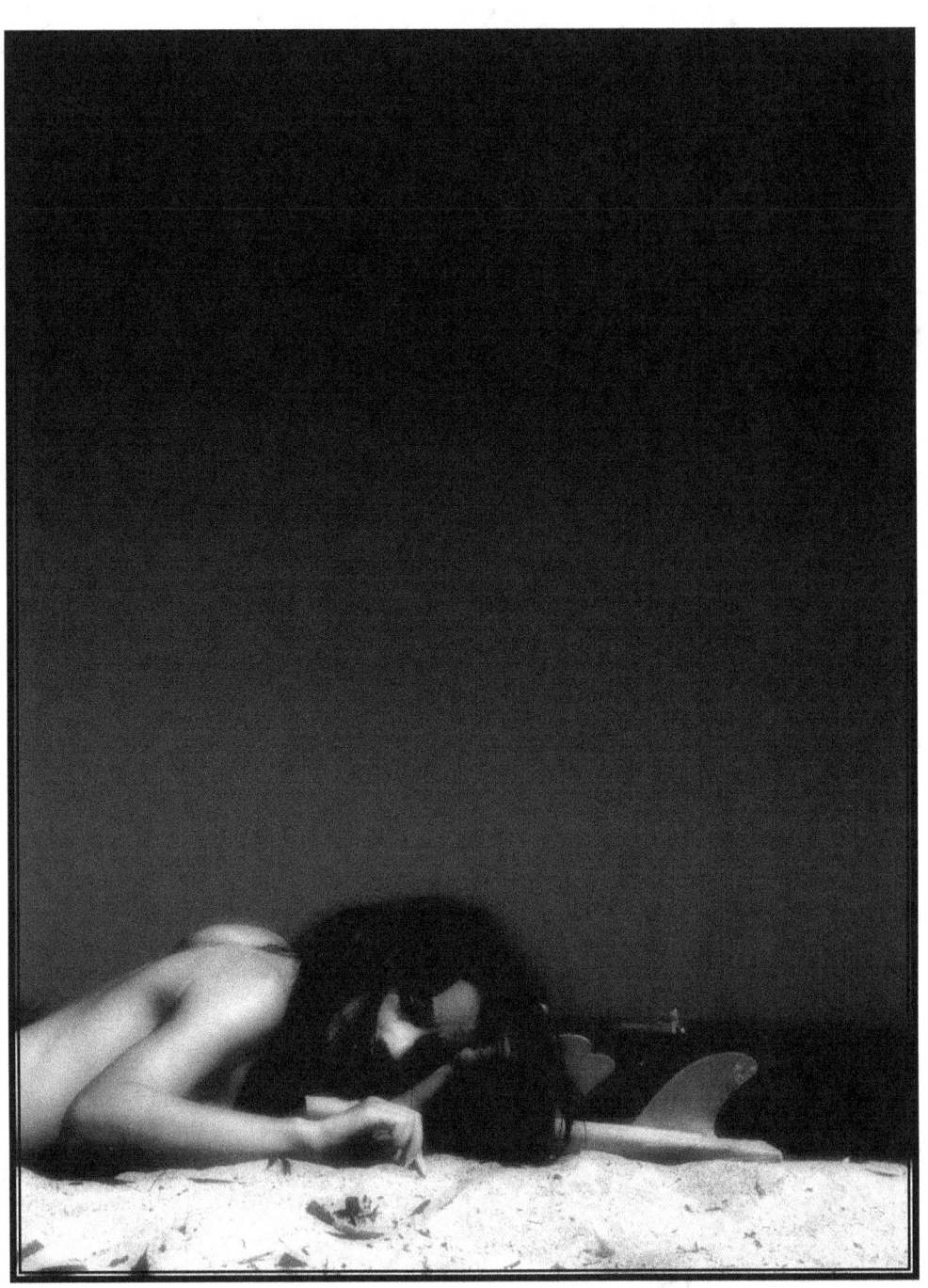

"What started as a "perfect world" image for advertising and fashion magazines, has spilled into our own art and most shots you look at these days are nothing more than lies!"

What started as a perfect or manufactured concept image for advertising and fashion magazines, has spilled into normal photography and many (if not most) shots you look at these days are nothing more than lies. They are not photographs, they are "photo reproductions".

With the introduction of globalisation, made possible by technolgy, the world has become the same. And the manufacturers now tell us how our photos should look.

They are mostly, no longer real or credible.

And as for the the term photographer!?

Look up the word! There is no mention of computer manipulation or graphic redesign or reproduction. It seems anyone that can afford a camera is now a photographer. The manufacturers have brought the technology into the hands of anyone that wants it, to "point and shoot", brilliant pictures, with no real understanding of what just happened. It's great!

But this has now reduced the commercial viability of yet another industry with cheap technology solutions that make the art worthless and everyone the same again.

Shoot RAW they say, so that if you screw it up or the shot wasn't really on, you can fix it!

Or better still, start from scratch and redesign it. What a sound philosopy! I hope the surgeons don't follow this path!

Retouching has become reconstruction, colour correction has become complete re - colouring and even the cut and pasted content has become mostly a lie. If there was telegraph pole there, so be it!
Work around it, get creative, use it! Notice it!

We have dozens of people visit our gallery each day who stand there and argue with my staff about the degree of photoshop we have used in images. We say to them, if we used *photoshop* how could we sell these as photographs?

It's sad that the world no longer celebrates, believes or recognises how to separate "real" from "virtual" or "surreal". Our creative skills and craft has been compromised and cheapened. Anything is "virtually" possible and nothing less than perfection is tolerated, the creative recognition and credit shifts from the photographer to the manufacturers.

Don't get me wrong, in my opinion, I believe software can be a welcome addition for commercial shoots where photographs were never the aim and concept was always the intention.

And given that cameras are now digital, it is fair to swap the darkroom for a digital darkroom.

So if you use *photoshop* or the like as your darkroom and stay true to what you shot, slightly adjusting things like contrast and brightness a bit, then you have merely enhanced your work and created a photograph to be proud of. (Good or bad!)

The moment you start manipulating or modifying a photo and the airbrush comes out, the shot is completely re-exposed, colour graded, elements composited or the backgrounds tampered with, you may well be a good photographer, but this is no longer your photo. It has now been changed and has become "software art or a reproduction" and should be labelled as such.

So that's the end of my "old school" ramblings for the moment!

The models I work with, are "real" people and so are my photographs, good or bad. I believe it is an insult to "fix" a person with software, as this means that the world did not like the way they looked and who are we to say how they "should" look.

If they don't look how you want, why did you choose them? This just makes you a bad talent scout.

For standard artistic concept work, I do not computer manipulate any images to create a software masterpiece or polish photographic terds..

At the end of a shoot, I want to be able to sign a shot as my own and the model to be able to sign it as her.

Beauty is how nature designed it, not a computer.

Like I mentioned, if you are doing a commercial shoot for advertising purposes and the original intent was to get an immpossible shot or create a lie, it's a whole different world and ball game! It was always just a basis for a concept or design job.

I believe, if you are true to your passion and the craft, "keep it real" and do your best to get it right on the day!

I use "on camera" filters (often too many at once) and natural light wherever possible. The talent is real, the locations are real and I deal with whatever comes along on the day.

Everyone has their style, mine is contrasty, gutsy, bold, sometimes a little tragic, but reflective and real. "If it's your photo, your art, why would you let a computer program change it?"

The satisfaction is enormous and who knows, maybe one day people will look at photos again and start to believe them....

Keep it real, know your style and love it...

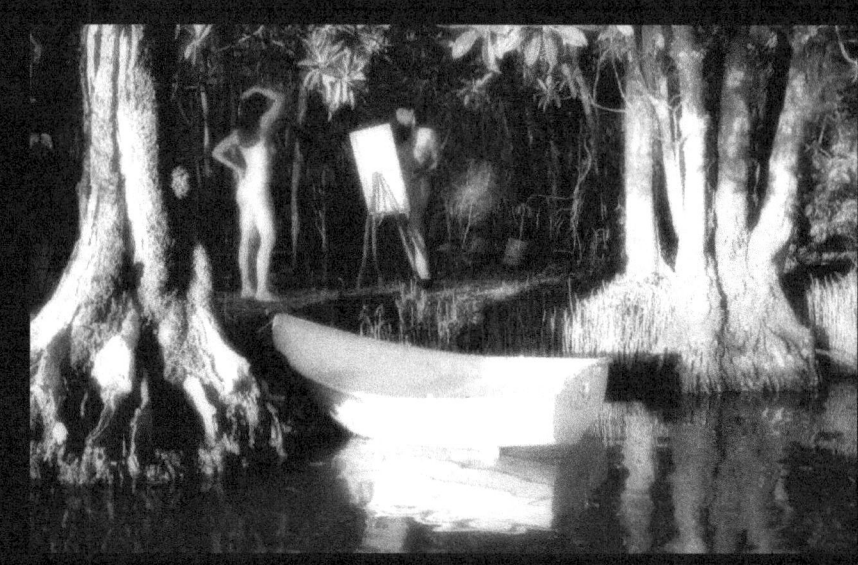

DEVELOPING THE STORY

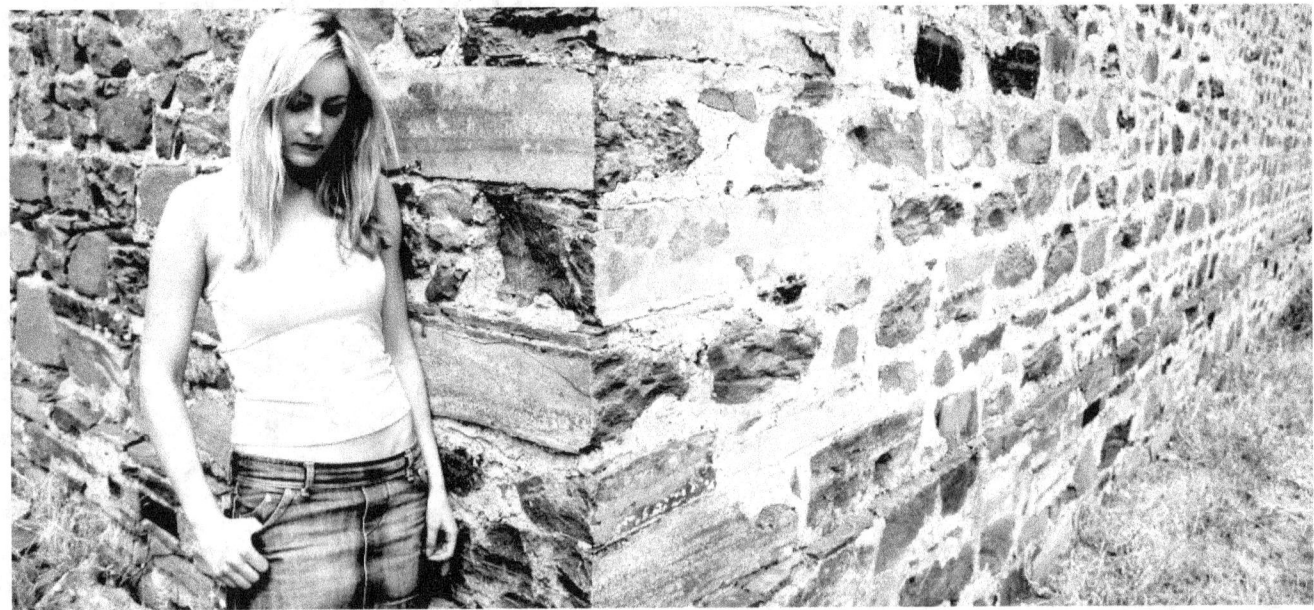

Everything that's not fact, starts with a creative thought process, a concept, or a story.

Lock the door and let the mind run free!

Write down your ideas and then revisit them, to sort it all out. I have a list of over a hundred shots, concepts or ideas I have dreamed up, most of which will never see the light of day. Some are too complicated, some are just flat out dumb! But some I like and when I walk into a location, they come to life!

So what do you shoot?

Many photographers are content to just grab a model and their camera and head down to an awesome subway drain they found last week while fishing.

And that's fine if that's your thing.

Arrive, shoot the crap out of it and then spend the next 5 days on your computer looking at lots and lots of "girl in subway" shots!

In my mind, when someone sees your shot, it should create a definite emotional response. Maybe they would love to be there, maybe they think its stunning, maybe it saddens them, they wonder why ... or maybe they are a little shocked. No matter what it is, if it creates an appropriate and expected response, it triggered an emotion and you have achieved.

If they look at your work and say "what a spunk" or "that's a good location" you have failed artistically, in my opinion. They only saw the subject, not the photograph.

Do people like what you shot?
Does it create the intended emotion?

How many *non* industry people (and presumably this is who you shoot for) are going to say "mmm that would have been great, but pity about that digital artifact!" If you re-moved the digital artifact would they buy it?

Of course not!
It's about the image, the story, the composition.

Personally, in it's most simple form, I like to create a bit of a concept about why is she there and what is her overall feeling. Is she hot, cold, sad, suicidal, happy, reflective or bored? Is there something going on? Will the shot pose a question that can be answered, do I want the shot to be uncomfortable and confronting to the viewer or strangely comforting.
Once I have grouped a number of "like" shots, I create a "series" that will compliment them. For example, this book features a lot of simple images shot in ruins, with rusty backdrops, rotten timbers and old brick textures.

The "series" has a double meaning and is called "RUINED" and each image was given a concept and title that fitted within this.

Obviously, you always see and shoot a few frames during these sessions that did not fit into your theme and consequently, to avoid any inconsistency, these "extra" images should never appear under your series title.

So sit down and write a little story, maybe it starts with the location and write it around this and then find a model to suit, or maybe it starts with the actual models look and find a location to match their look.

For it to work well as a photograph, the location, model and theme must fit together like a glove. Or maybe in contrast, it should be completely opposites, creating a juxtaposition. Which in itself maybe complimentary. Break the rules, but know what they are first.

Generally, I do not do any full frontal work. It's just not my thing. I love the female form blended with complimentary textures or perhaps an incidental landscape. It's rarely big and often a little complicated.

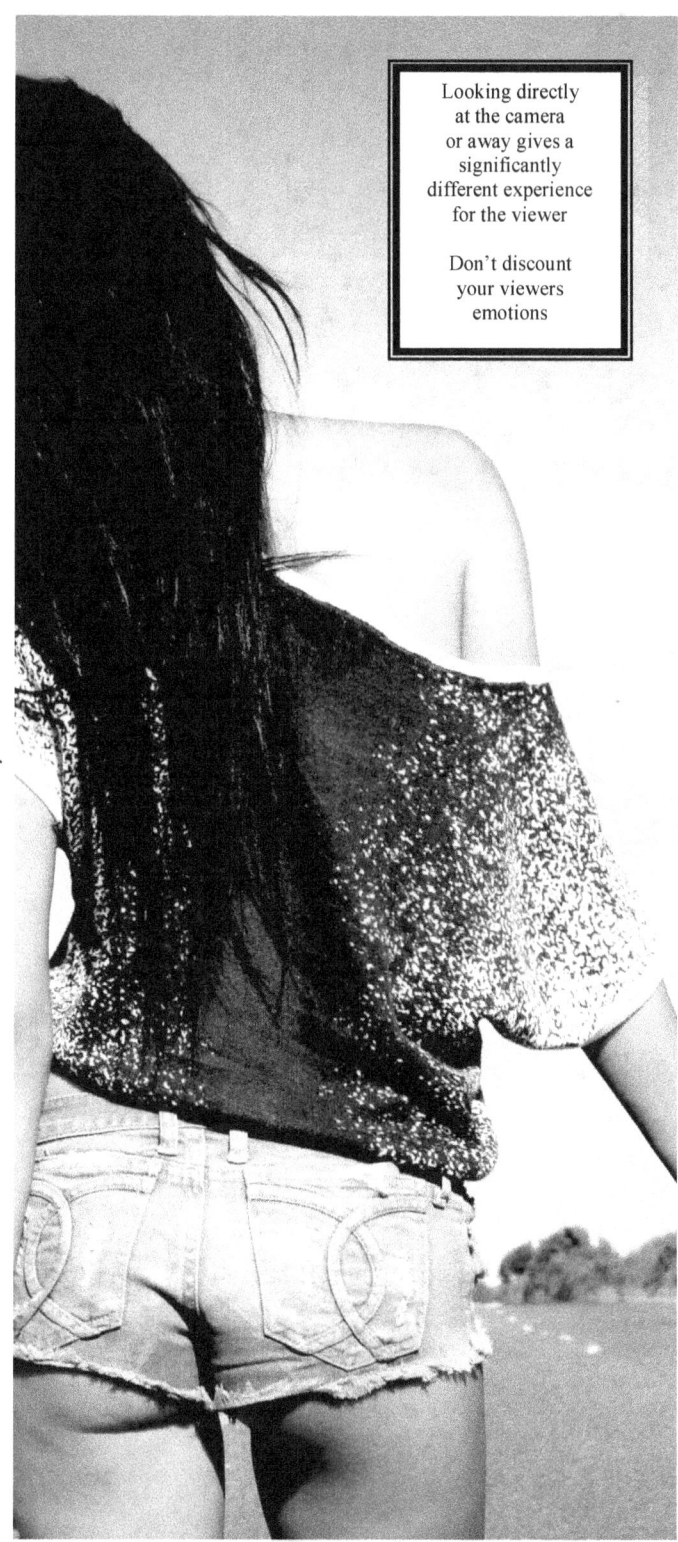

Looking directly
at the camera
or away gives a
significantly
different experience
for the viewer

Don't discount
your viewers
emotions

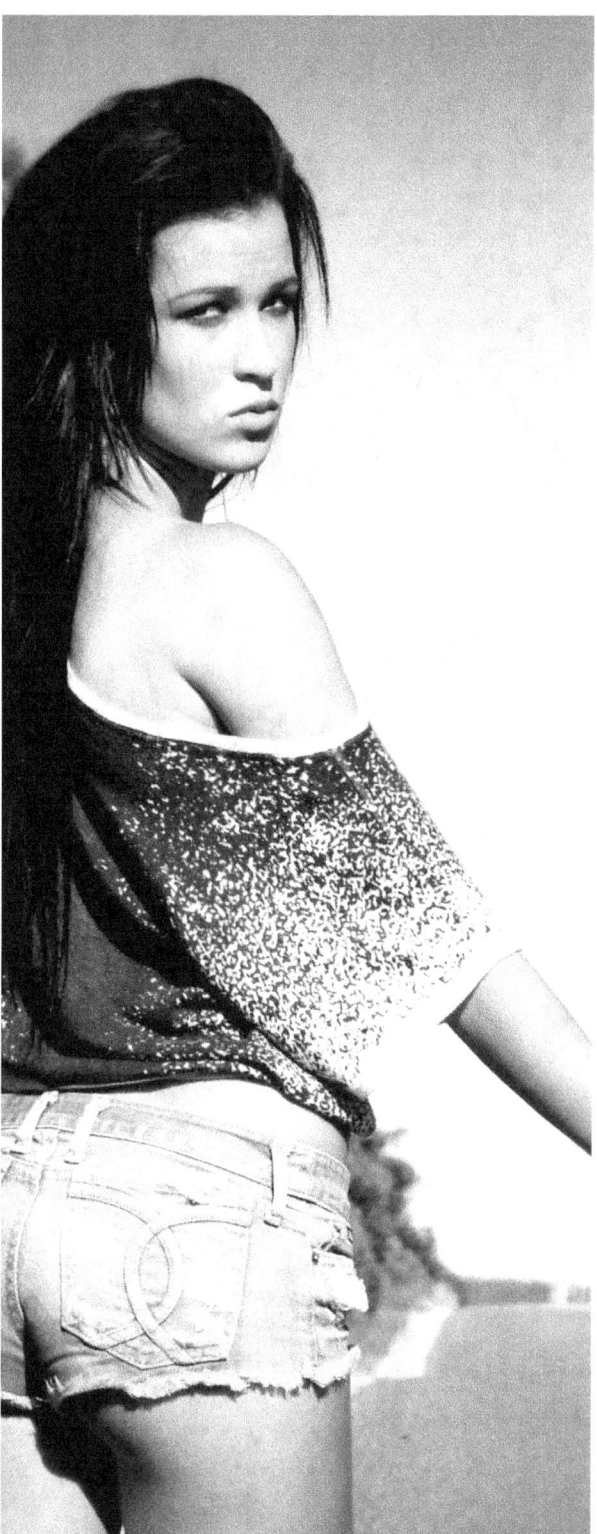

As a rule, I avoid showing the models face, to create a sense of mystery and aloofness, keeping the image humble and avoiding confrontation or embarrassment for my audience.

If a nude model is looking at the viewer, they can find it a little intimidating.

Your style might be to shock or embarrass the viewer, but unless you just like shooting art forms on your camera, know what your intention is, prior to starting the shoot.

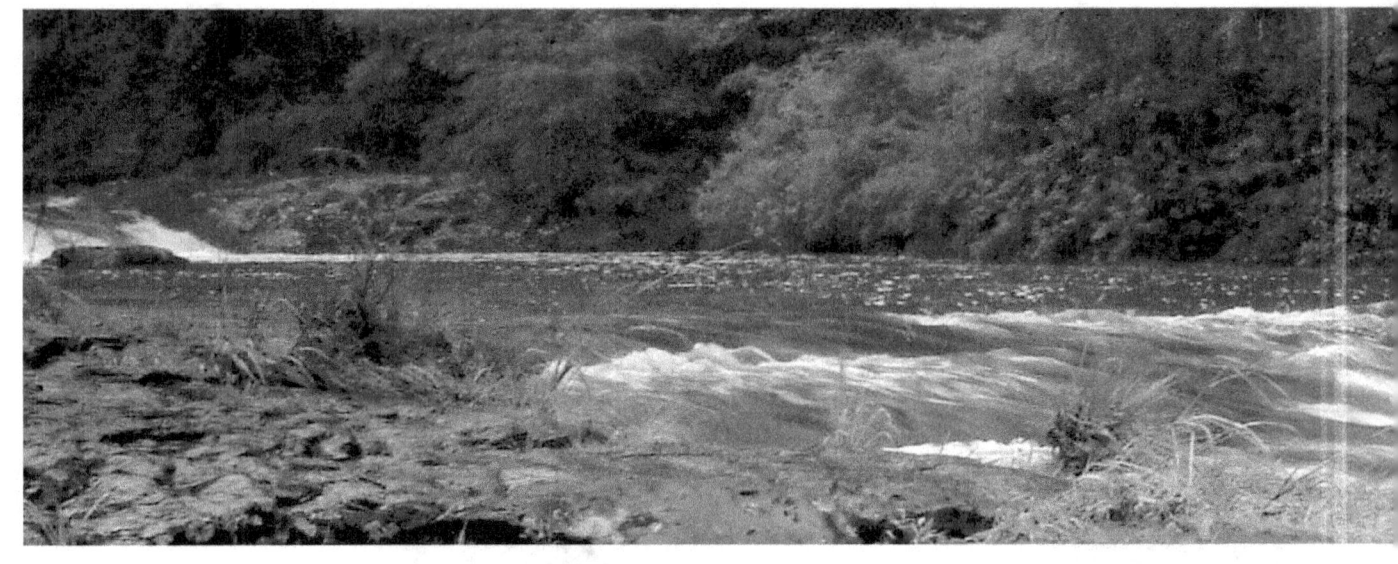

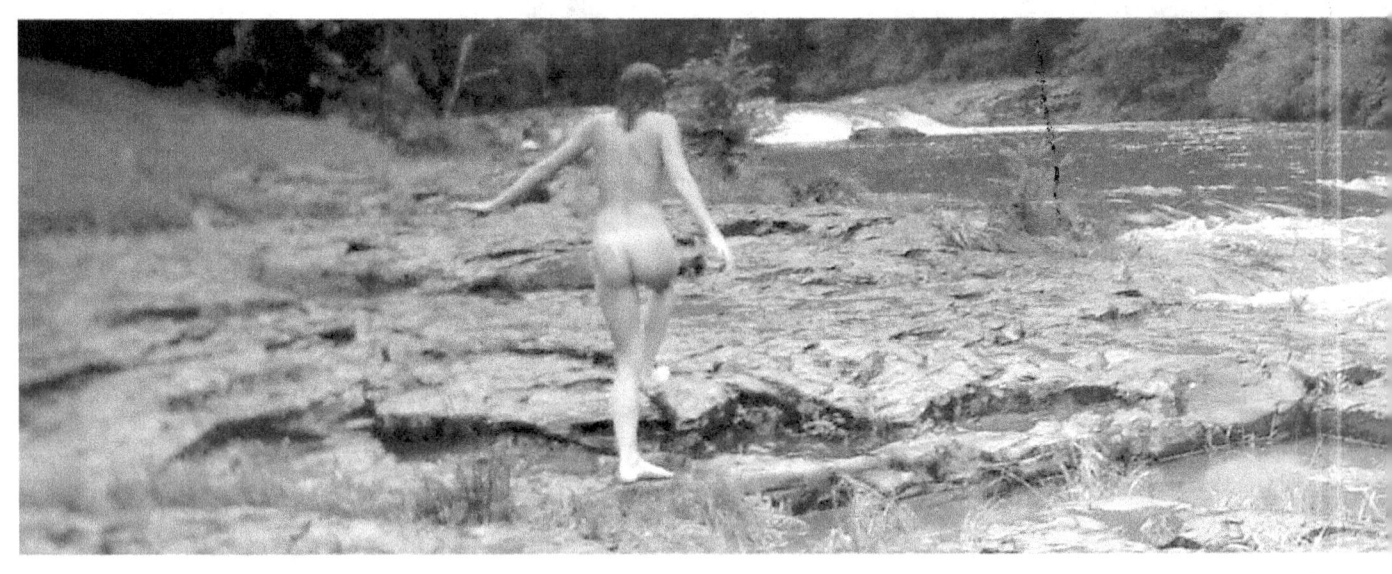

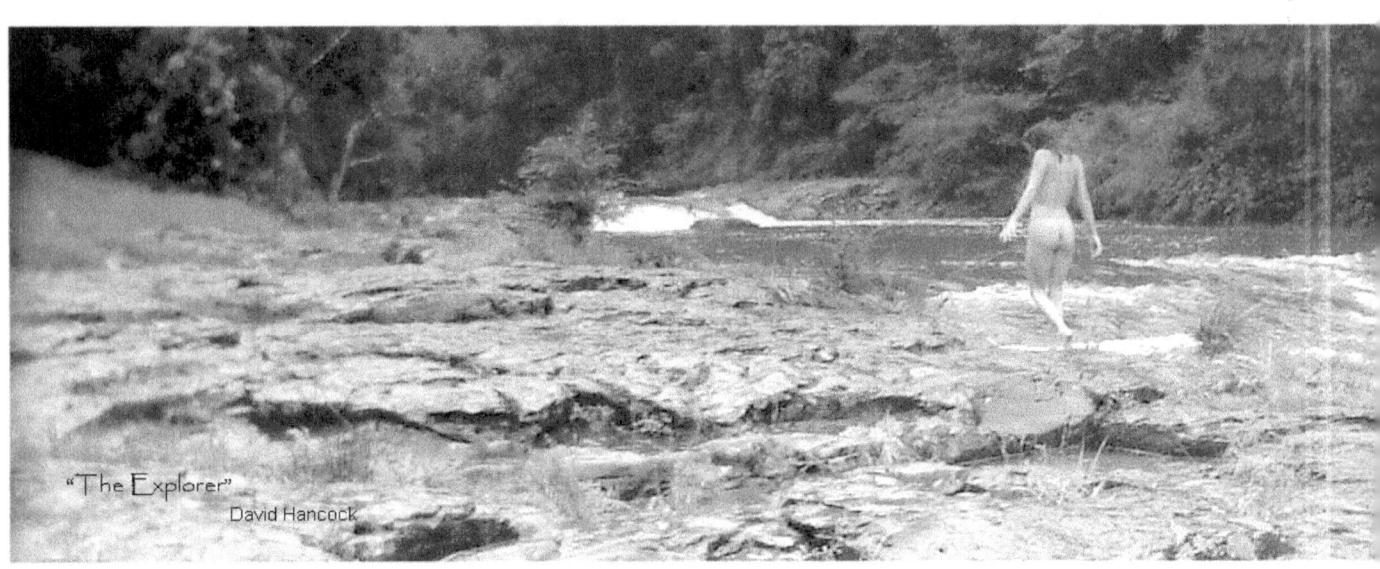

"The Explorer"
David Hancock

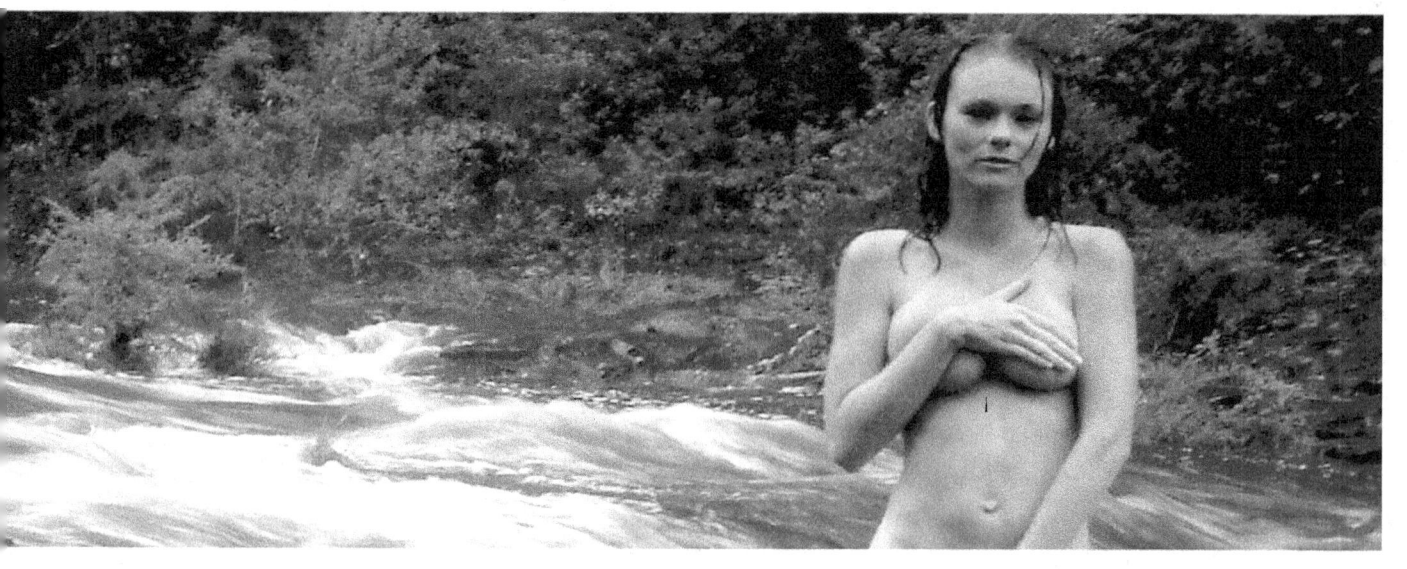

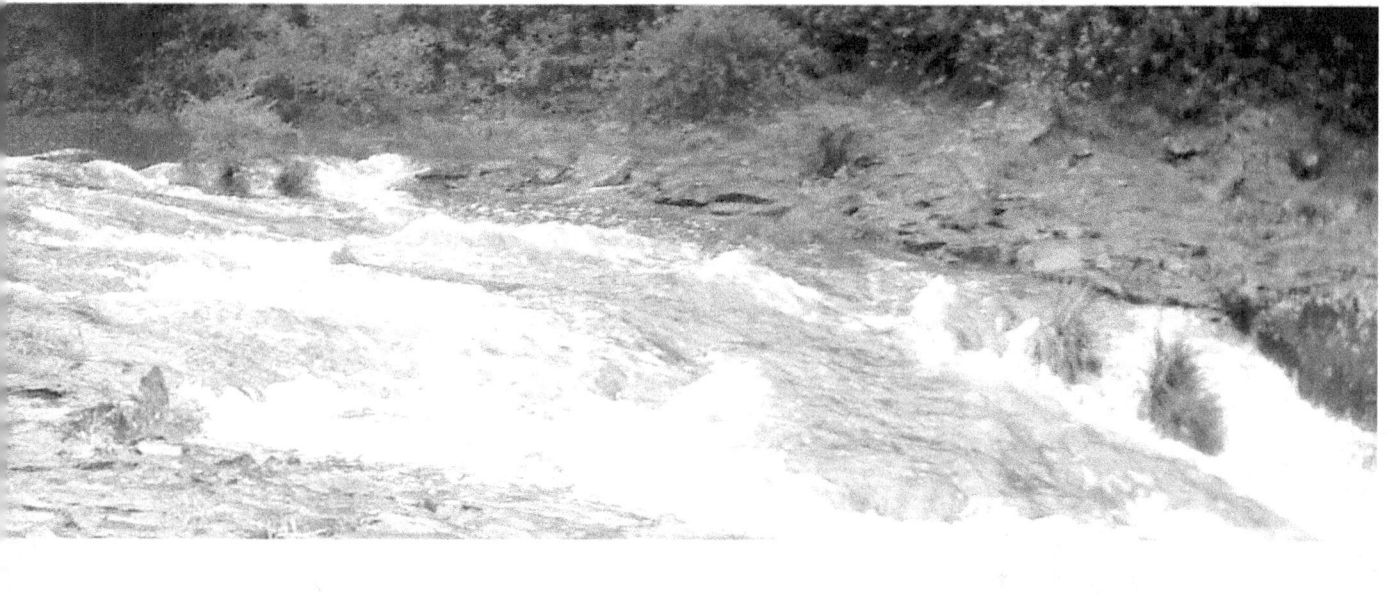

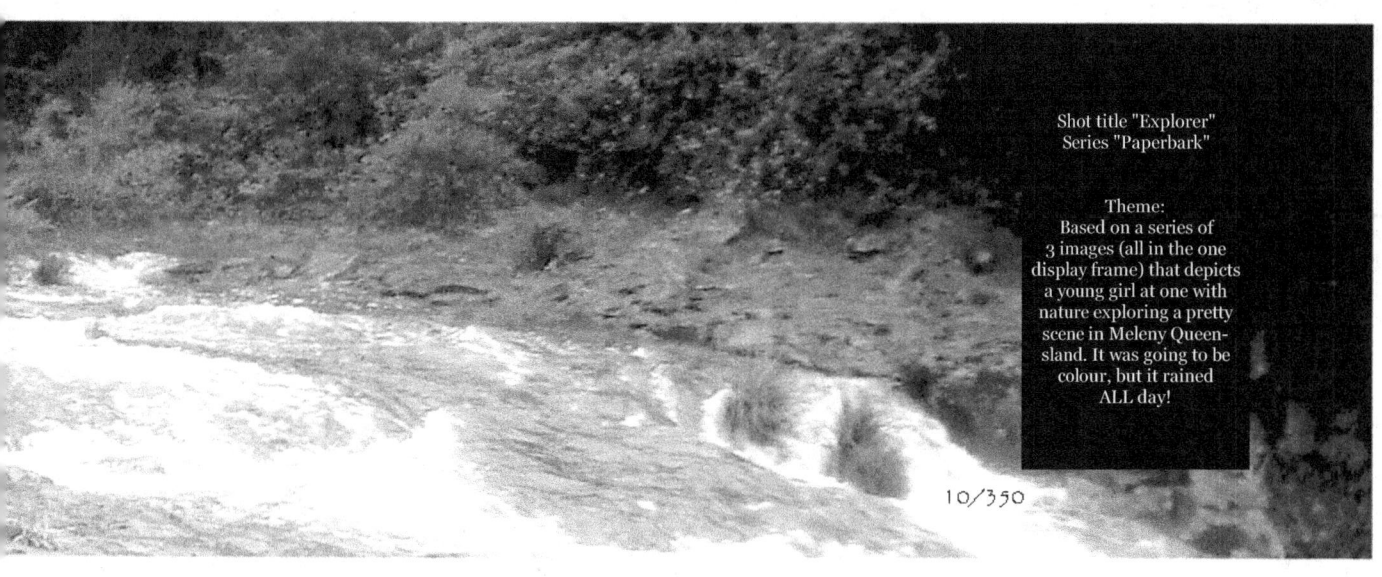

Shot title "Explorer"
Series "Paperbark"

Theme:
Based on a series of
3 images (all in the one
display frame) that depicts
a young girl at one with
nature exploring a pretty
scene in Meleny Queen-
sland. It was going to be
colour, but it rained
ALL day!

10/350

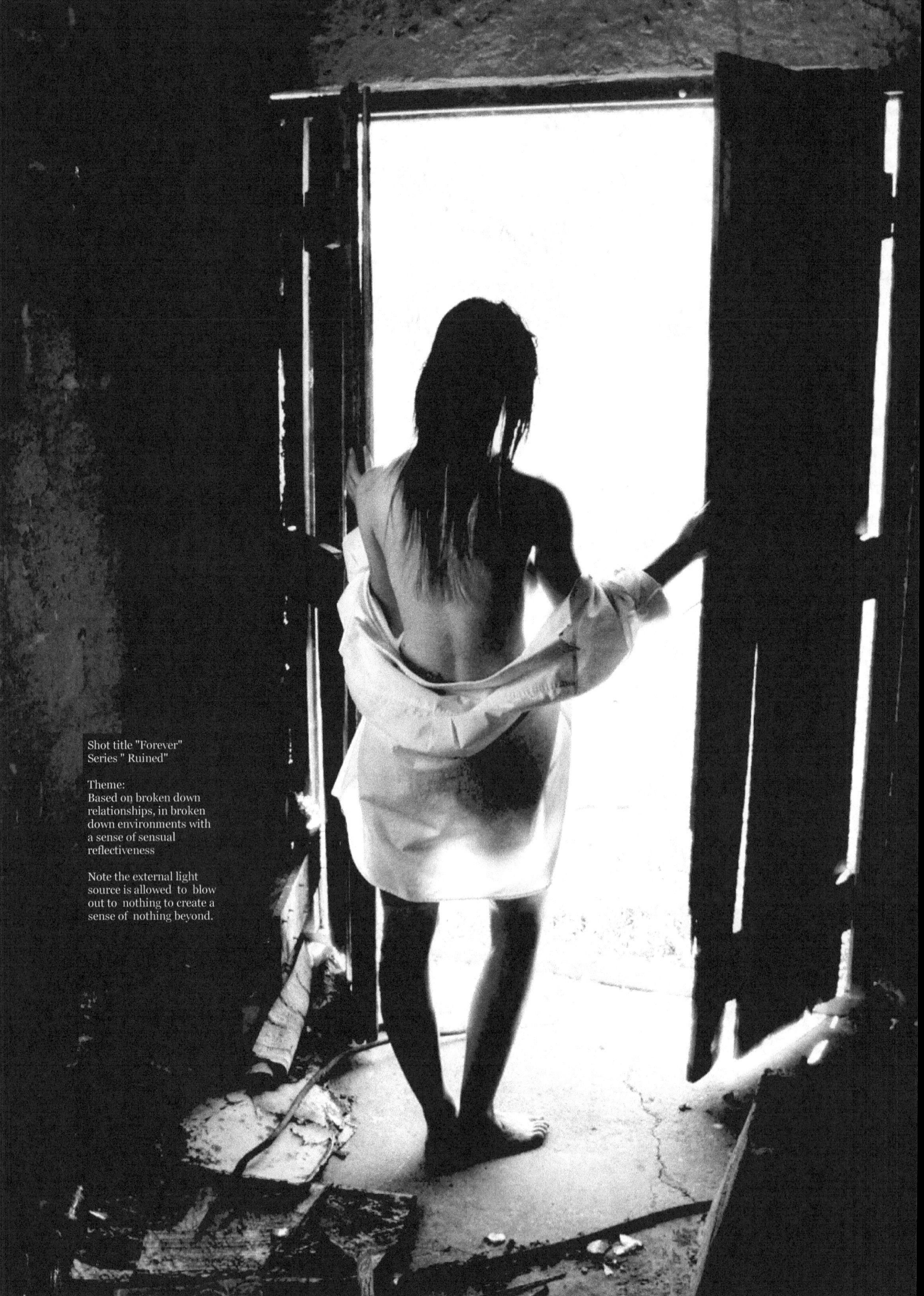

Shot title "Forever"
Series " Ruined"

Theme:
Based on broken down
relationships, in broken
down environments with
a sense of sensual
reflectiveness

Note the external light
source is allowed to blow
out to nothing to create a
sense of nothing beyond.

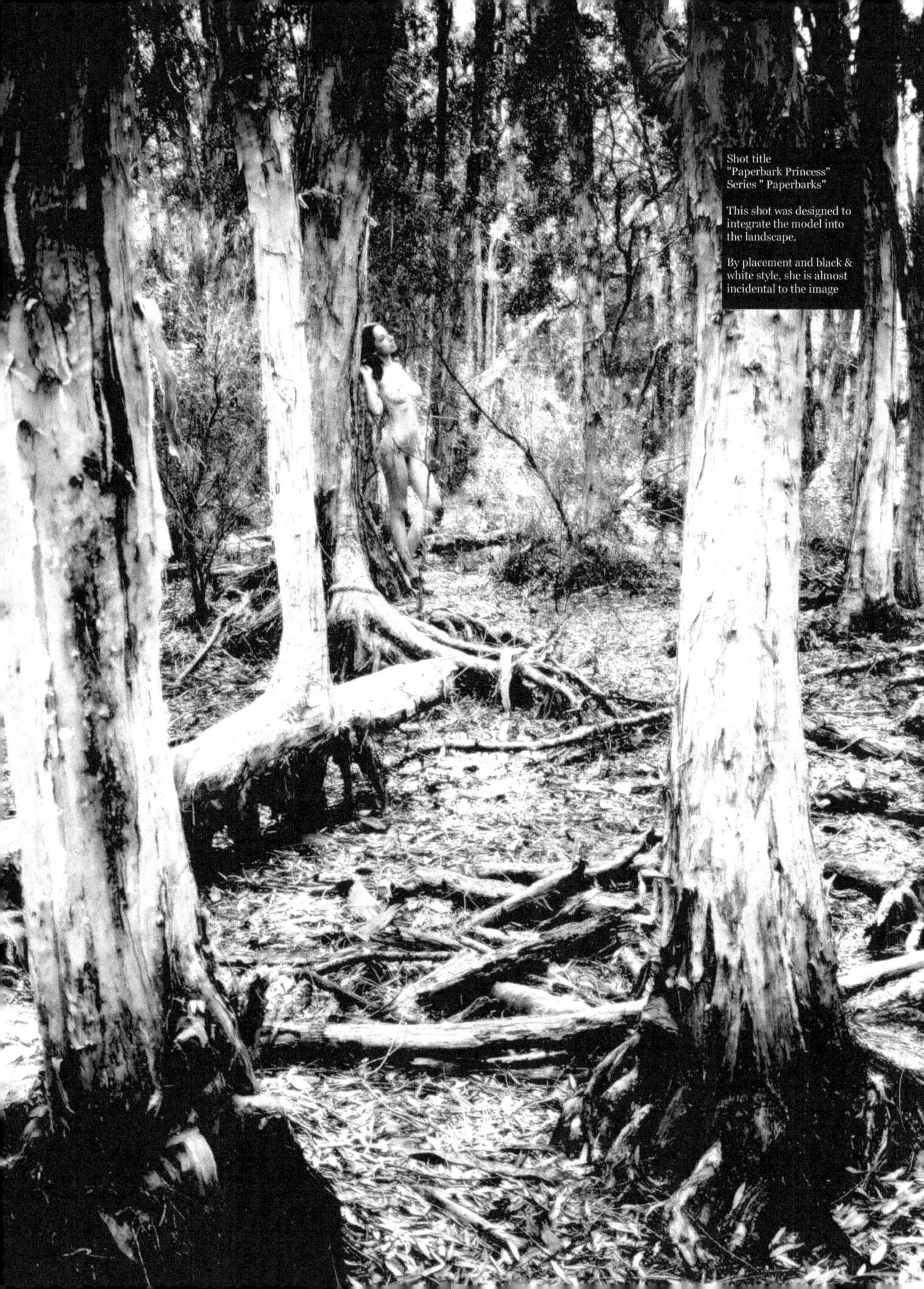

Shot title
"Paperbark Princess"
Series " Paperbarks"

This shot was designed to
integrate the model into
the landscape.

By placement and black &
white style, she is almost
incidental to the image

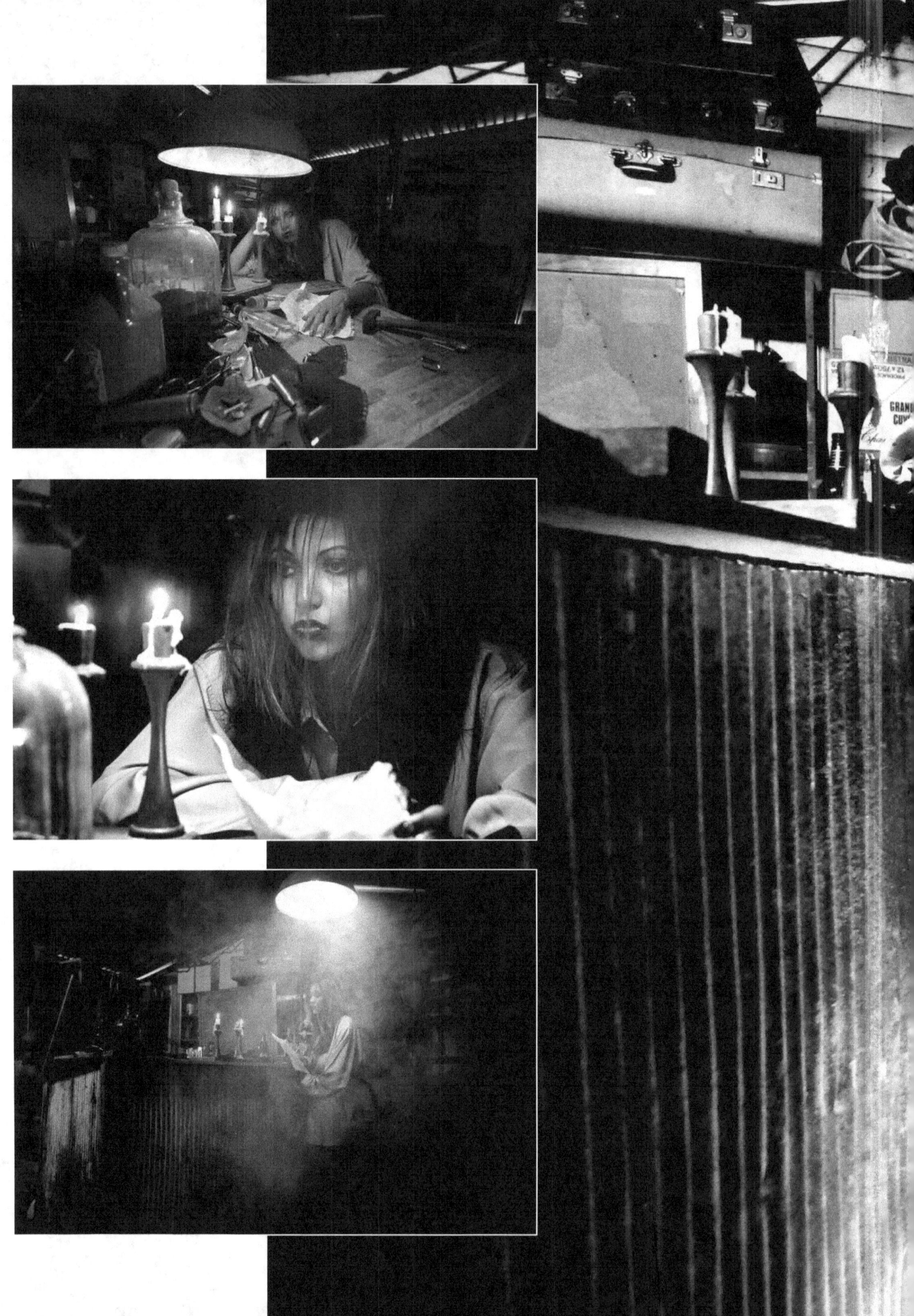

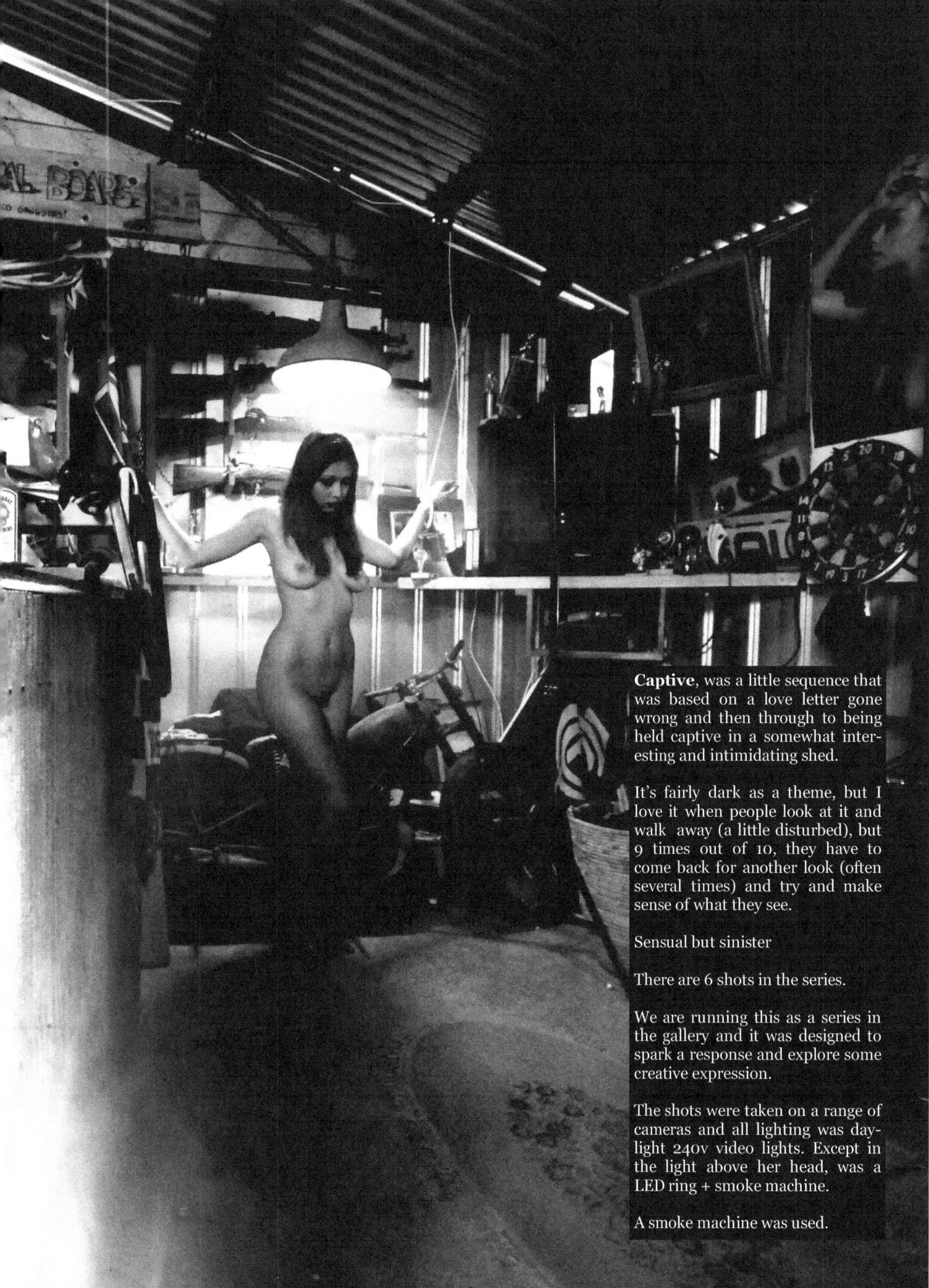

Captive, was a little sequence that was based on a love letter gone wrong and then through to being held captive in a somewhat interesting and intimidating shed.

It's fairly dark as a theme, but I love it when people look at it and walk away (a little disturbed), but 9 times out of 10, they have to come back for another look (often several times) and try and make sense of what they see.

Sensual but sinister

There are 6 shots in the series.

We are running this as a series in the gallery and it was designed to spark a response and explore some creative expression.

The shots were taken on a range of cameras and all lighting was daylight 240v video lights. Except in the light above her head, was a LED ring + smoke machine.

A smoke machine was used.

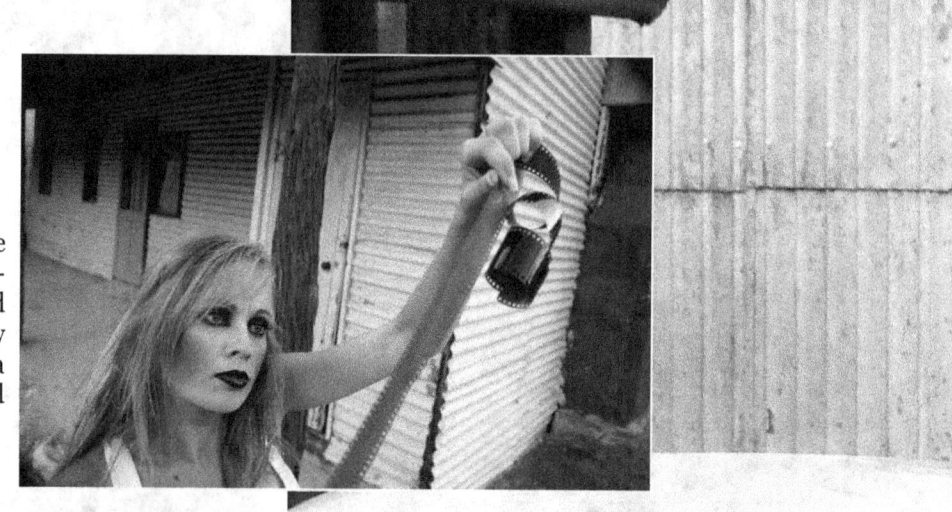

The Dark Bride, was a little sequence I worked up that was based on and depicted a ruined wedding that started from exposed negatives, through a few anger emotions, the other woman, a disgruntled father and then finally and ending.

There are 14 shots in the series.

We are running this as a series in the gallery and it is a great talking piece. A number of other shots were taken at the same time that are more saleable, but it works as a creative piece of expression and a bit of fun.

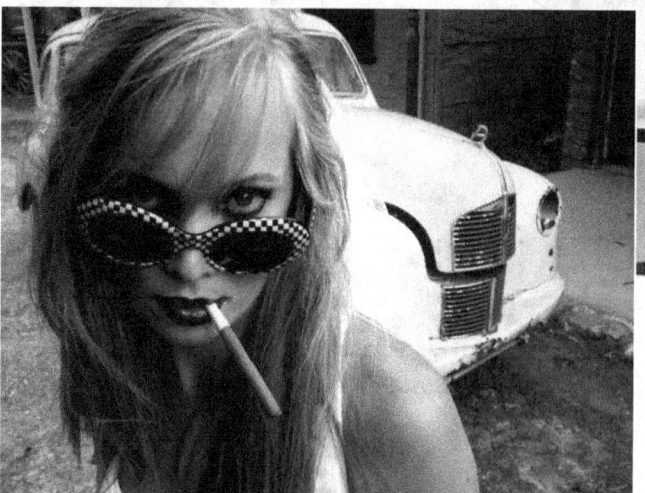

The shots were taken on a range of cameras, all in the last 2 hours of light and the first hour of darkness. I have used quite a few props with this shoot and found an excellent location that gave me close proximity to each shot (given the time frame) and good vehicle access as I needed a number of 240v and battery lights.

I tend to use a lot of powered lights, rather than flash when I can, as I find them more predictable with digital cameras and chip sets. I guess also as my background is TV, I am just more comfortable with them.

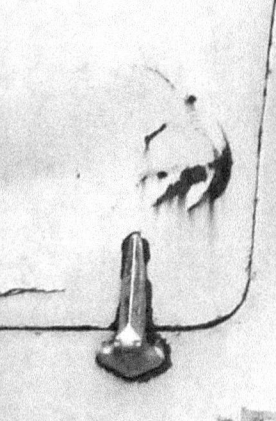

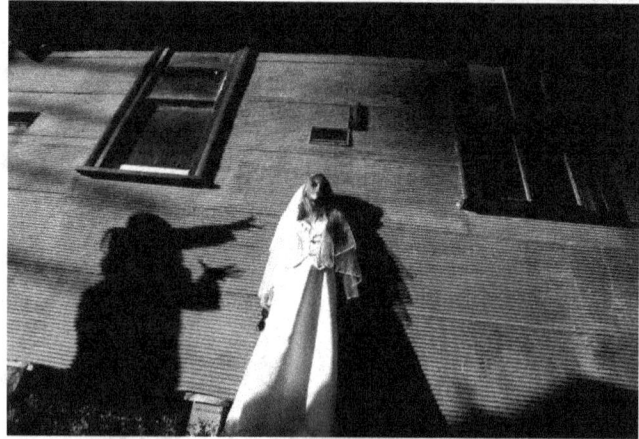

All shots were hand held except the night scene and this was painted with a torch. I put a few small LEDs on the ground around the tombstones and up the walls, with a smoke machine and simply painted the railing and model with torch light over a 10 second exposure time.

The breeze was an issue with the smoke out doors, but some patience paid off and we eventually got there!

Note: I also shot a G rated version while I was there so it had greater application in the future and for advertising purposes.

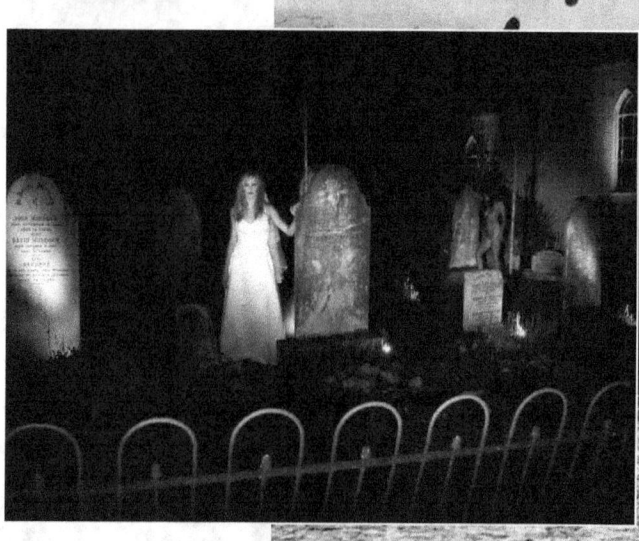

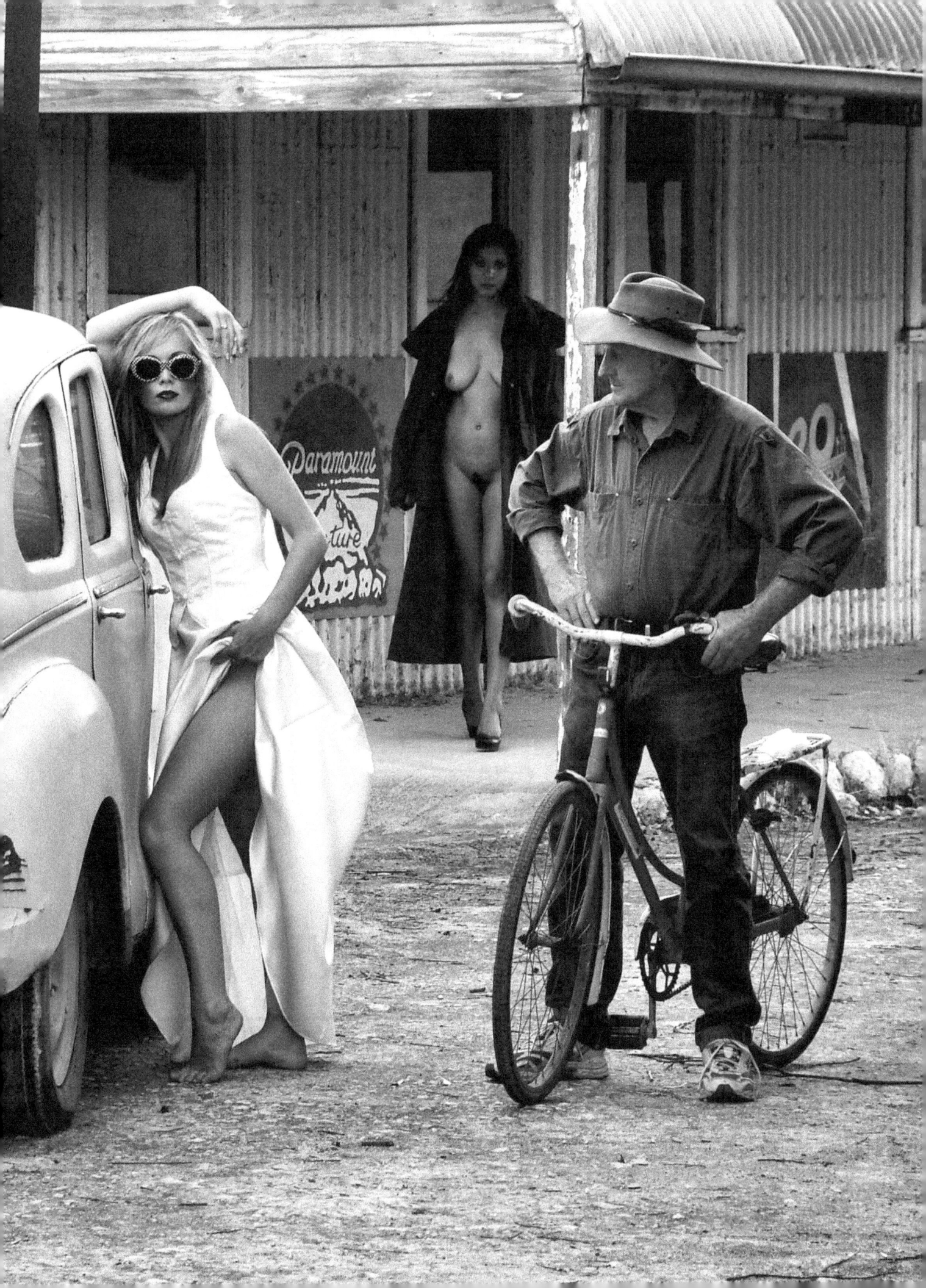

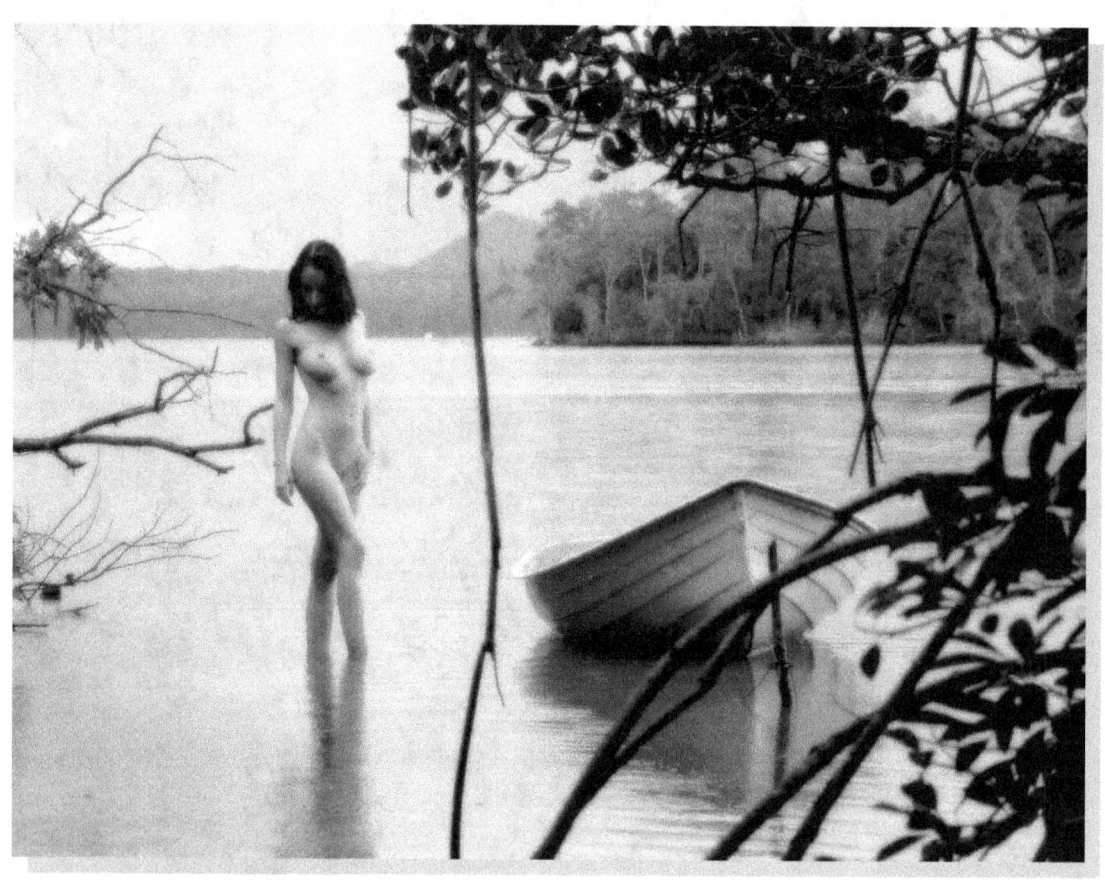

Shot title "Calm"
Location: Noosa, Queensland"

Theme: Based first and foremost on the serene location. Series features soft pictures (shot with a promist), with beautiful bodies that have a sense of calm, confident, voyeuristic, vulnerability. I often avoid showing a models face to create a sense of mystery.

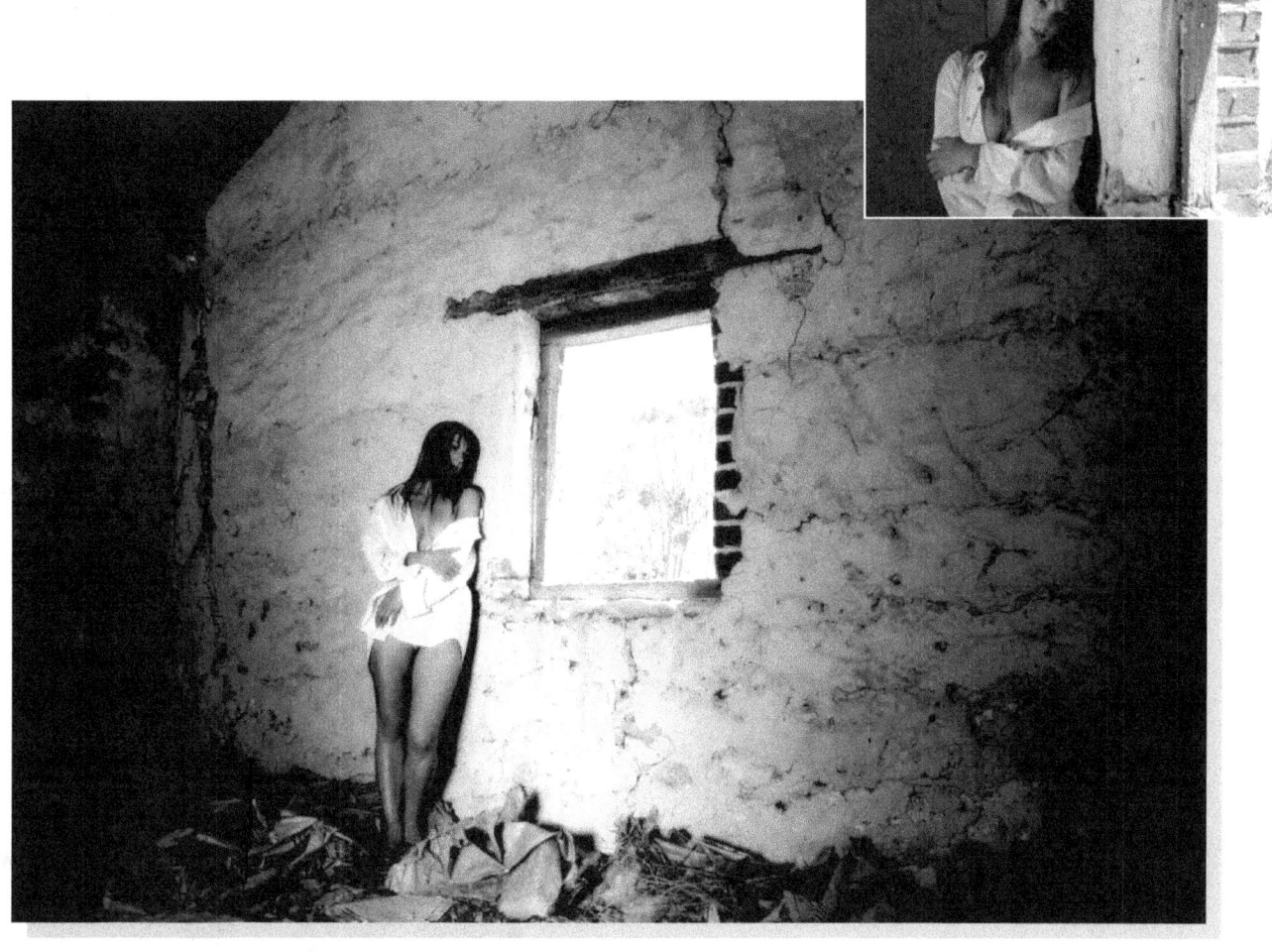

Shot title "Angry"
Series " Ruined"
Location: Country South Australia

Theme: Based on broken relationships in broken down areas. Simple but vulnerable.
A little less exposure in the window to create a sense of distance, but allowing the light source to fall off
around her to create intimacy of location and keep the shot tidy. (The location was a disgrace)

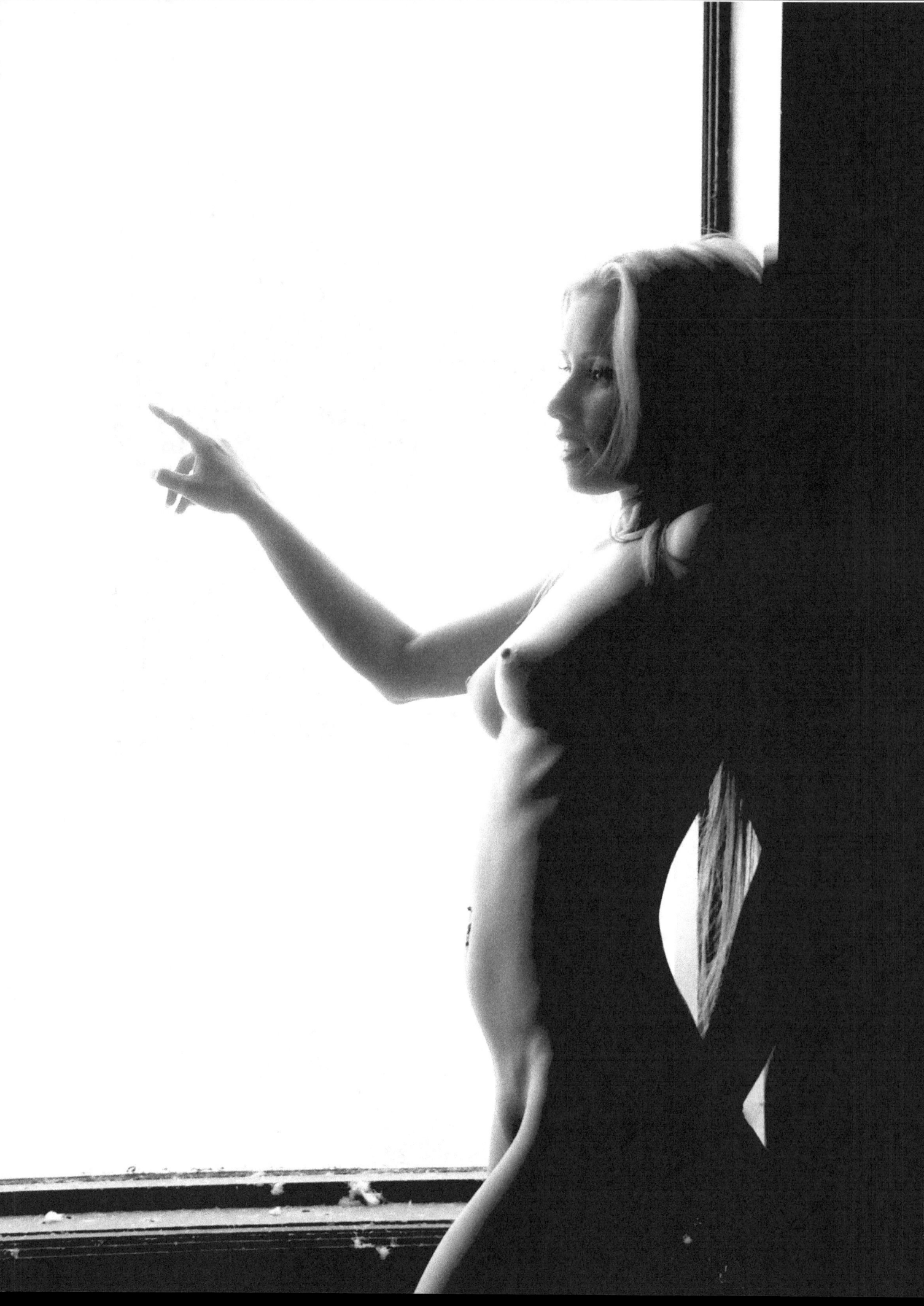

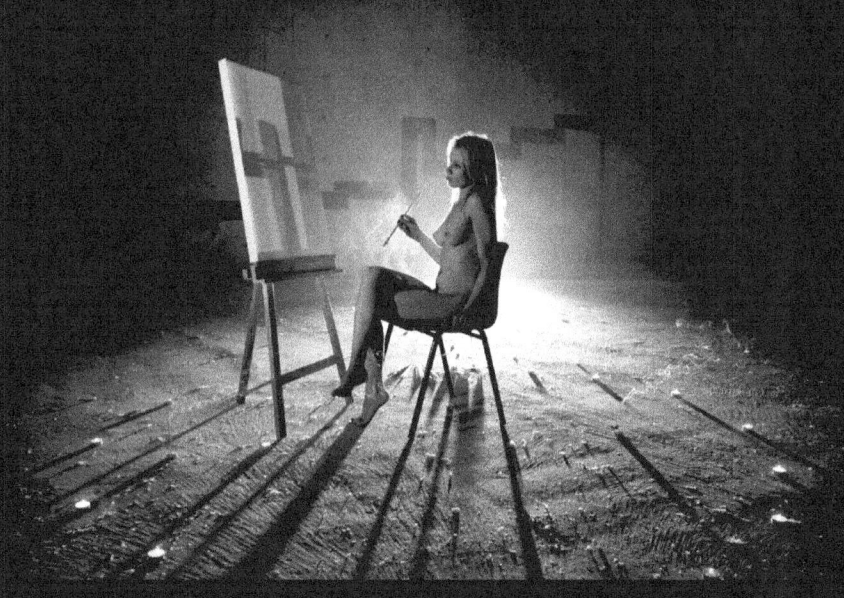

COLOUR
OR
BLACK & WHITE?

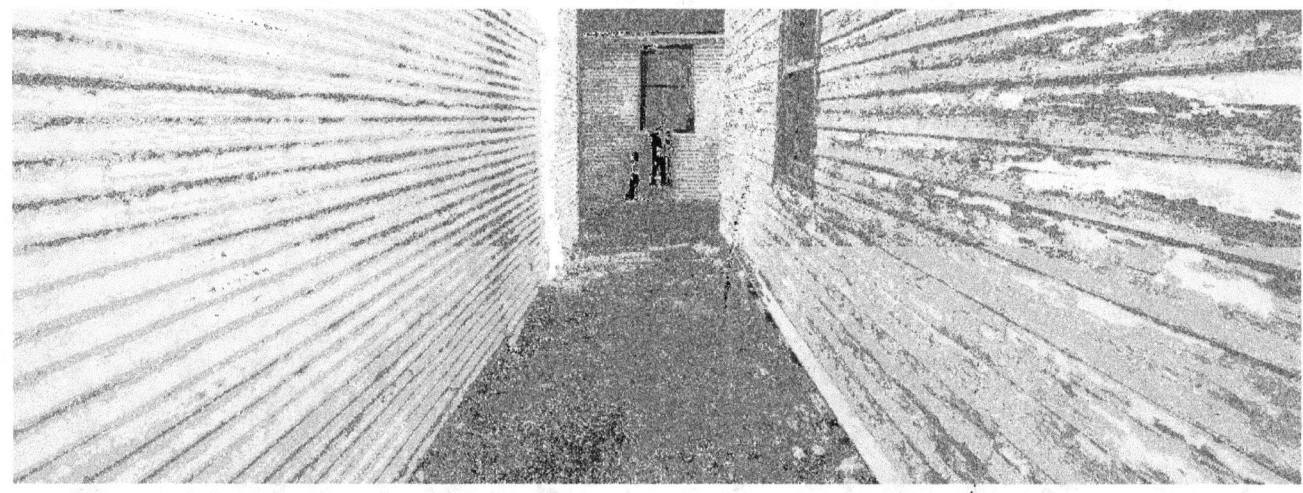

I love colour! The world is a colourful place and I love to accentuate it and over exaggerate it most of the time. We all see the world differently, but this doesn't mean you should.

Black and white has become quite the art form in recent years, but I think much of this has been due to lack of talent. People's inability to work with colour.

I get so bored of people using black and white imagery, as a cop out and a way to make a boring "no idea" style more interesting. We all know that a terd looks good in black & white , but try and make it look good in colour... there's the challenge!

Look another crap shot! Let's turn it black and white! Crank up the "everything" and ...WoW! Doesn't it look great now!

A terd is always a terd, no matter how much you polish it, and whilst a few of your ignorant friends and peers might sing your praises, does it really make you feel good about what you shot and the planning or thought that went into it?

Placing your talent on a rock, hanging them upside down or draping them uncomfortably over a massive tree root and then switching it to black and white or sepia is hardly artistic, it's more autistic (photographically speaking).

If you are going to go for black and white or a colour grade, shoot for it. Plan for it, learn for it, or at least experiment with it. Use red filters, work your highlights / shadows and make the dramatic contrasts work for you. Don't just use it as a patch up after the shoot. Black & white looks fantastic, if you know how to shoot for it.

Why not turn the sky black with a polarizer, or your talent white with over exposure. Use those shadows!

So why not shoot colour for artistic work?

Granted, it's harder to add that arty style, but who sets the rules anyway? Isn't it you? The trouble with colour is can often look a bit too real and people don't like real!

If you go out of your way to create a photograph art work that conforms to all the rules and everything you have been taught, it will look exactly the same as everybody else's that was taught at your college or club. Especially the moment you click the Photofix button on your computer!

Nothing is visually illegal technically anymore printwise, so go for it! Blow out your whites if that's what you intended to do, lose her face in the shadows, wind in too much ISO grain, over expose it to a solar flare or underexpose it to milk. But just be clear about the final objective.

On the shots (opposite pages) I have put 2 shots side by side to demonstrate the vastly different overall feel between colour and B&W.

Both quite soft & beautiful, but both with a very different outcome and final style.

The image on the left is soft, warm and accessible to the viewer, perhaps even a little voyeuristic.

In the right hand version, notice how the tree is no longer a feature in the Black & White image, it's been lost. The light has flattened out through the whole shot and become quite wishy washy. That said, the talent is less of a feature, possibly making the photo more palatable to some.

The shot was designed to be shot and viewed in colour.

It's your call how you tackle it, so enjoy it.

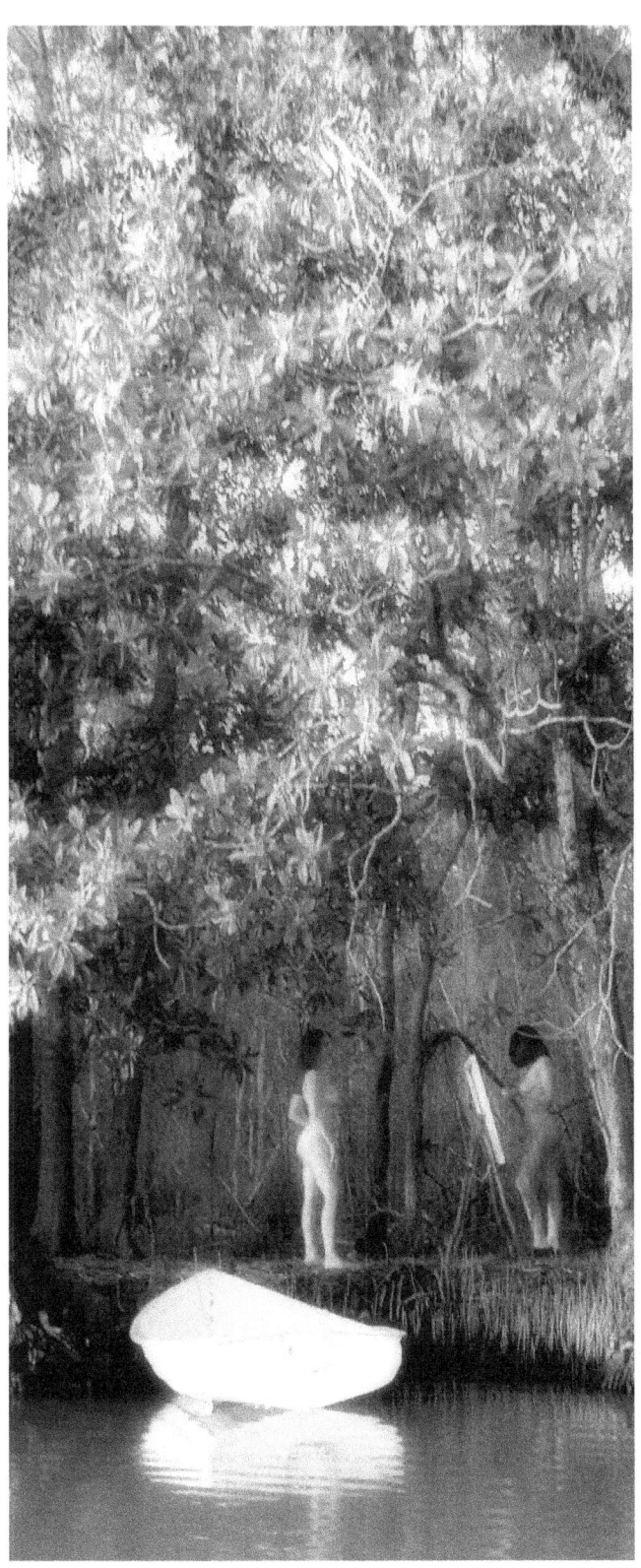
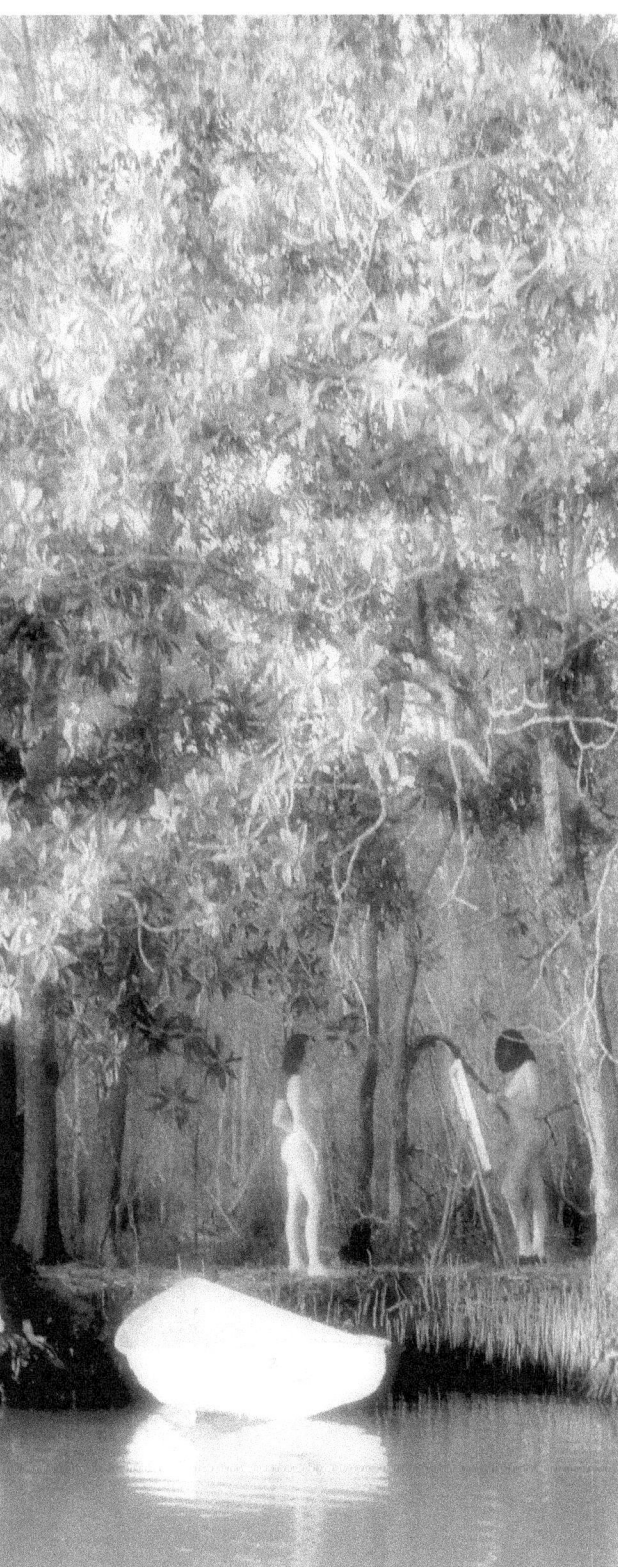

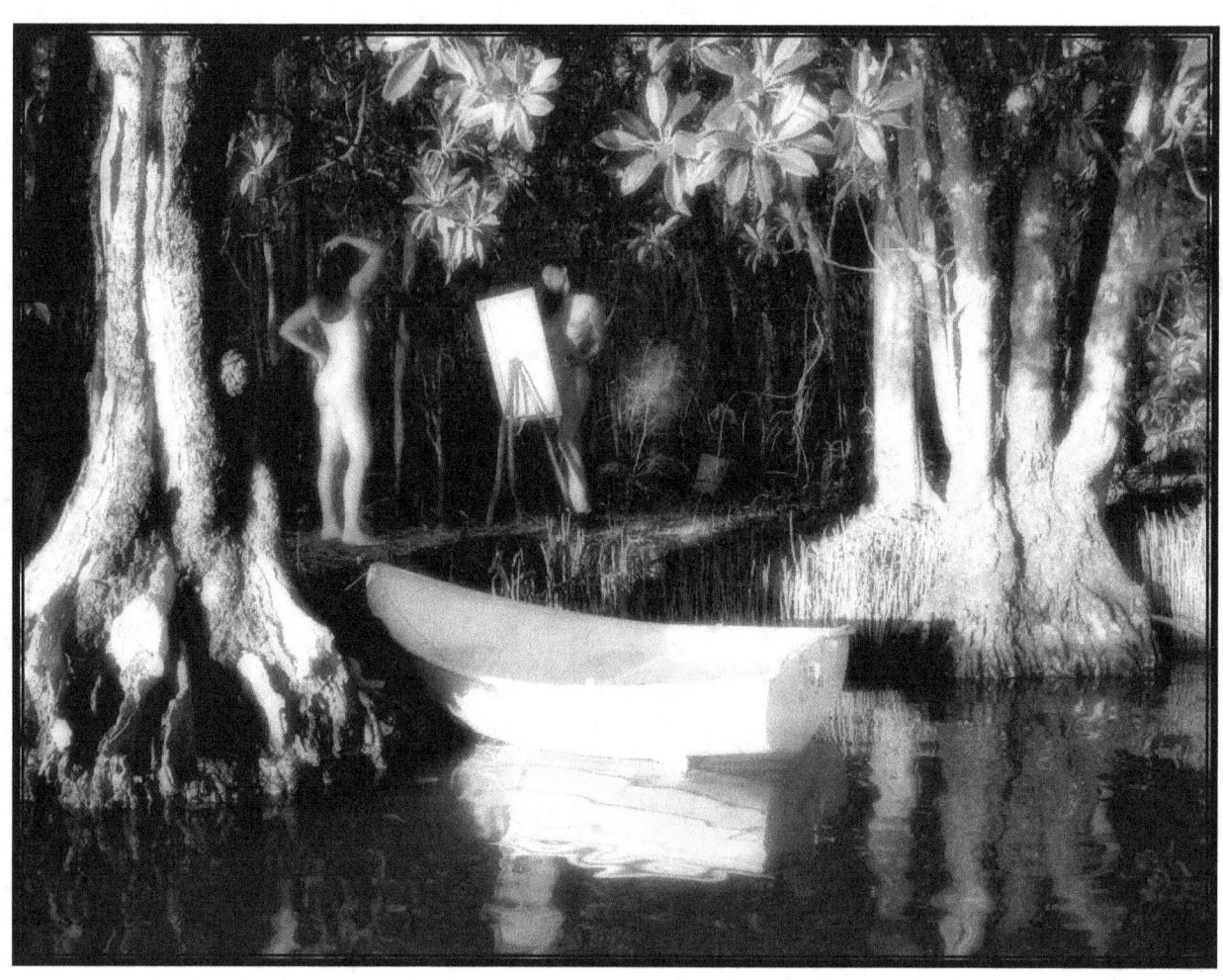

Shot title "The Artists"
Series " Everglades"
Location: Noosa, Queensland

This is an alternative version from the previous page.
The shot as it was intended, calm, beautiful, colourful, voyeuristic, peaceful

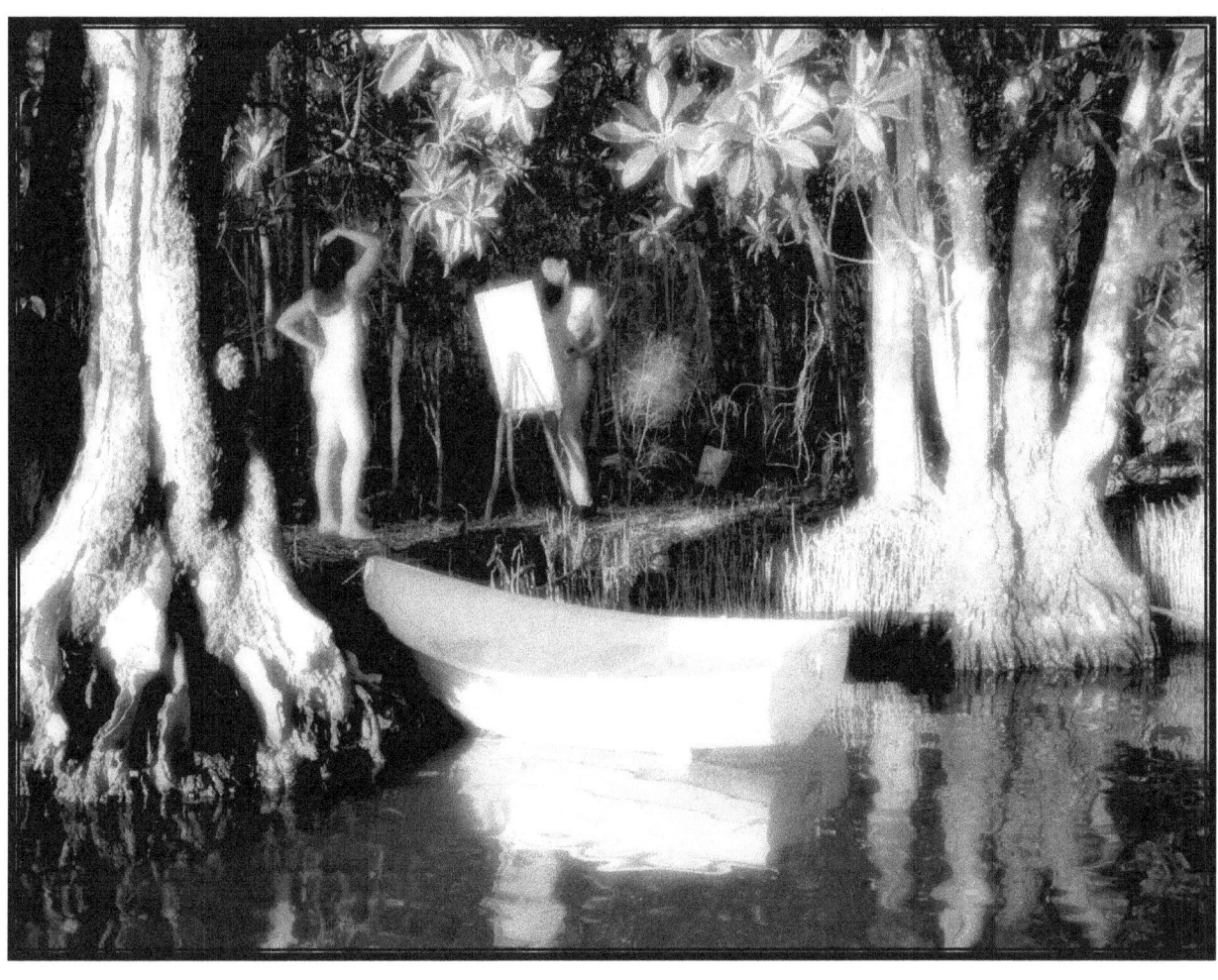

As an example, the black and white conversion, whilst "arty", robs the image of realness (skin colours),
it also removes the big powerful canopy of green that gives the artists their feeling of intimacy and protection.
The reflections are now somewhat irrelevant and the strength of the landscape weakened.
But perhaps.... A little less real and offers different appeal?

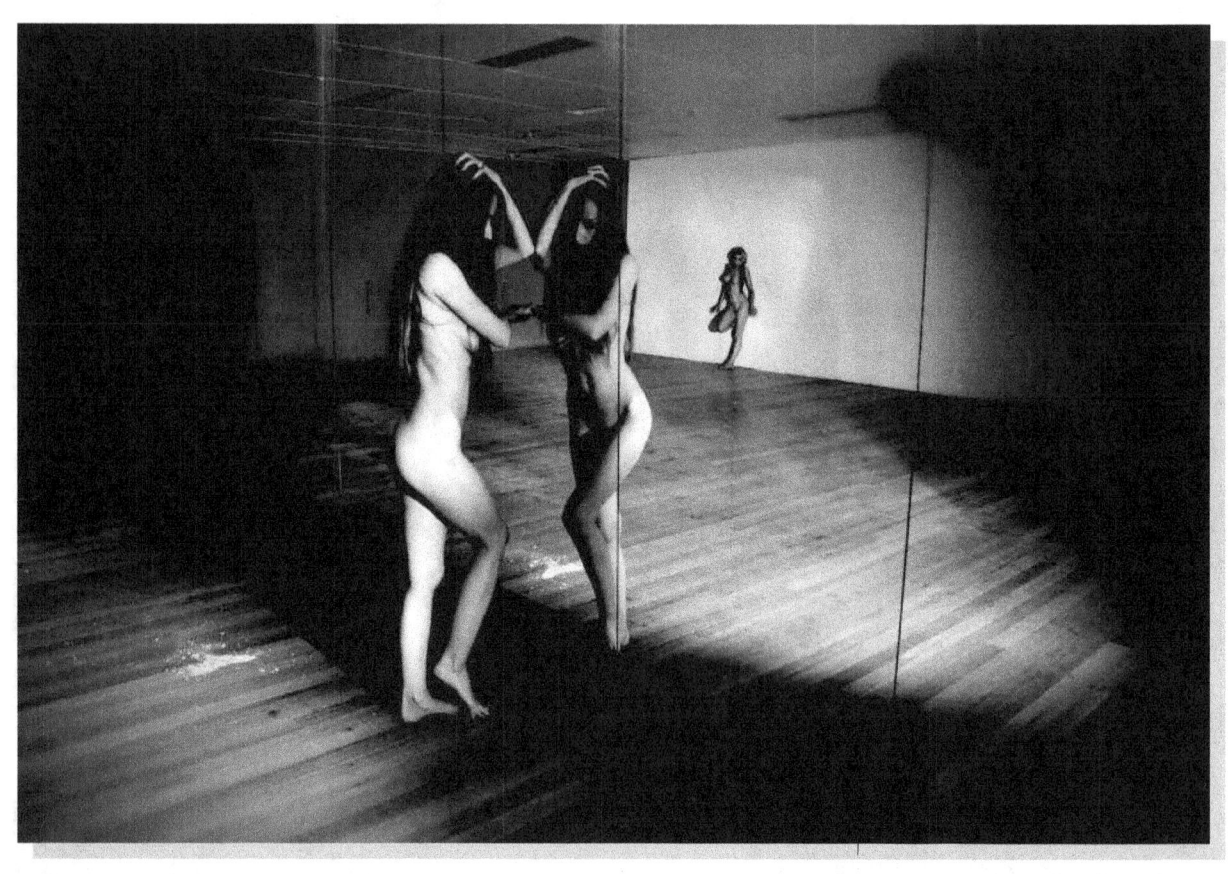

Shot title "Last Dancers"
Series "Art House"

*Again, Black & White adds an element of mystery and style
when there is really no colours of interest in the scene.
It also creates lots of interesting black holes into the shadows if lit carefully*

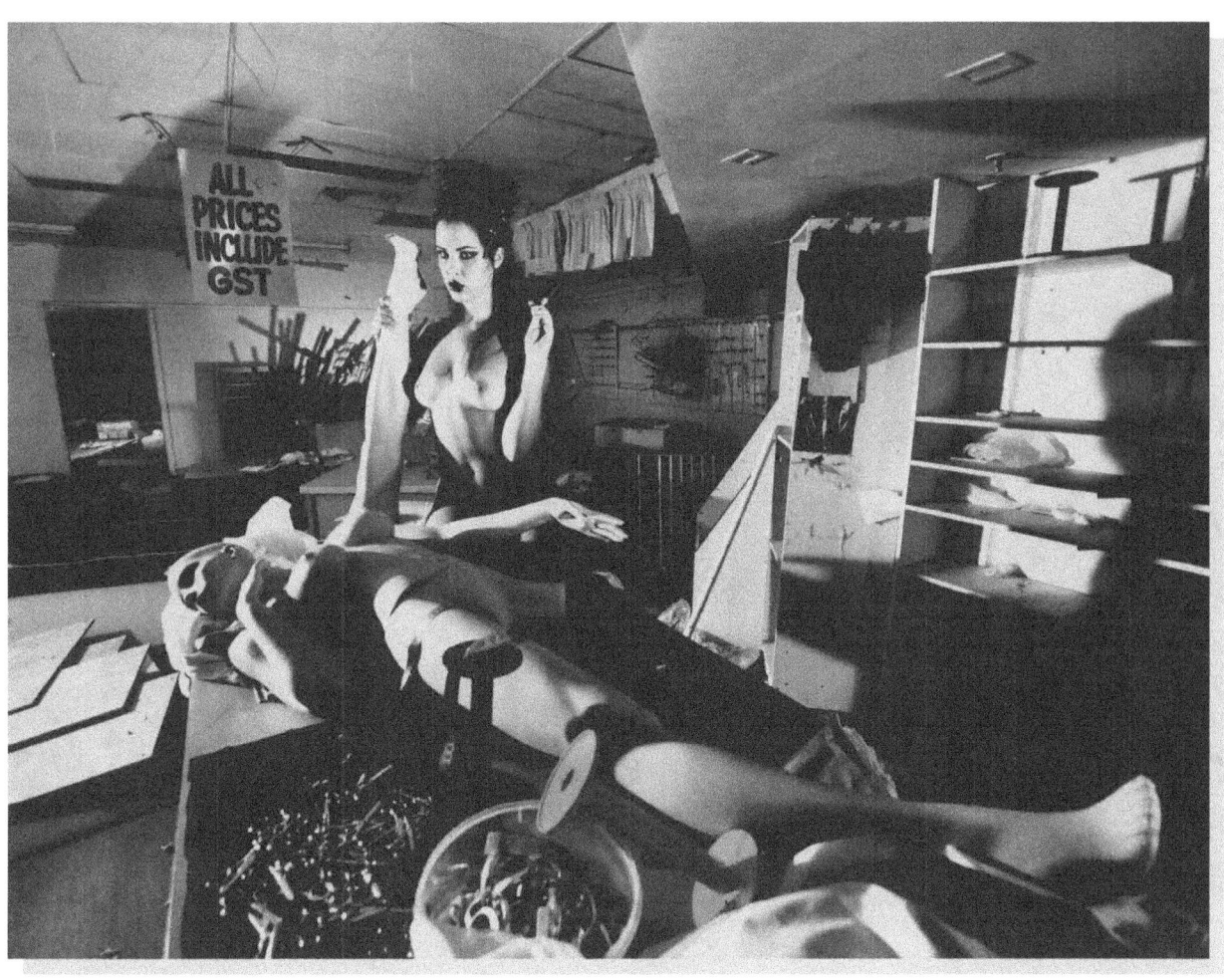

Shot title "Midnight Dressmaker"
Series "Art House"
Location: Melbourne

A little bit crazy, but none the less interesting?

- Nominated for Black & White Spider Awards -

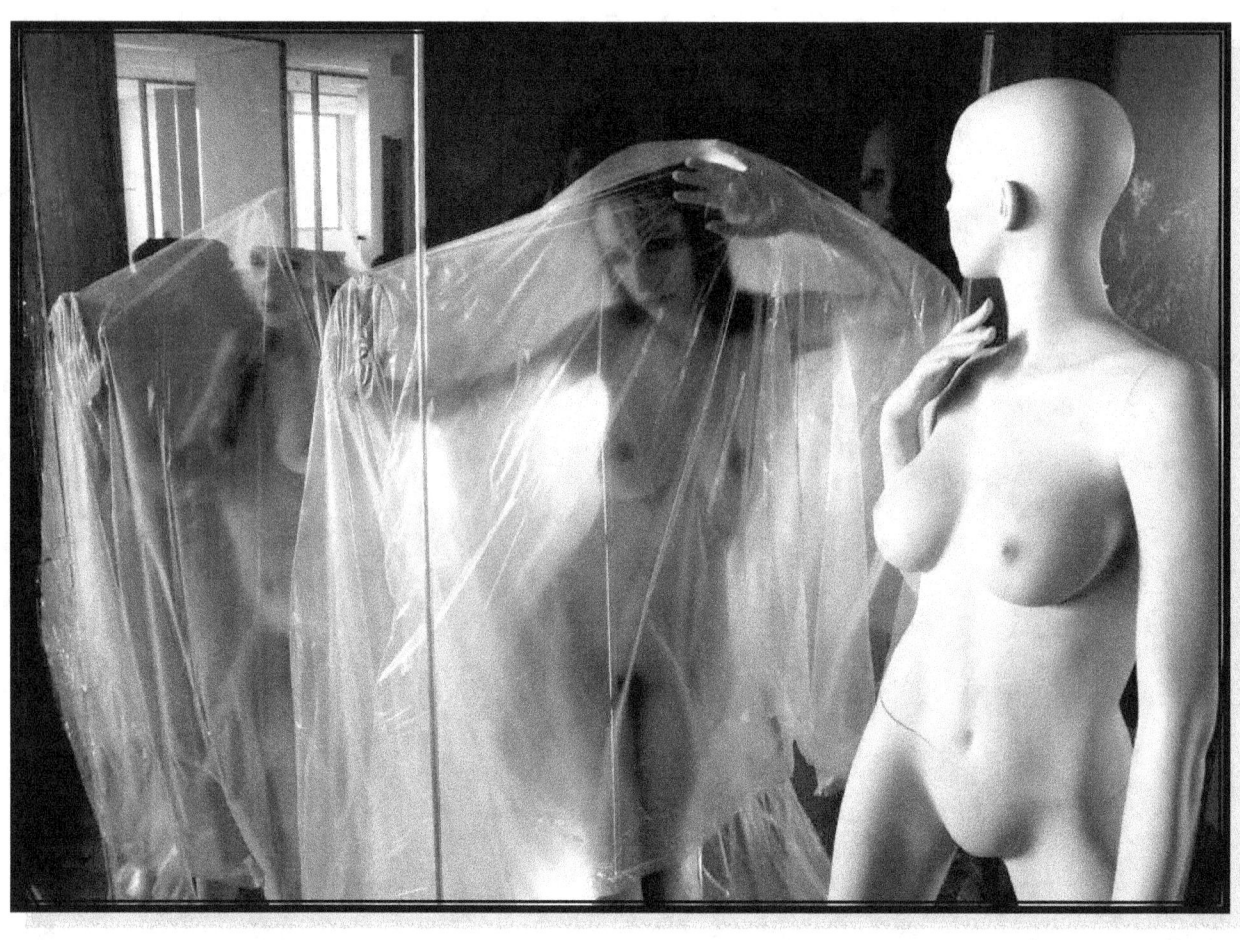

Shot title "Window Shopping"
Series "Art House"

Black & white can be used very effectively to add an element
of interest and style when there is really no colours of interest present

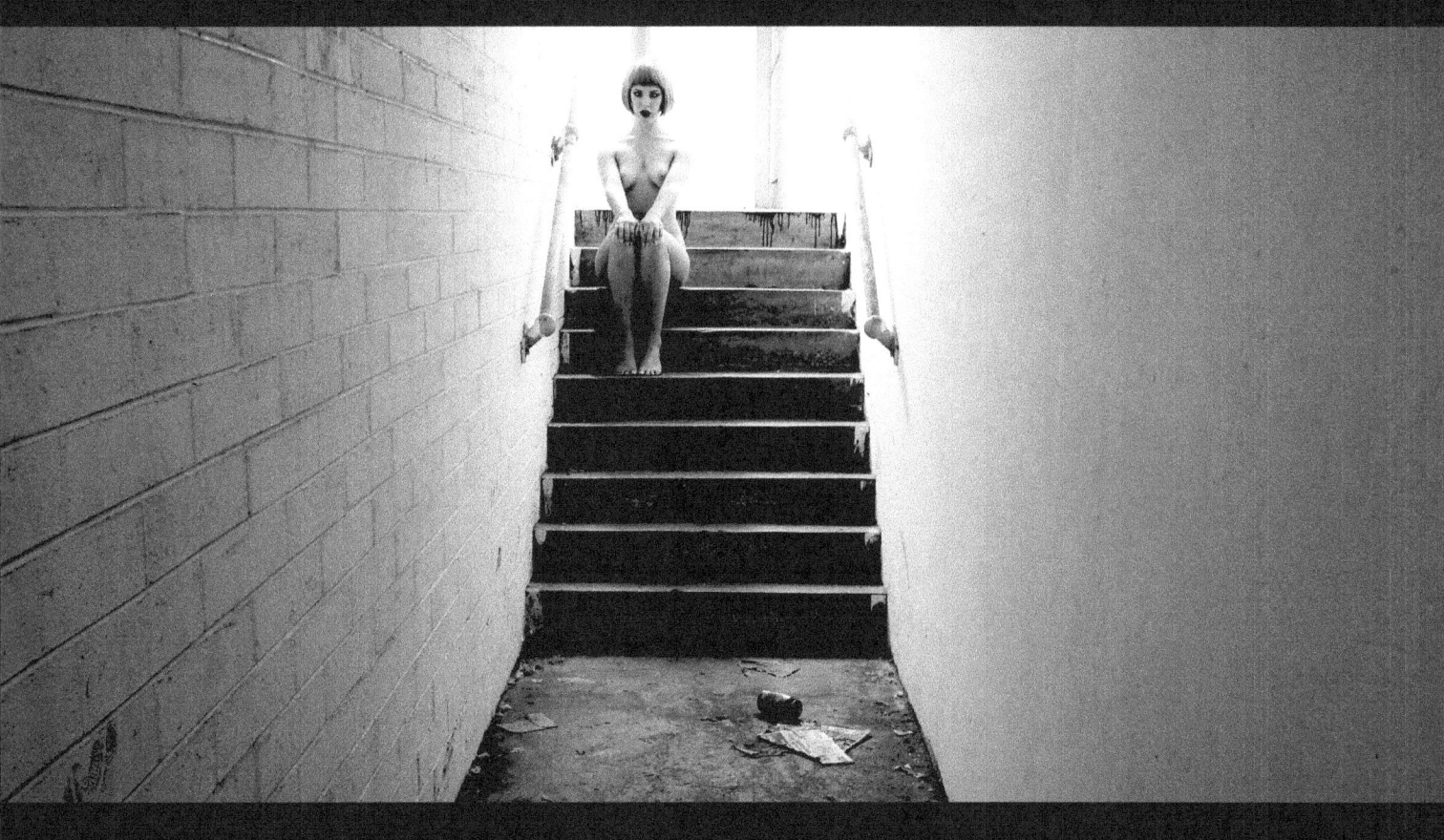

Shot title "Blank Stair II"
Series "Art House"

Symmetrical, gutsy, powerful

Black and white is used here to
separate the subject from the
background and accentuate the
tattoo and striking colours.

A good use of black and white
in my opinion.

The shot was designed
for advertising prior to
shooting and kept simple
and exposed accordingly.

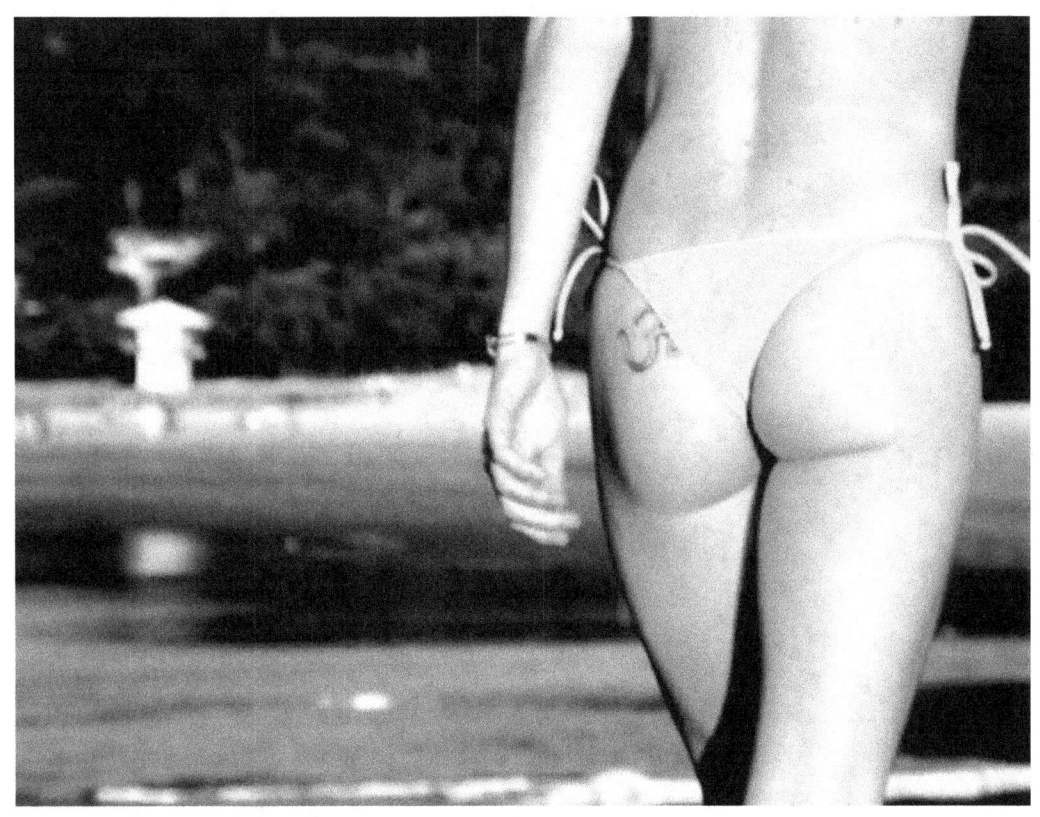

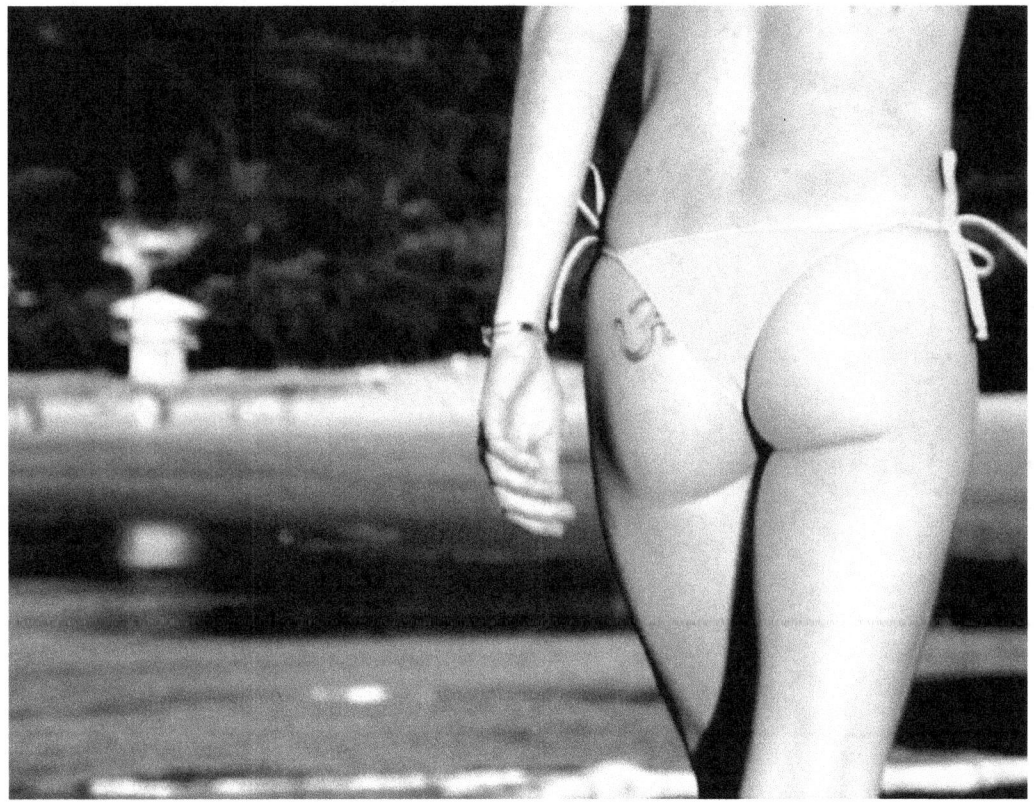

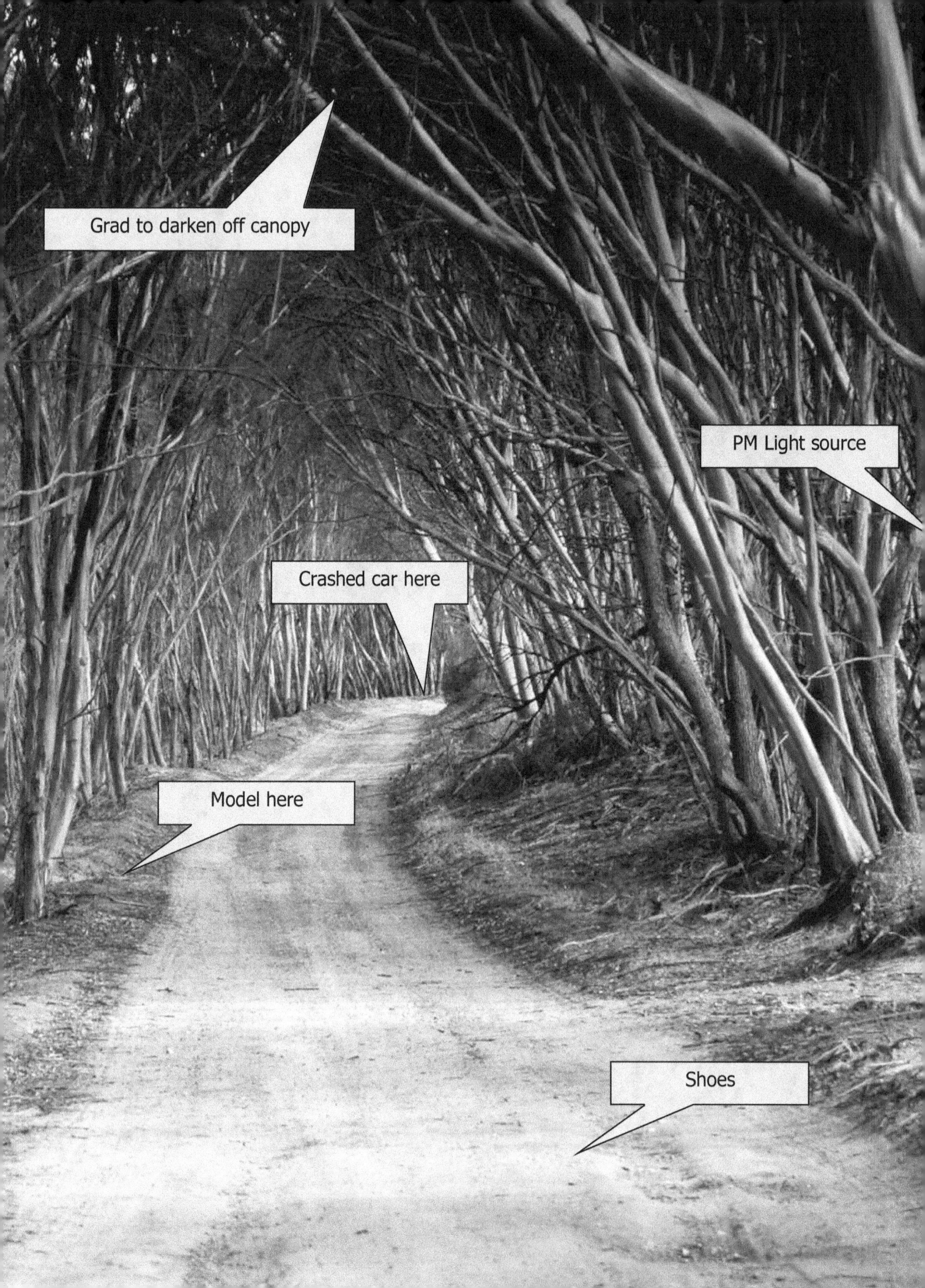

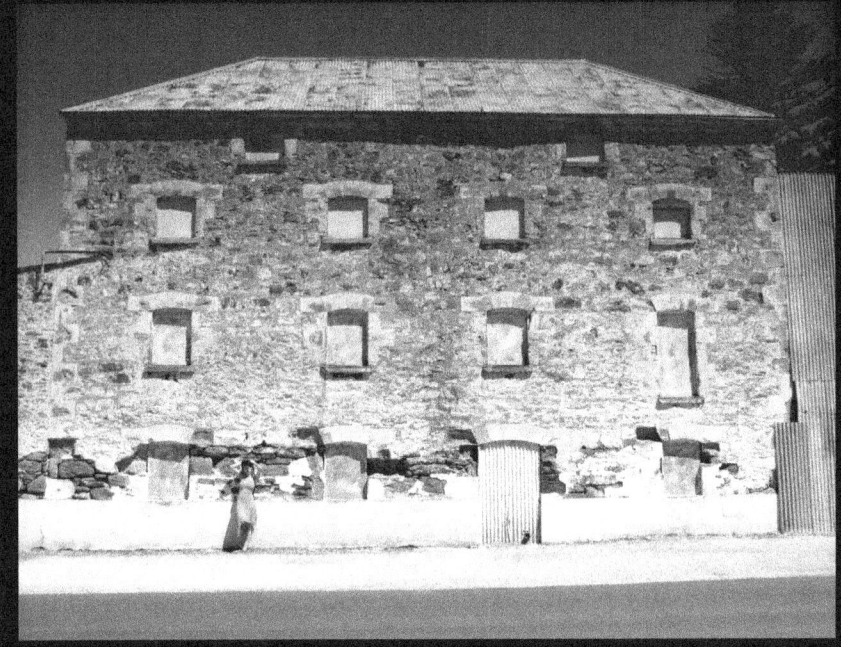

THE LOCATION

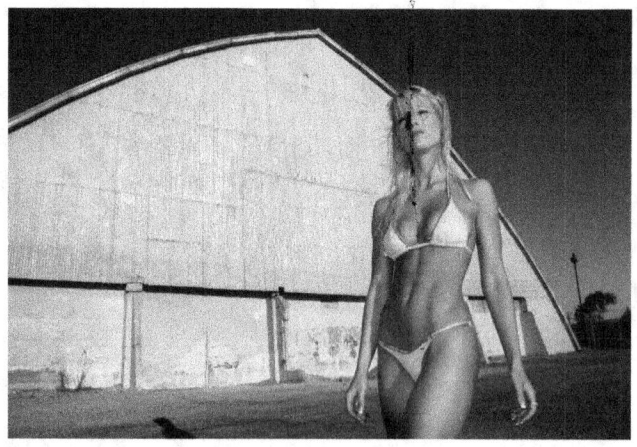

What is a location anyway?

Is it the focus of the shot, or is it simply a background? Be clear before you start. In a lot of my work, the location is the main point of the image and the character is there to add an extra element only, a focal point, accentuate it or compliment it. Rarely is the talent the reason for me.

Does the location suit your intended vision or more importantly your model? There is little point in arriving with a *stunning and glamorous* model and slumping her on the floor and telling her to pose like a refugee, nor is there much point in trying to squeeze a *sad* and *sultry soul* into tight, brightly coloured leather or a G String.

Location is so important and is often closer than you think.

Personally, I love textures. Doesn't matter what, maybe ripples on a beach, old bricks, a galv fence, a zebra crossing, timber, whatever takes my fancy and of course, I love gutsy colour… I'm a man, so this means I will likely go for symmetry (I'm told) where as the women will try perhaps a little less symmetry and more beauty.

Once you have picked your location, go there at the time of day that you are planning to shoot or at the very least, stand back and see what the sun, shade, tides or wind is doing, when will it look it's best for your purpose?

Long shadows, bright colours or maybe dim and dark is what you are looking for. It might be a great location, but will it light up the way you want at the time of shooting?

In my opinion, light is the key to all great shots. Even a great location can look dull, colourless and boring in drab light. It creates more interest and brings out the colour and saturation. I would rather have great light, than a great location. Both is perfect!

Imagine walking out into a flat, vast, open, freshly cut paddock, with nothing around for miles at midday and the client says "ok lets shoot this!" You will most likely come back with a dozen shots of zip.

Go back to that paddock 1 hour before dark and shove a dead branch in or on the ground and the world changes. You now have bags of warm colour, long shadows and a focal point.

After you have picked your location, shut down the creative process for a moment and take a long second look for logistics, what else is wrong or needs doing? It's time to take out the pen and notebook!

Rubbish bins unlocked and moved, power poles covered by props, if you are coming back in December will it be covered in Christmas decorations?

If it's near water, will the tide be in or out when you return? What if the wind comes up, will the reflections be gone?

It looks great right now, but how about when you are coming back to shoot? Do you have a plan B nearby?

Do the windows need cleaning?
Do you need a permit or permission?
Vehicle access and parking?

No point in taking the shot of a lifetime if you are forbidden to sell or exhibit it.

Do you need some ground cover or shade for you or your crew? Will your model? Is it dusty? flyspray, hats, sun cream, water?

Where will the models get changed or make up done?
If they are doing their own, is there a suitable place?

Sit down, take the time and have a good think....

Forget the shot for a minute and consider only logistics. Maybe you are dead keen on doing a nude, but this awesome location is better suited to something else!? A car, clothed person, product shot or sunset maybe…

Many a time, I have arrived on location to photograph a nude and ended up with no clothes off for anyone! (Except me when I get hot!)

Just because it's an awesome location doesn't mean it's well suited to an artistic nude location.

Then, think about some extra props that might compliment what and where you are going to shoot.

Props can be simple.

Clothing, hats, furniture, a stick, fishing rod, antique radio, maybe just a texture pen or some chalk. A can of paint or maybe a bucket of water? Look around you, what can you see that would work ? Stones, rubbish, textures.

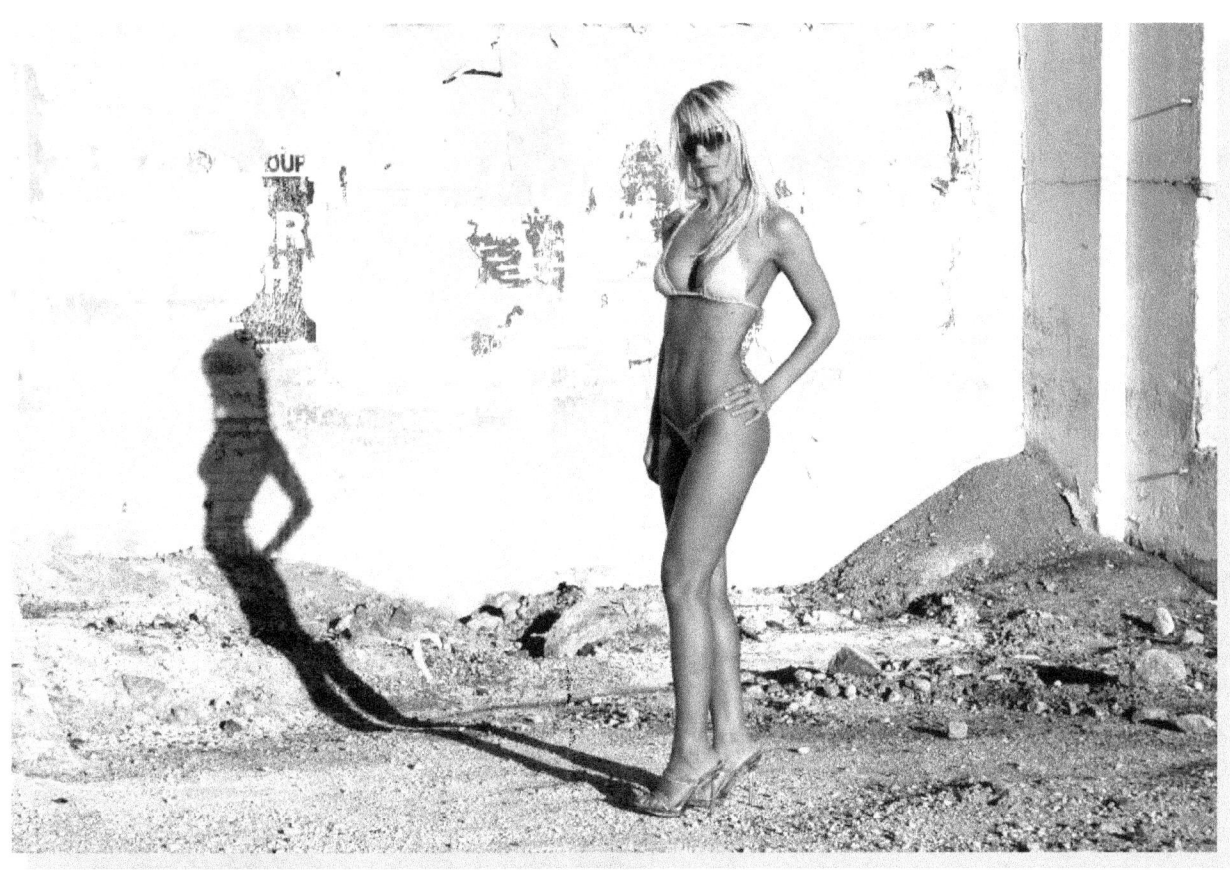

Shot title "Private Commission"
Location: A wall somewhere

Note: This model wanted gutsy glam'. The location sets her off. Again, I could have put a shopping trolley there in place of her.
But she looks sensational against the stark building, utilising her shadow for figure emphasis.

Planning and being organized is everything when it comes to a successful shoot, we use a *"photographers shoot notebook"* for each shoot, which we find excellent for keeping shoot information together.

It comes with a check list and allows you to keep each shoot separated.

Check out www.pronotes.com.au, definitely worth the few extra tax deductible dollars.

This location was great, as it was a run down old cabin and the colours and rustic timbers added an element of realism.

It was originally planned as a full nude scene, but it looked wrong, awkward and out of place. What was supposed to be soft and pretty, suddenly looked blatant and token.

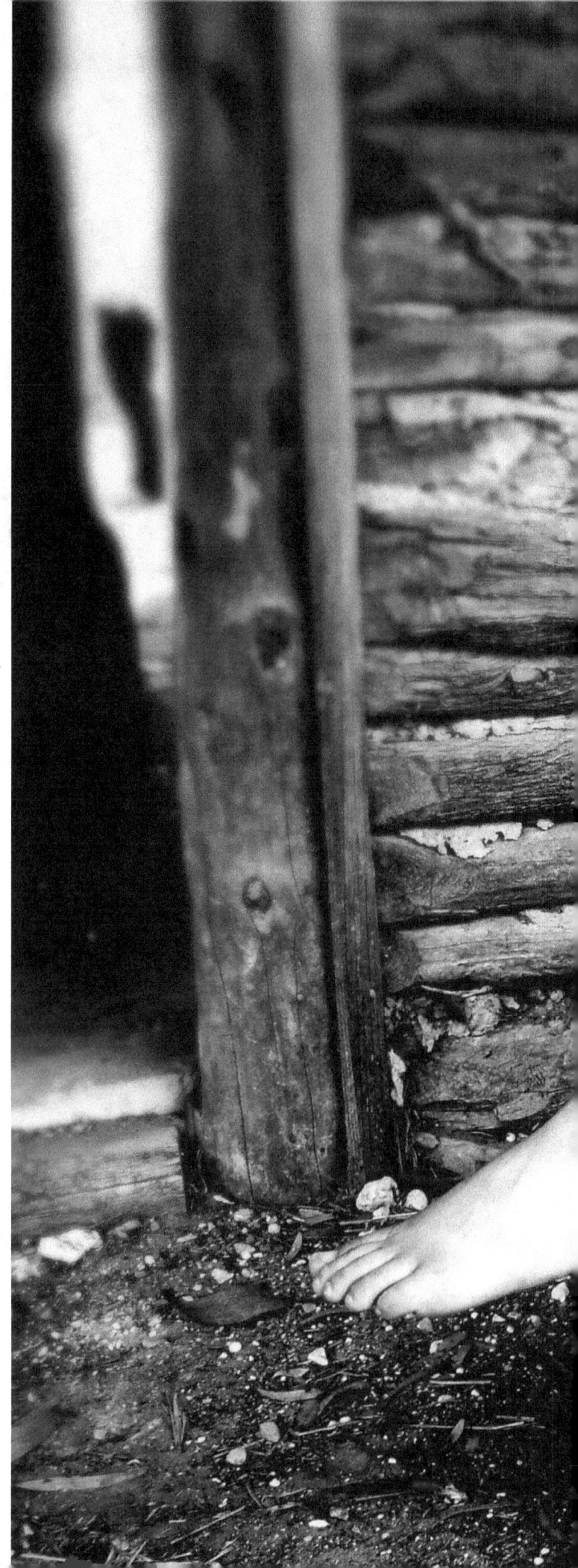

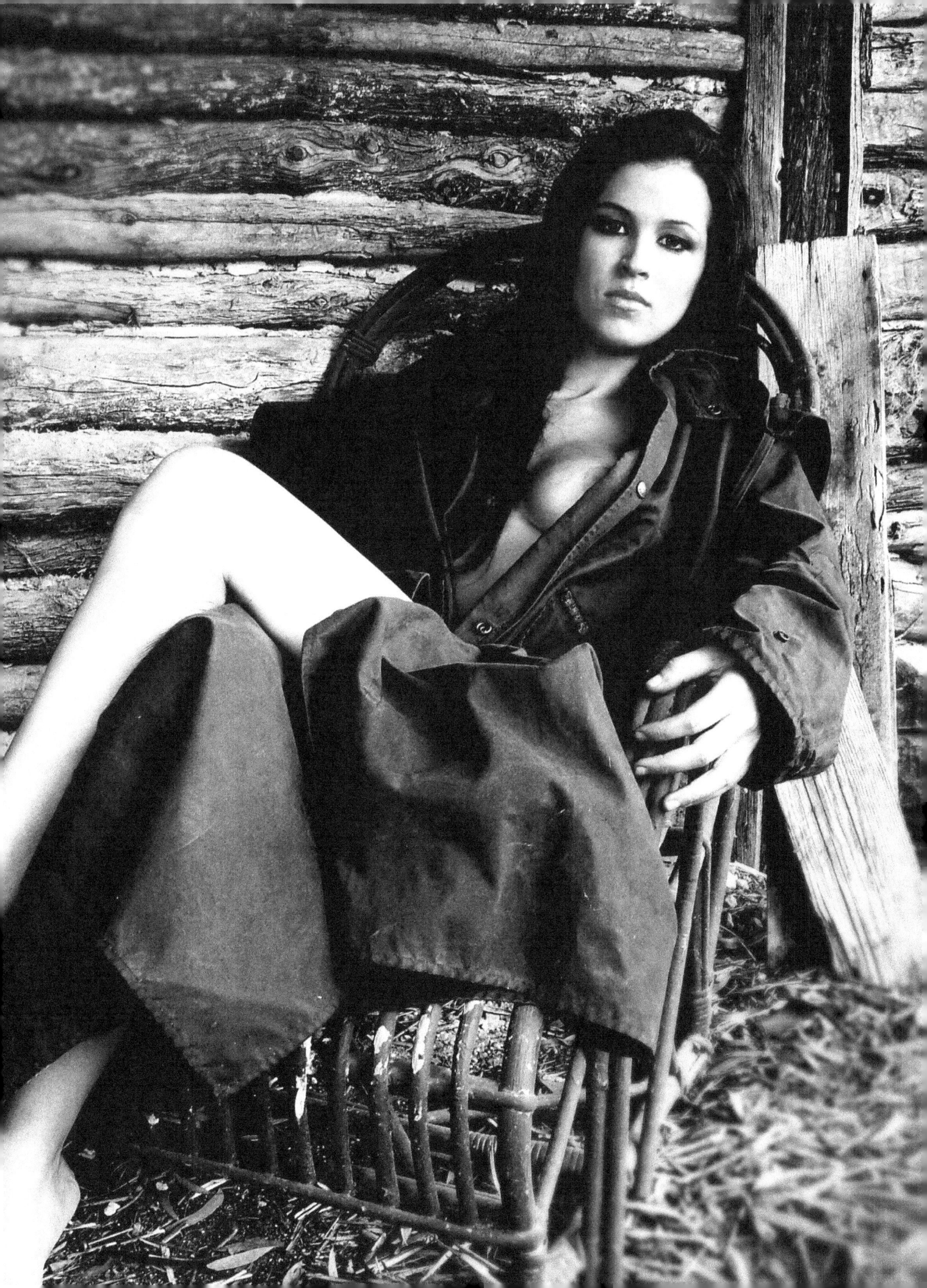

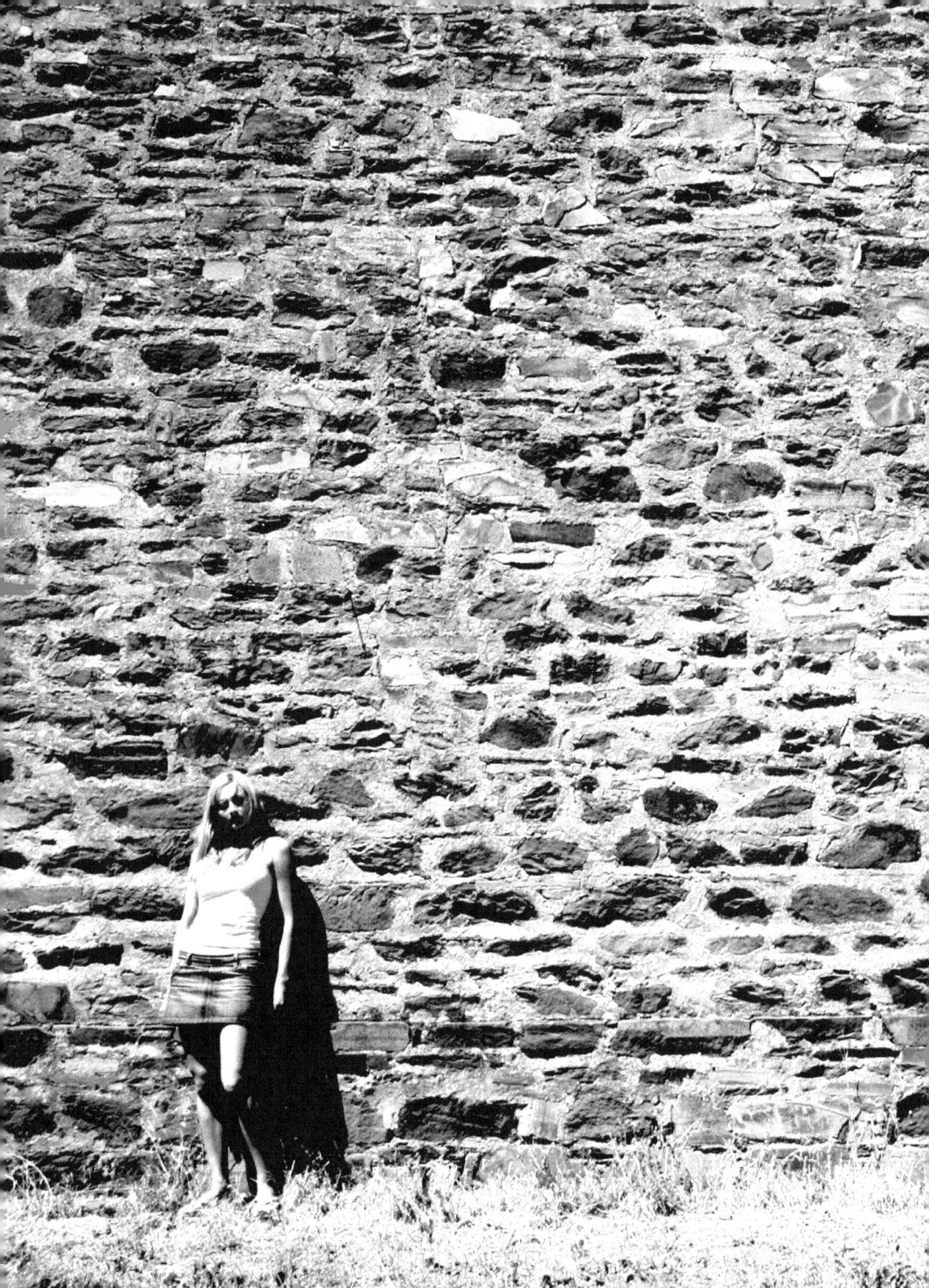

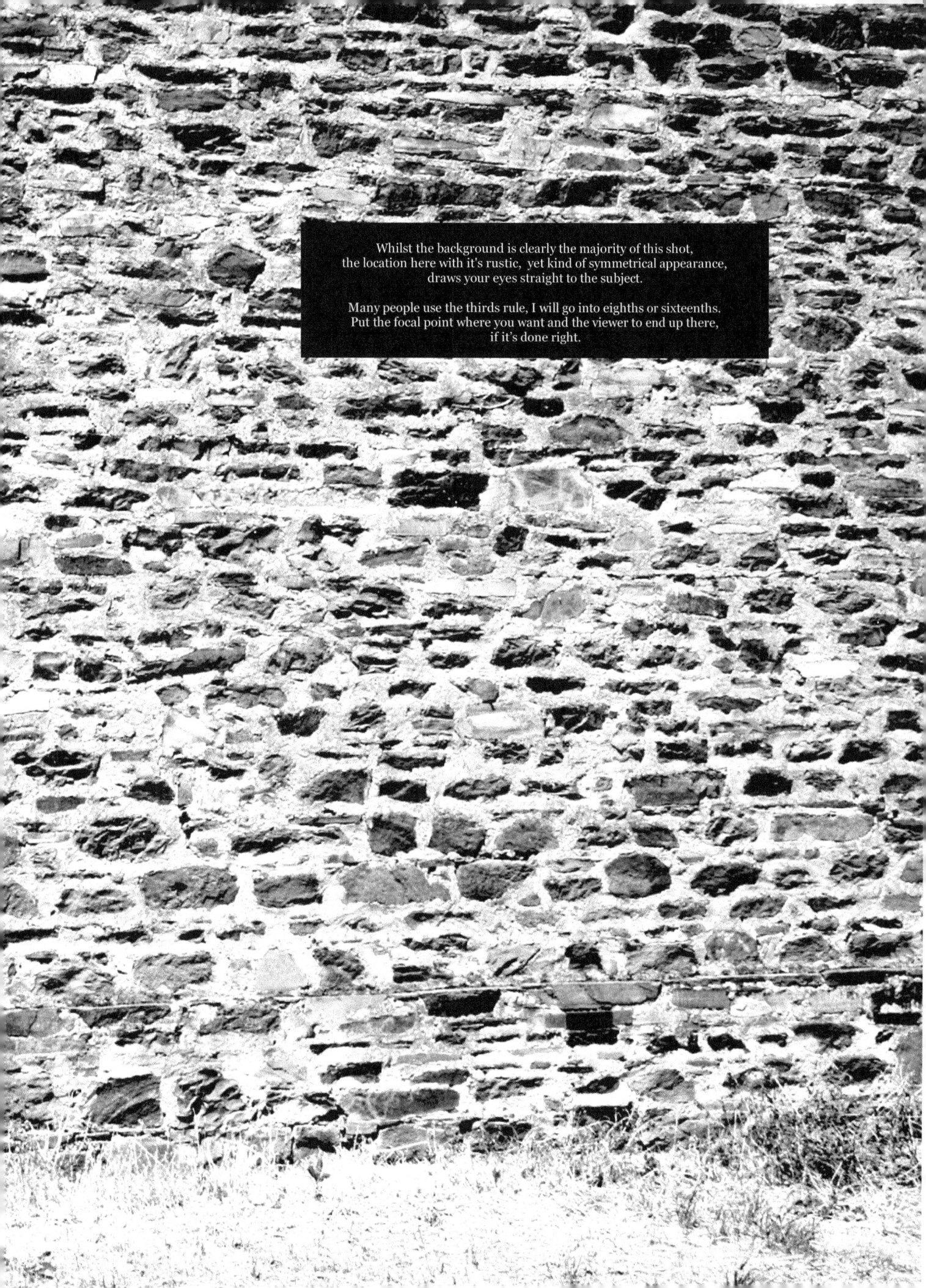

Whilst the background is clearly the majority of this shot,
the location here with it's rustic, yet kind of symmetrical appearance,
draws your eyes straight to the subject.

Many people use the thirds rule, I will go into eighths or sixteenths.
Put the focal point where you want and the viewer to end up there,
if it's done right.

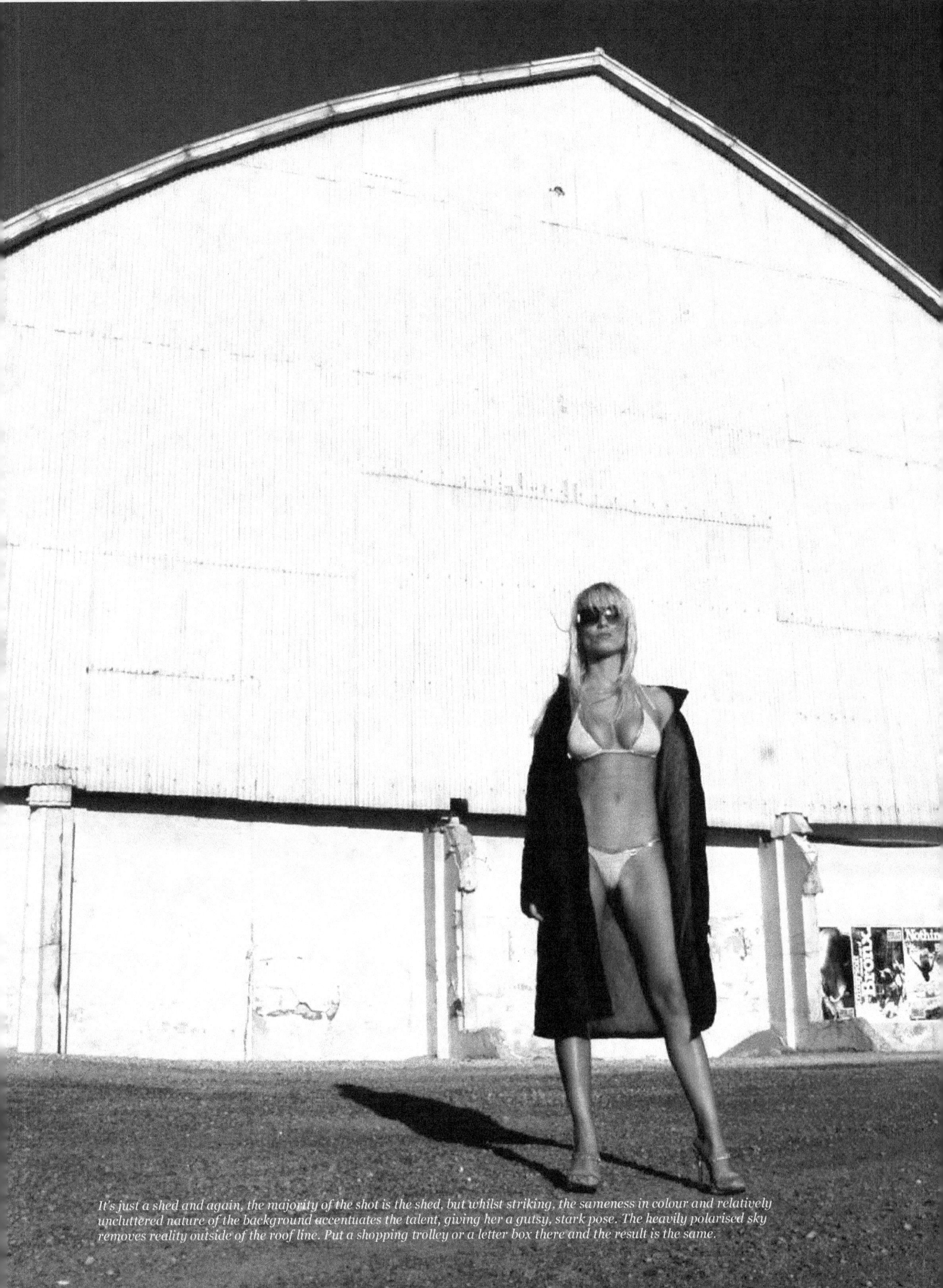

It's just a shed and again, the majority of the shot is the shed, but whilst striking, the sameness in colour and relatively uncluttered nature of the background accentuates the talent, giving her a gutsy, stark pose. The heavily polarised sky removes reality outside of the roof line. Put a shopping trolley or a letter box there and the result is the same.

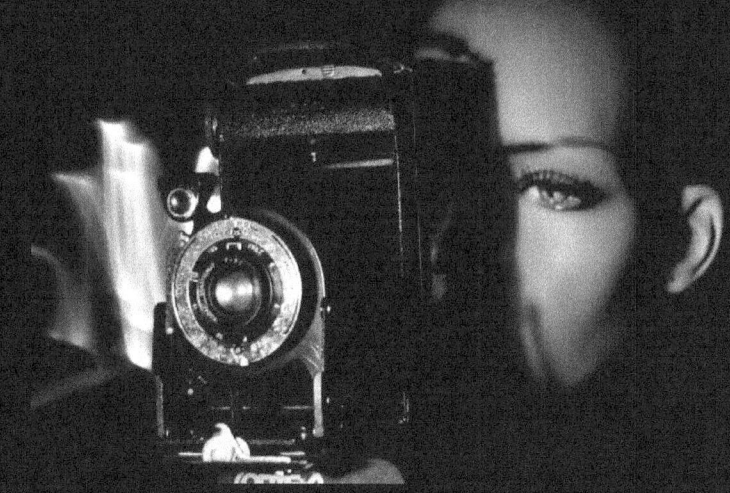

THE GEAR

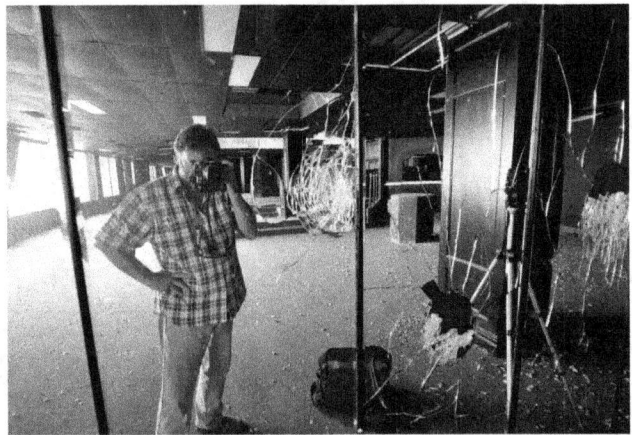

Always the big talking point, but rarely the reason!

Megapixel madness through to image manipulation! What a mess and still such a new and ever changing frontier. We believe and consistently produce pictures that the manufacturers tell us are consistently good and assure us we need their equipment and software, but often not what is true to our purpose or our creative selves.

Don't get me wrong, I am a new technology junkie and I have every gadget known to man. But I think that's why it saddens and frustrates me to see people "building" photos these days instead of capturing what they saw.

I'm no spun out purist, but I am also not a software compositor either. A lot of people these days are not really photographers, they are digital acquisition experts, graphic designers or image compositors that have perfected the electronic art of image manipulation or creation.

Do not confuse the two! Who are you?
If you are a computer whiz, that's great, but this little book may not be for you, as I have no interest in what you do.

Even the very soul of a photographer, good or bad is different! Photographers see the world a little differently, everything is a picture, everywhere you go and everything you do. It's almost an incurable disease.

Software! It's all PART of the process they tell us! But sadly, to a large extent, it's *become the actual* process for many!

As mentioned earlier, I do not manipulate any artistic images, except to push the contrast into a range that my camera fell a bit short of or perhaps to bury a dead pixel or filter shoot off. I intentionally do not use or own a copy of Photoshop.

Anyway, enough of the rambling's...

What cameras do I use?

I should qualify that, as what do I choose?

I will only talk digital, as 35mm is possibly not relevant in this book.

I have a number of cameras ranging from 1 mega pixel to 20+. Each camera delivers a different result. Just as a painter would choose brushes for a specific purpose, I choose cameras for a look. Sometimes a painter might put down their nice oils and brushes and pick up a leaf or a stick. It matters not, it's about the art and achieving what they set out to do.

Knowing what the shot will end up on, is extremely important to me, as different cameras have different methods of storage and when uncompressed, introduce different artifacting that can be part of the intended look.

The composition is also completely different knowing the end result. For example, if it's going to end up 4 inches square, the picture needs to be big, simple and uncluttered, whereas a 1 or 2 metre print is often more interesting if the image can be explored for a while.

One of my old faithful favourite cameras is an old Digital Fuji 7000. It's not even an SLR and its only about 4 megapixel, but it's gritty, highly meshed in grain, crazy contrasted, but often suits my style of figure shooting. Fuji do a good job with their glass (Lenses) and always have. It has a meshy grain when blown up and if put on canvas, works in really well with the texture, even up to a metre. It doesn't matter what the camera is, what matters, is what you have shot.

Remember who you are shooting for!
Not the industry presumably, but for you or your clients.

I will pick this old camera up often in highly textured backgrounds. I bought it's subsequent replacements, but was not impressed and took them back. Seems manufacturers don't always build on what they have started. Don't be fooled, every model of camera is different. Same brand, different model and each will have different characteristics and glass (lenses) than the last model!

I loved this camera so much I bought 6 (Just in case)
Old fashioned? Maybe... but go tell that to a musician when he picks up that old guitar he's been carrying around the world for 40 years or the sculpture that doesn't want his or her statues machine pressed.

It's not about the technology, It's all about a love of the art. The process and the result. When it becomes about the technology, it just became about money!

I use Nikon's a lot also, with a number of bodies and numerous lenses. Nikon tends to under expose everything a bit in my opinion, but isn't that new way?

Shoot RAW, underexpose and then find it all in post, so that you have everything covered?

Not my way, I'm afraid ...

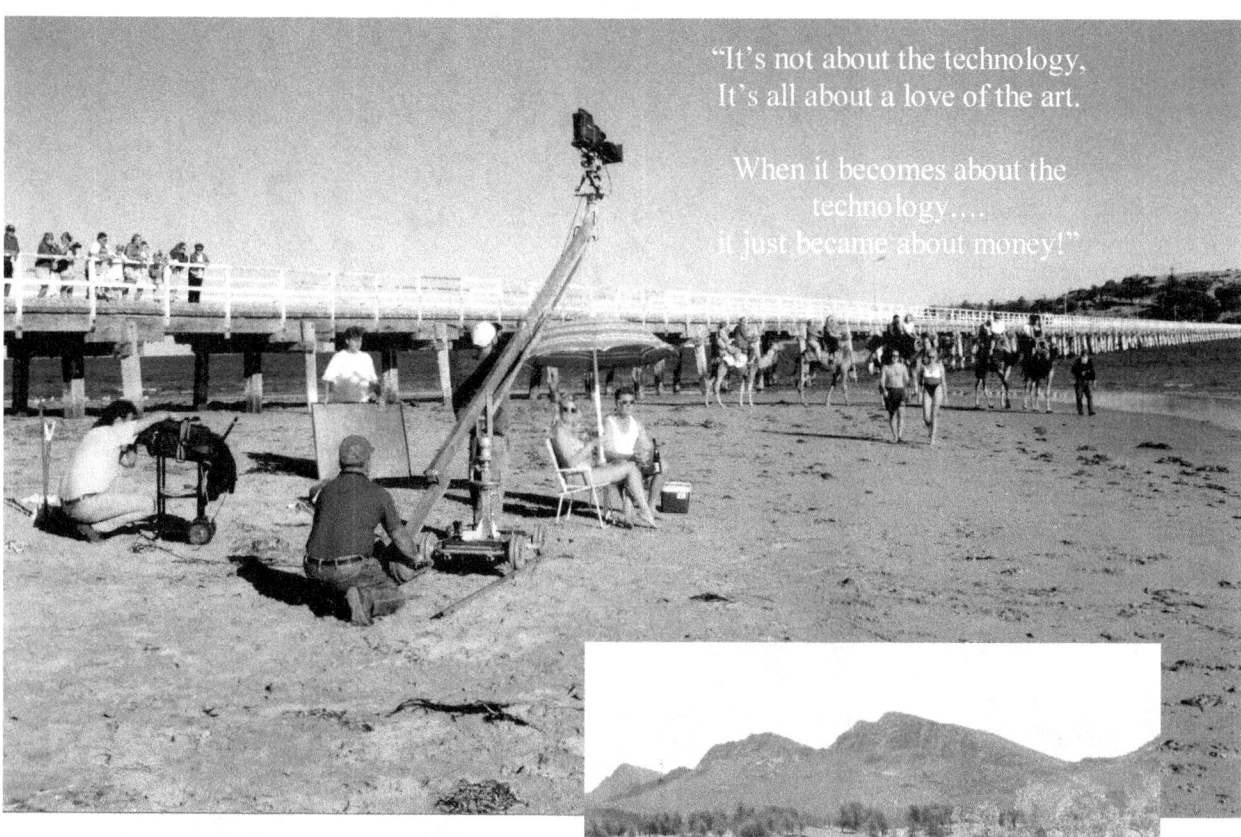

"It's not about the technology,
It's all about a love of the art.

When it becomes about the
technology....
it just became about money!"

Having come from an industry with so much equipment, stills is so much more liberating and when the shot is on, it's on!

Do what you need to! Yes, I got caught with my new tripod and Chinese work boots!

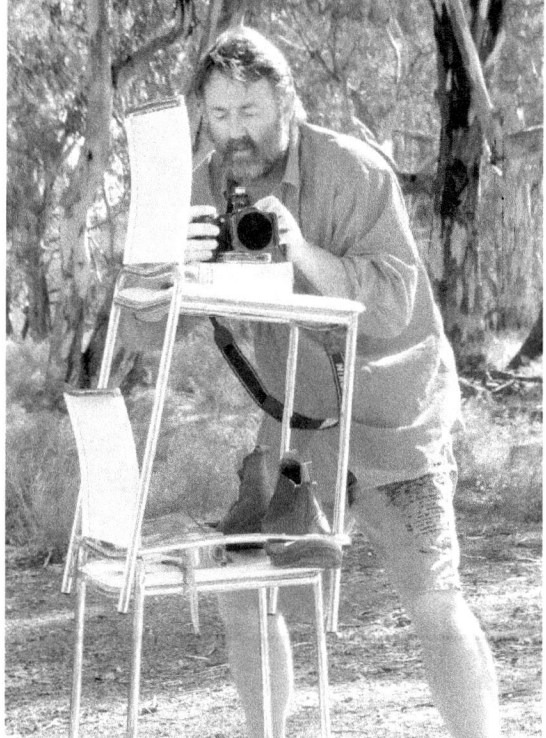

I still use a lot of filters and make the sensors work hard in the camera, I pretty much leave the polariser on everywhere (often even indoors), so that it acts like an ND filter, making the camera work that bit harder and open up, giving less depth of field and saturated colours.

To me, filters are paramount on the day, allowing you to come back with what you intended and forcing the camera to work harder or even a little less hard in many situations.

Sure you can add a grad in software, but it still won't fix convergence issues accurately on the file.

Generally I carry a few reflectors and a bit of portable lighting. Often just ordinary halogens or leds with filter gels. You can use flood lights, it really doesn't matter.

There's lots of ways to achieve great results.

Sadly, people will stand and argue with us that this shot is not real and that it was done in photo shop!

We had to shoot a second shot, to prove to our clients that the model was there and so was the frame!

As a photoshop piece, this print is worth about $10, as a creative piece of fine art, it sells for around $1200

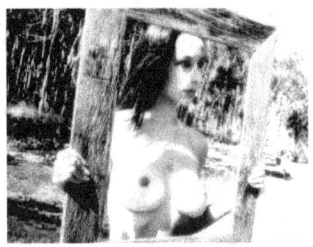

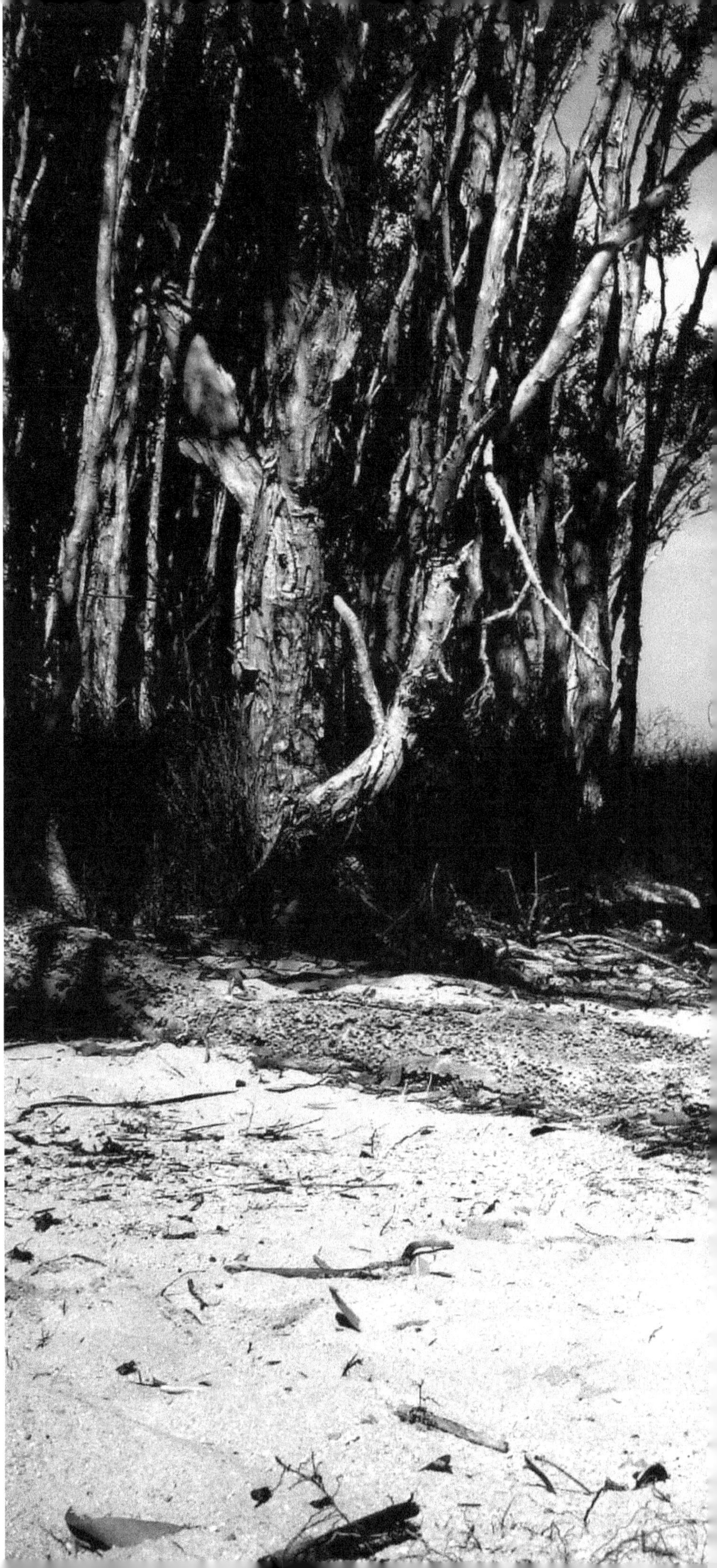

Shot title "Framed"
Series " Sunshine"
Location: Noosa, Australia

*This is a real frame
with real glass
on a real beach
and a real sky.*

No software required

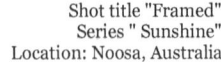

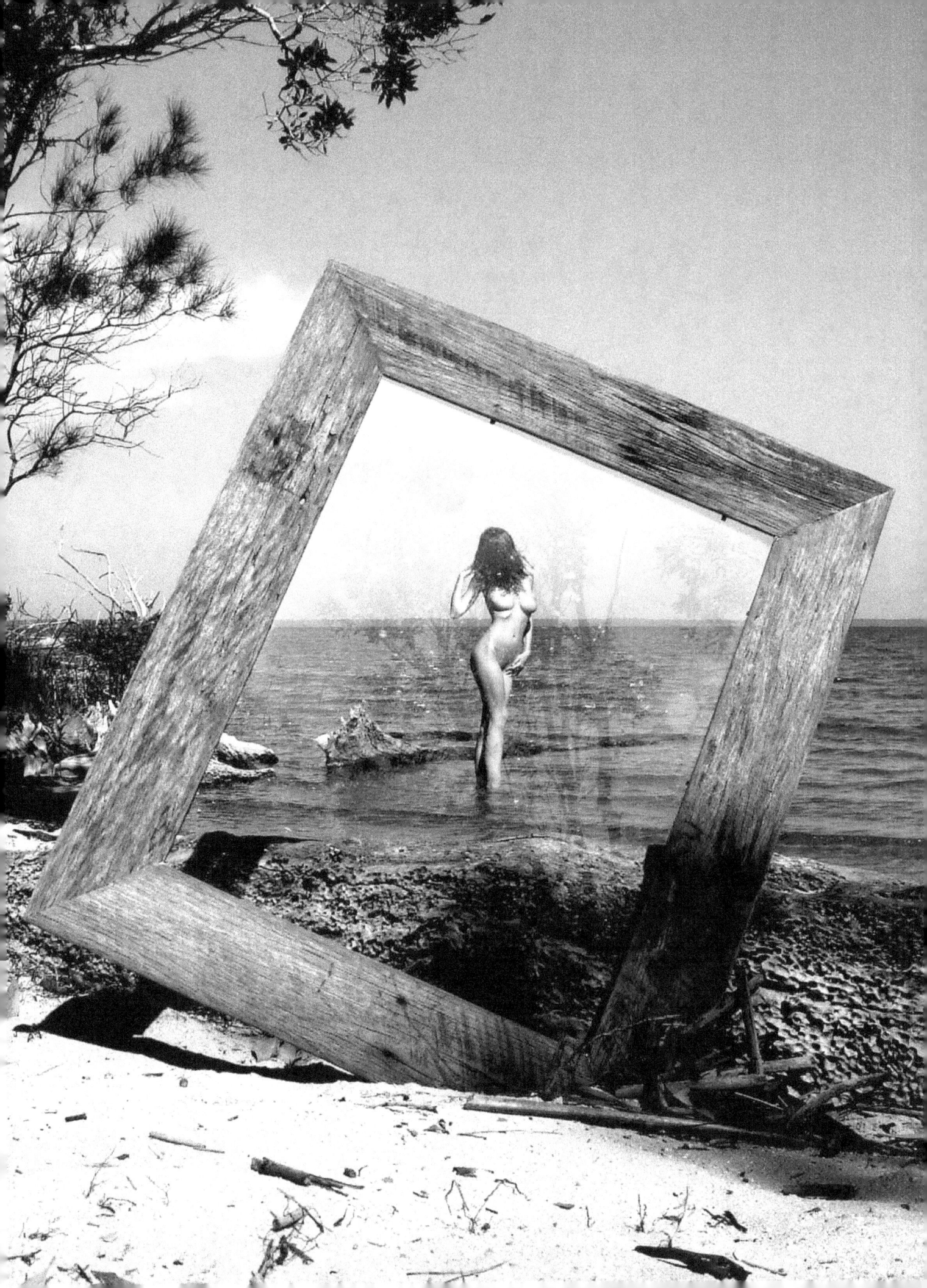

"It doesn't matter what your camera is...

what matters,

is what you have shot"

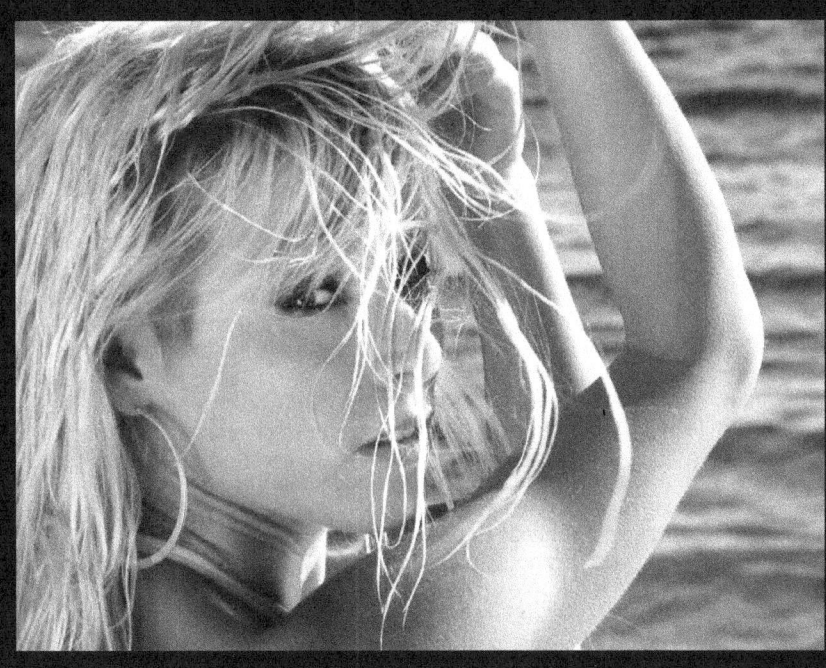

THE LOOK
& SELECTING TALENT

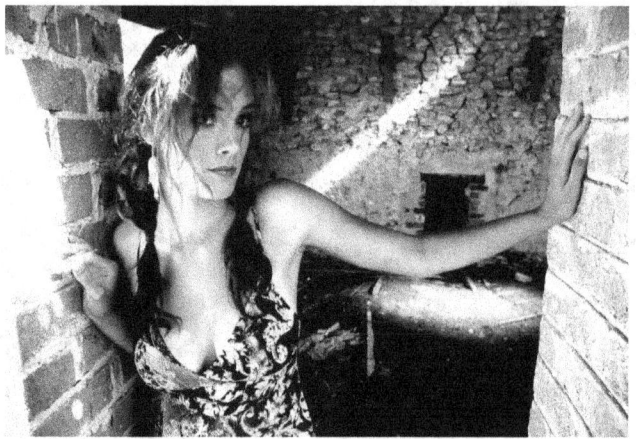

Models! What a mine field....

Many, (the majority, I think) just want to be glamour queens or magazine covers. Often the models that have the most abundance of beauty, are rarely up for the job and will let you down, time and time again. It's quite sad when you work with many of them and hear what they think has been sold to them as a twisted and false reality.

So don't make it worse by promising them the world and then not delivering. Selecting and working with models, nude or not, can be a great experience, but needs to be approached professionally and with consideration. Not just for you, but as a legacy and courtesy to the whole industry.

Most artistic models do it for their own reasons, be it artistic, nature based, universal freedom, fleeting beauty, or maybe self exploration and some ... just plain money. So don't ruin it for anyone. Why are you doing it?

Advertise your casting call realistically and do the right thing by them, yourself and the industry. The artistic ones will love you for it and sign on to be filmed by you forever!

Beauty can be but a fleeting moment for many and some people like to document or immortalise that part of their life and hold it sacred for ever. Honour and flatter the trust they place in you.

OK, so here comes part two of my "old school" opinions...

Software and portraiture!
If you don't want to shoot real people, why do it?
Go and shoot a mannequin!

I have just completed a series, photographing mannequins which look eerily real.... even though they weren't... what I shot *was* real!....even though clearly they weren't alive.

So why photograph a real person and turn them into a fake person .. A mannequin?

How will you or your models get any satisfaction from people saying, look! another *photoshopped picture that looks like a* girl or *computer model*! What a brilliant piece of software art! Most likely, you will hear "wow! She doesn't look that good" or "that looks nothing like her!"

So what have you achieved for either of you?

It's insulting that people want to constantly change a real persons (or models) look, I'm surprised the public allow it to happen. I guess it's the software manufacturers market research telling them that we just love virtual perfection and that we all want to look that good !

The camera is a *real* medium designed to capture real pictures and images. So why would you want to capture anything else for your own artistic shoots? An artist wouldn't paint a picture and then let someone modify it on a computer, what an insult!

Nor would a sculptor allow someone to throw a coat of paint on their work, paint in an eye or move an arm. If you are creating art, it is what it is. Good or bad. No wonder, the world no longer celebrates or pays much for photography, it's oversaturated and there's too many lies.

So assuming you are looking to create some art, your art, you need models that are this way inclined also.

Given you are are also presumably looking to create something that's a bit different, it will mean they need to be prepared to do something a bit different. Endure the cold, heat, dust, rain, walk a long way to the location, wait a long time for the right light, suffer adhoc make up facilities, etc

The moment they complain or get upset, your creativity will begin to dampen fast! Then when they finally see your creative genius in print, some will be disappointed as they expected more "Glam'" shots!

Finding the right models is essential. Just because a model is willing to disrobe for "art", is not a reason to film them.

Your models not a mannequin so don't expect them to look like one and don't turn them into a software mannequin

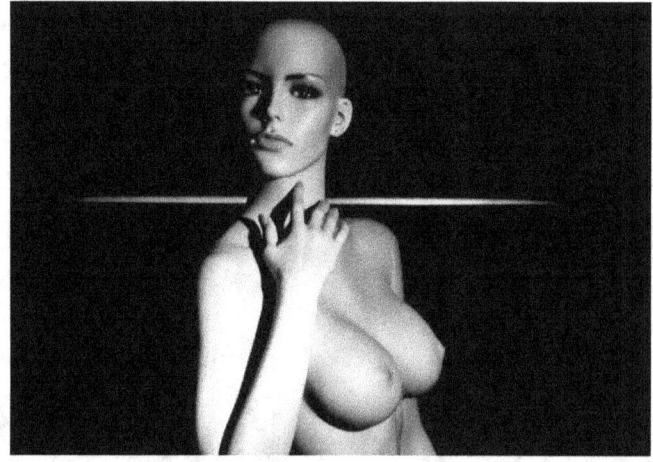

*Shadows can be a
great masquerade
or place of mystery
for the shot and
for the shy.*

*Sometimes
letting them see
what you are
getting in camera,
will help them relax.*

*I love seeing how
many different looks
I can get out of the
one model*

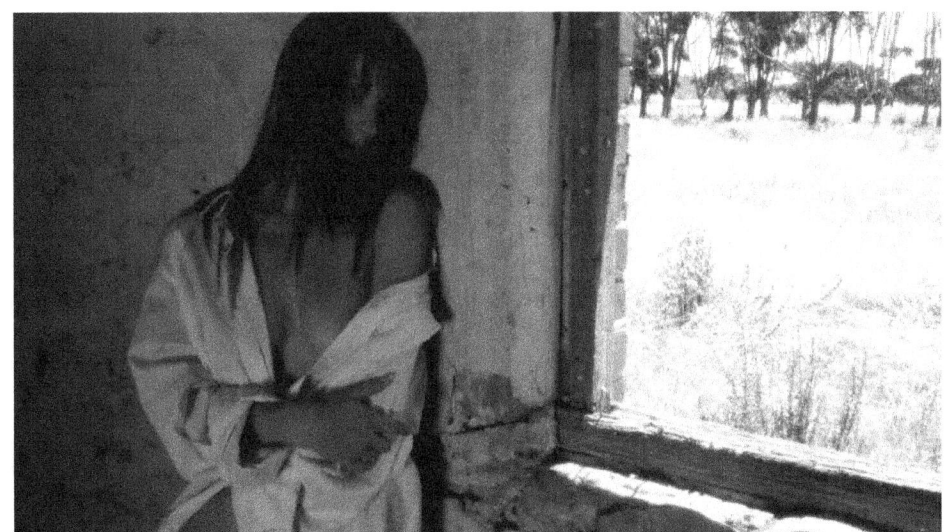

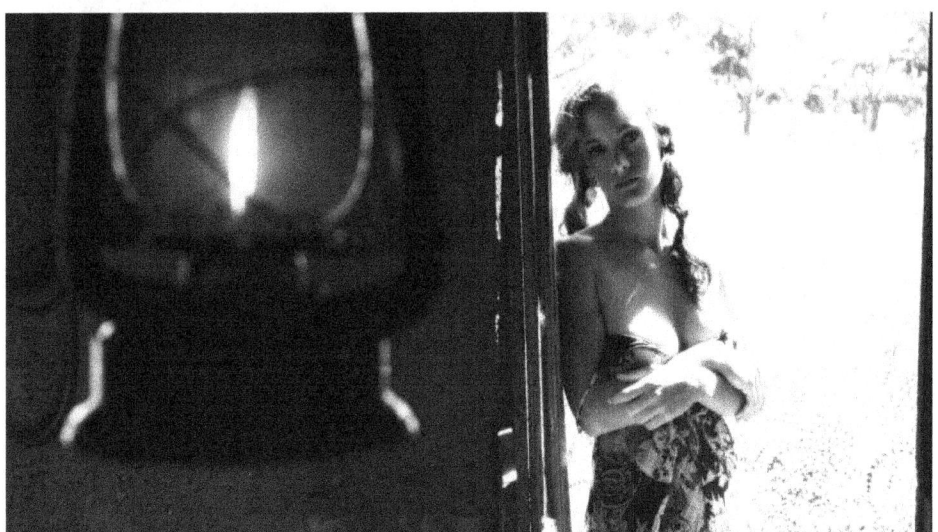

*When a model comments
that it doesn't even
look like them,
I love it"*

*Given they have not
been modified
in anyway...*

*I have achieved,
as it is them,
all them!*

*Any we all have a few
personalities within*

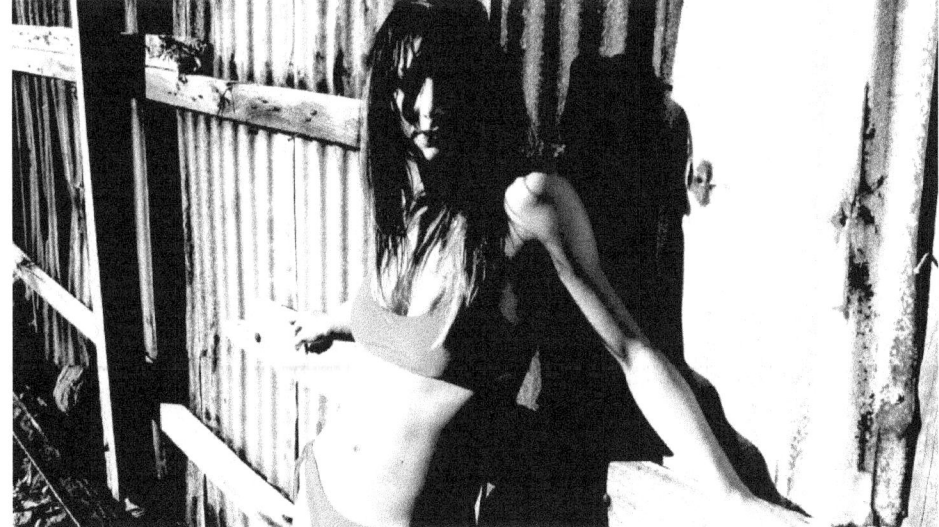

You need someone that fits your vision for the shoot. Their look, make up, attitude and stamina.

So you have found the perfect model and they arrive on set! Don't frighten them, (or yourself) when you get onto location! Don't jump straight into the "get your gear off" routine, it's uncomfortable and often intimidating even for experienced nude models.

If it's your first time with this model, and you have never filmed them before, maybe work them with your camera for a while first. Photograph them intimately clothed, to discover their look and make them work with the camera.

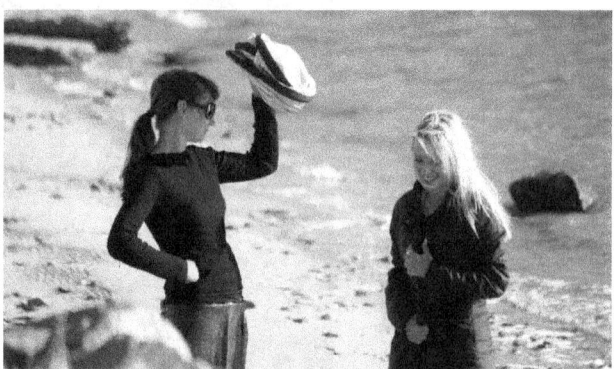

Photograph their face close up and see what they do with their eyes, are they shy? Photograph their features that you like and hate. Maybe a big forehead, or big ears, play around and see what their look is through your camera.

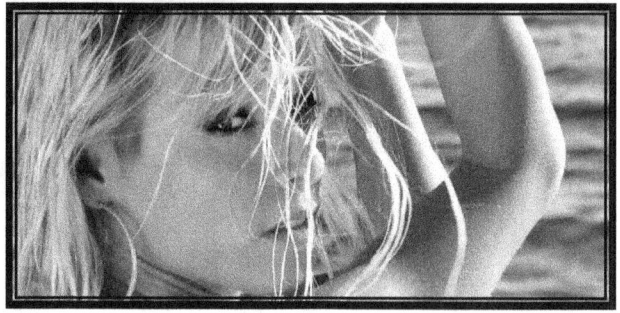

See what lens suits them! In makes a HUGE difference! Wide, close, medium, high or low .

Work out your models "on camera" features, what are they? Hair, eyes, back, breasts, whatever... work with them and use what they have, not what you want.

You will quickly see how the day is going to unfold, once you begin this process. Then sit back and take a look at what you do and don't like about their look. Work out a way to disguise the things you don't like and be aware of them. Emphasize the features you do like and work with them.

Above: Keep your models comfortable while you are fiddling around.

The sun, wind or the cold will affect all of you and your final pictures. It will also change the models experience and impact on future work.

If they turn out to be a bit shy, let them be shy and work with it, making it a feature of your images. If they are extroverted or a poser, so be it and become more flamboyant. But know your own limitations, strengths and weaknesses.

We aren't all good at everything.
My strength is composition and location emphasis.

As a rule, I like textures and I like gutsy, gritty, warts and all, you may like it warm and fuzzy. Just don't do it to the software manufacturers specified colour, softness and airbrushing. Do it to your liking.

How do you find your models?

I advertised the first time for people with an artistic interest and added "Glamour models need not apply".

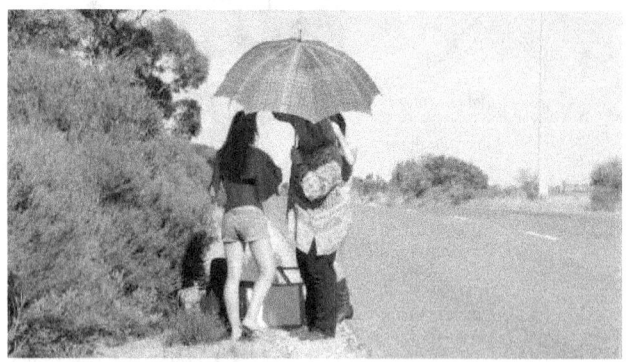

...After about 6 shoots, I seemed to get a bit of a following and they started to find me.

I currently have about 6 - 8 applications per week from models that want me to photograph them or have an artistic portfolio shot, artistic element added to their existing portfolios or pose for our galleries.

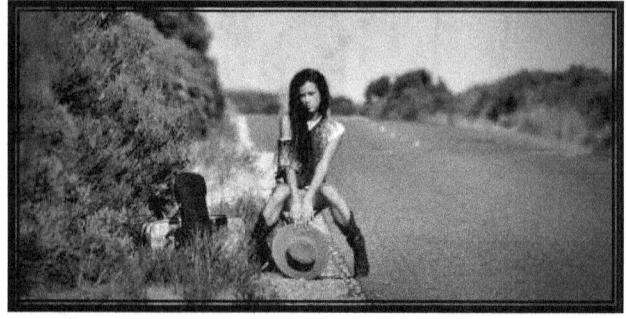

Many even pay *me* quite well, if I don't want to photograph them! I like using amateur models when I can for artistic shoots, as I think they are more fun and offer a more genuine creative desire to achieve with less baggage.

I will often take the models outside the front of the gallery before we even start or at the interview and play around with some shots to see what I get.

That way I already know their look prior to shooting.

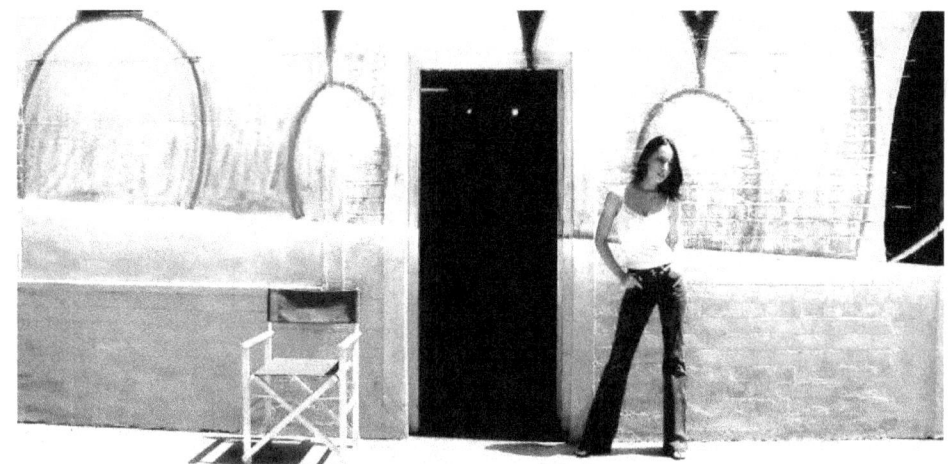

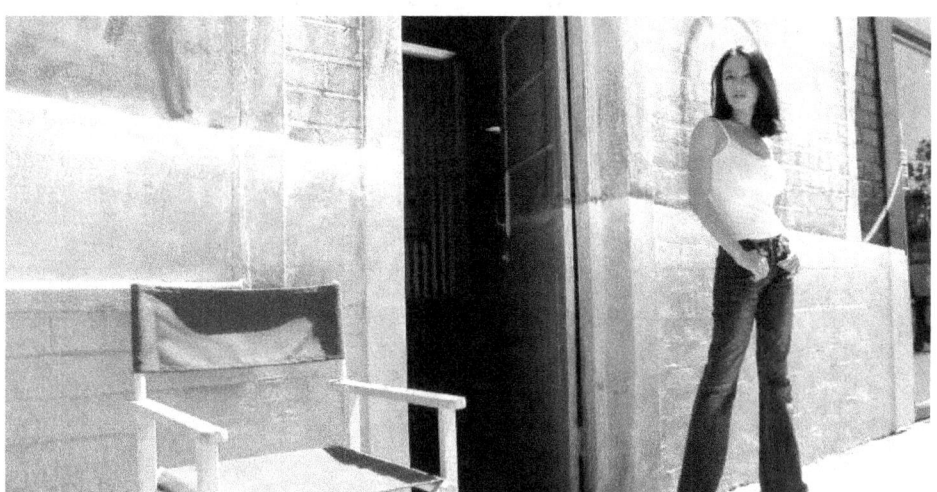

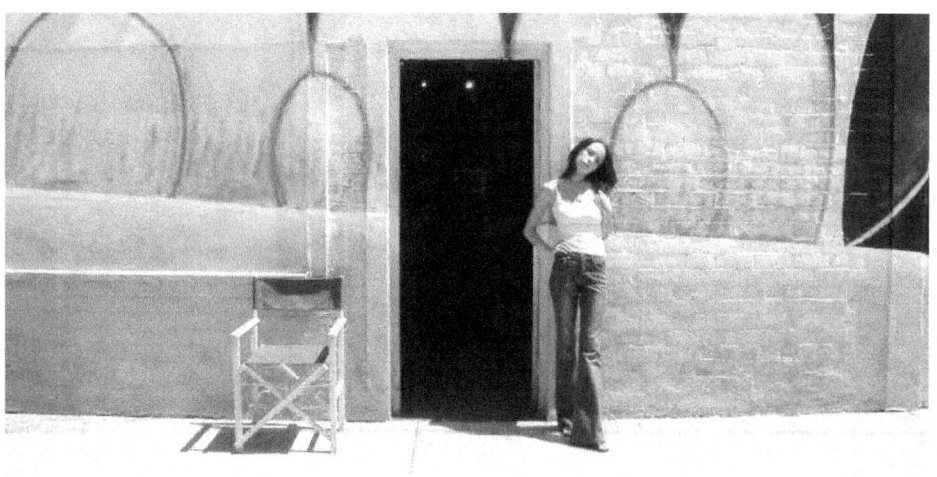

"I like using amateur models when I can for artistic shoots, as I think they are more fun and offer a more genuine creative desire to achieve"

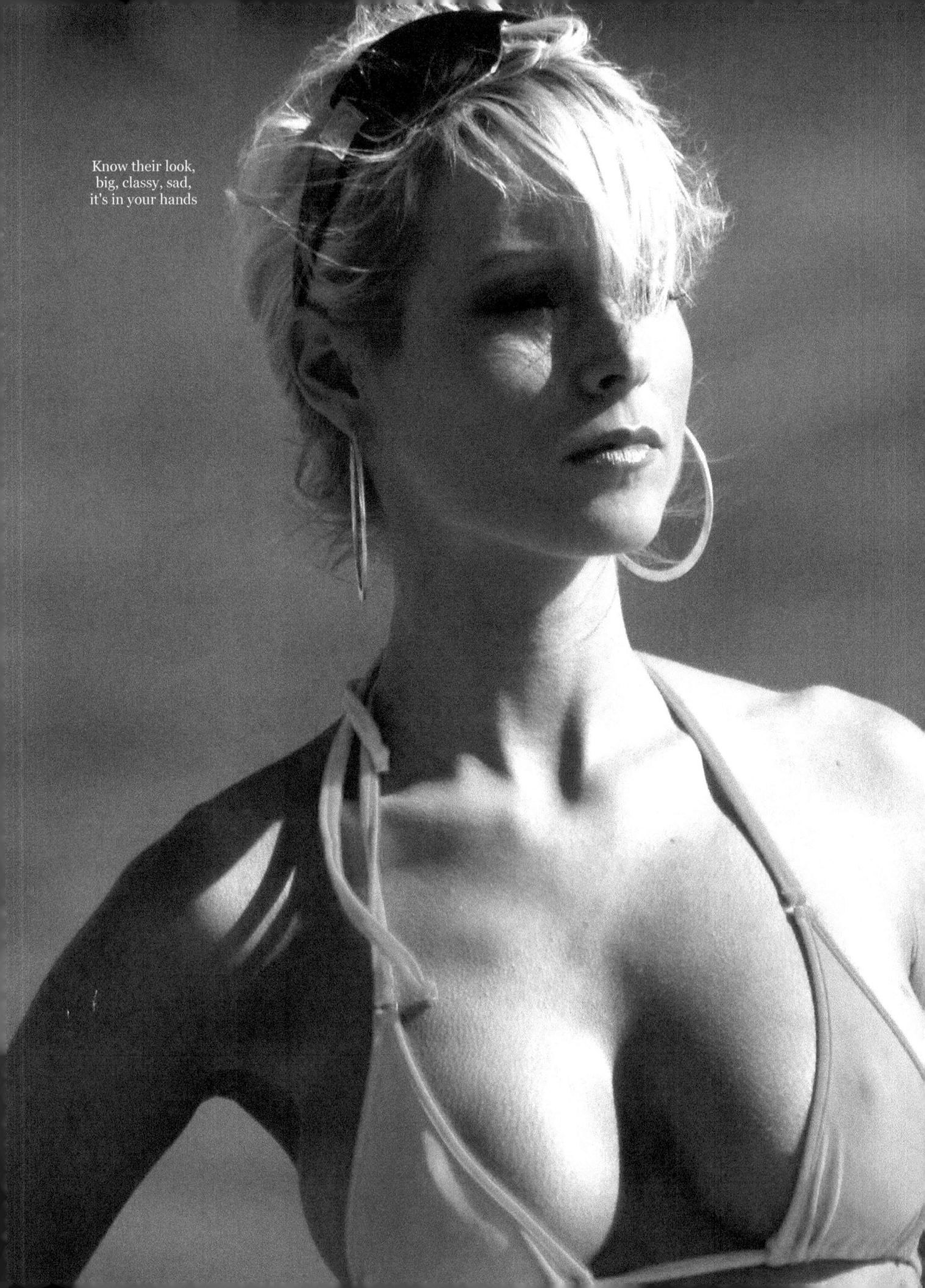

Know their look,
big, classy, sad,
it's in your hands

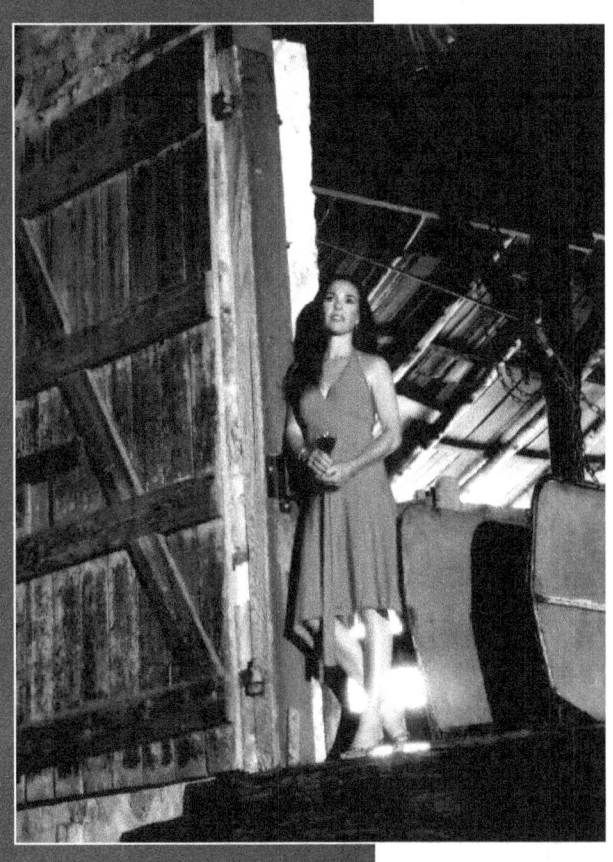

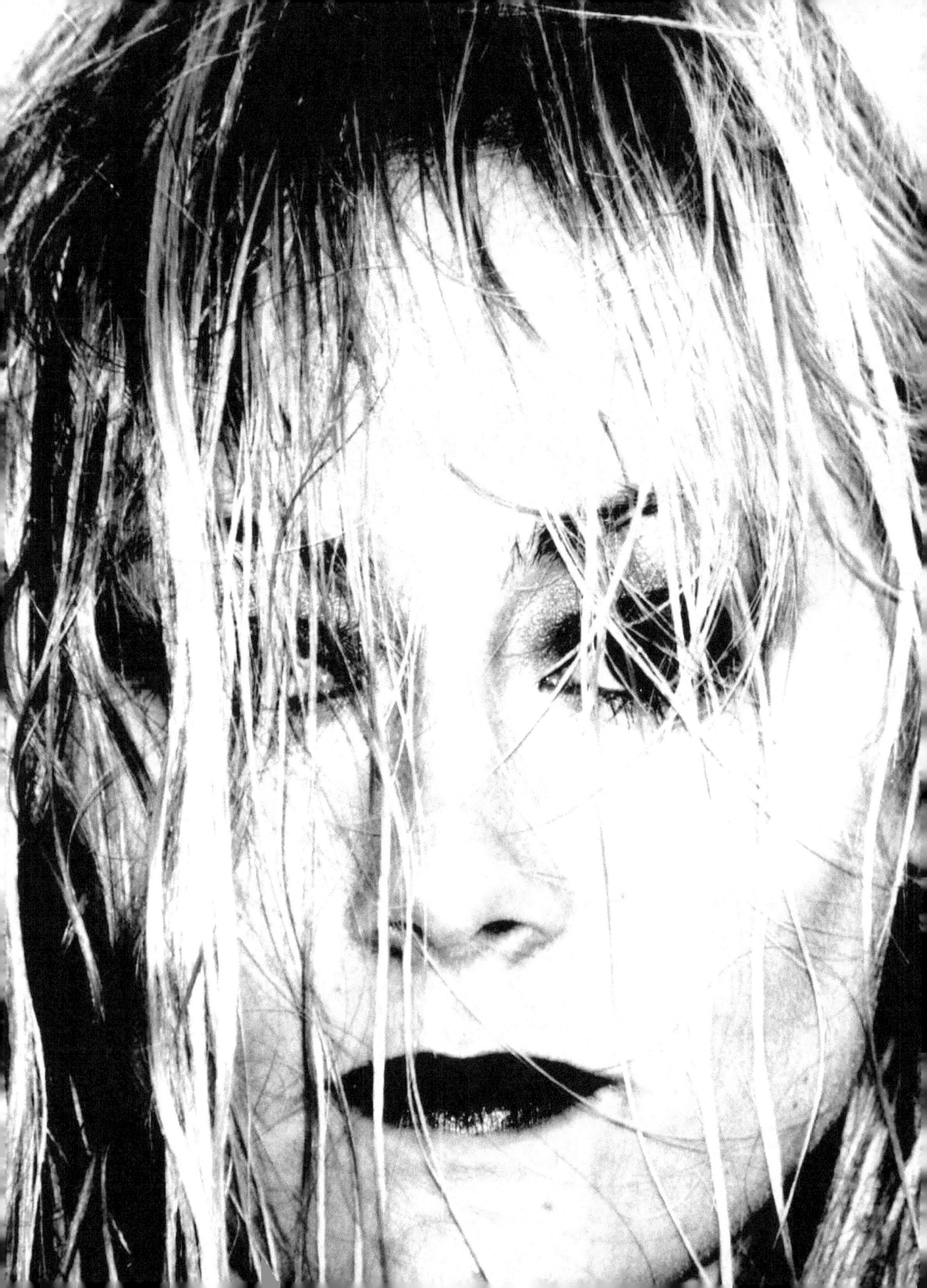

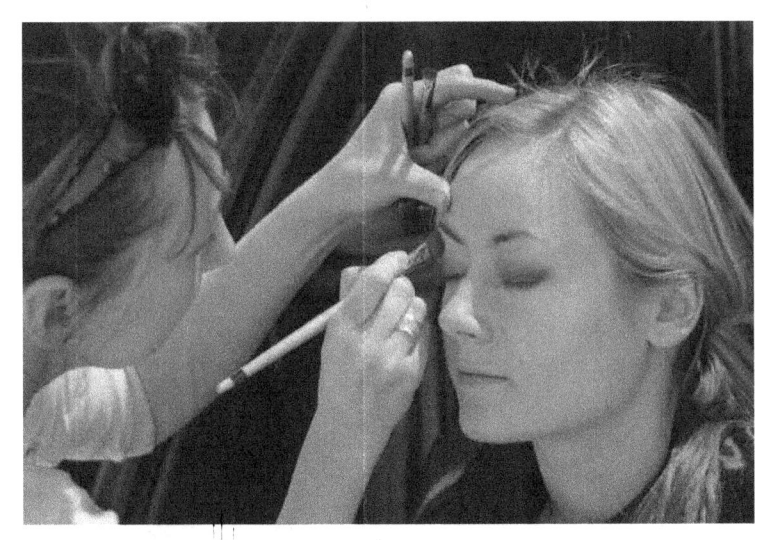

Whilst make up will help, the main transformation is in your camera.

Over exposed and a squirter bottle is all it took to change this look dramatically.

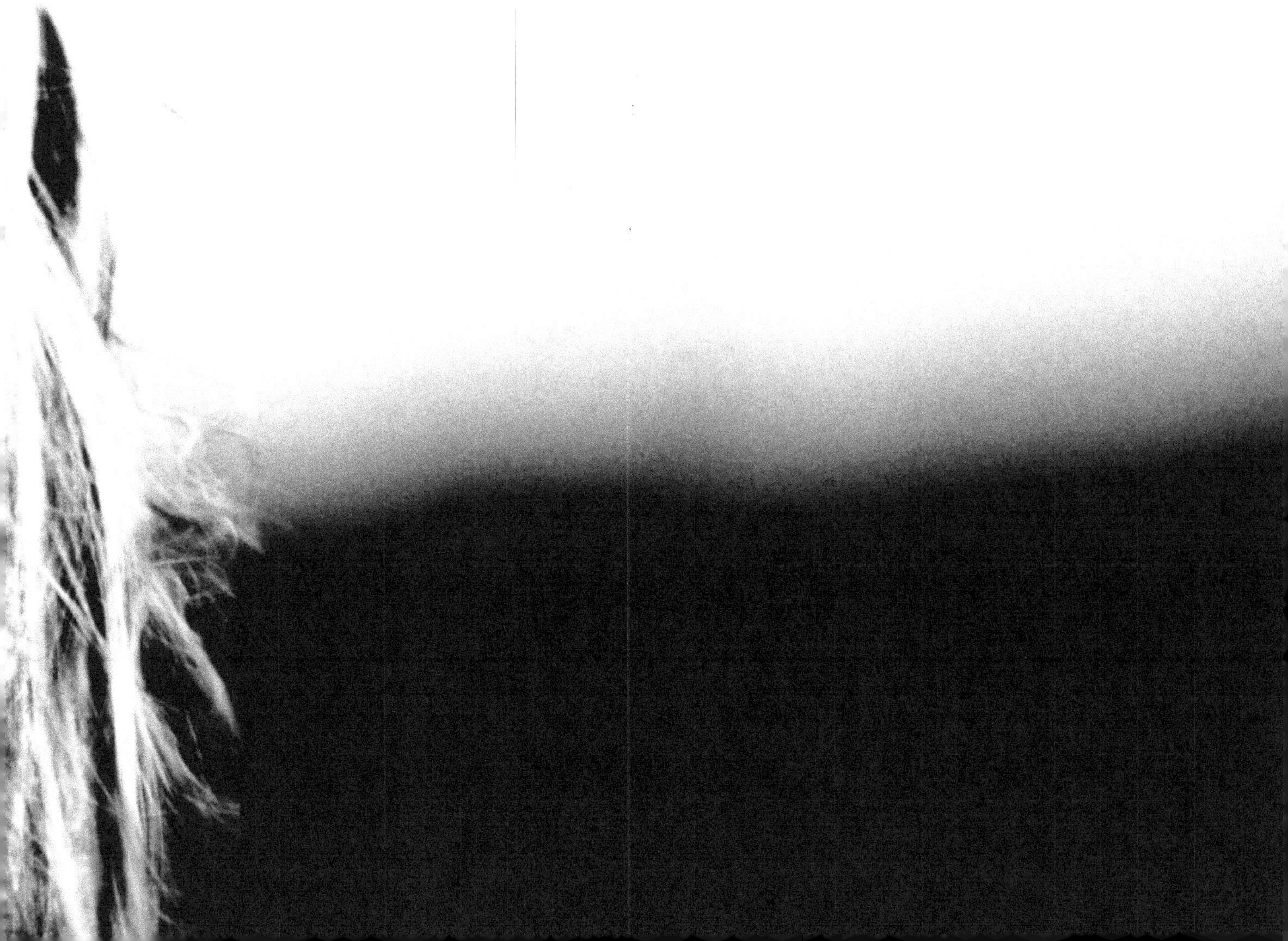

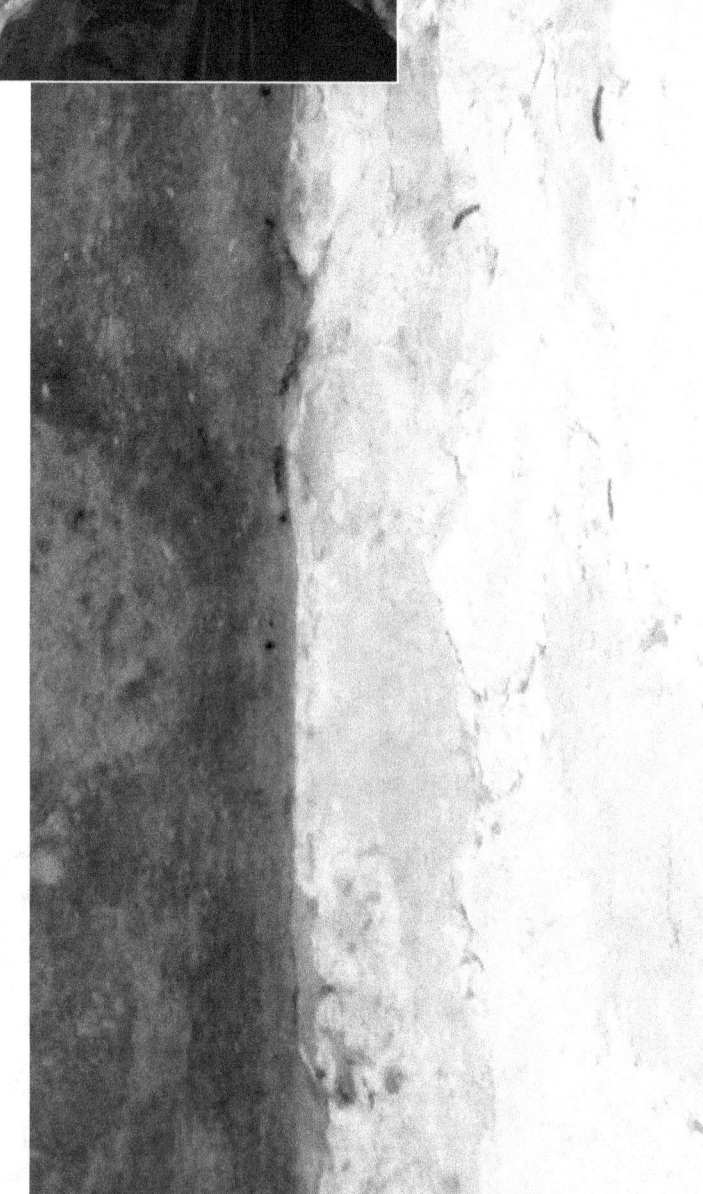

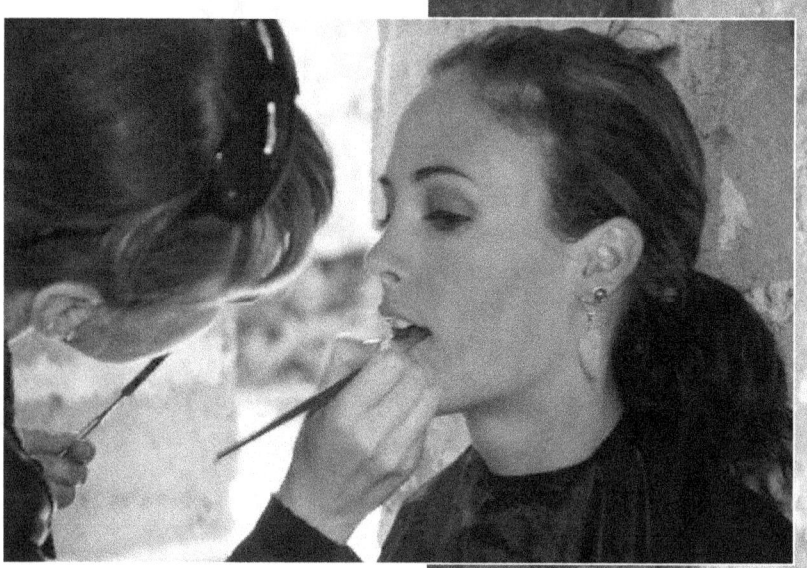

Normal people.

That's what I like!

They are untrained and
have no expectations
and often just love the
creative fun of it.

And it shows*!*

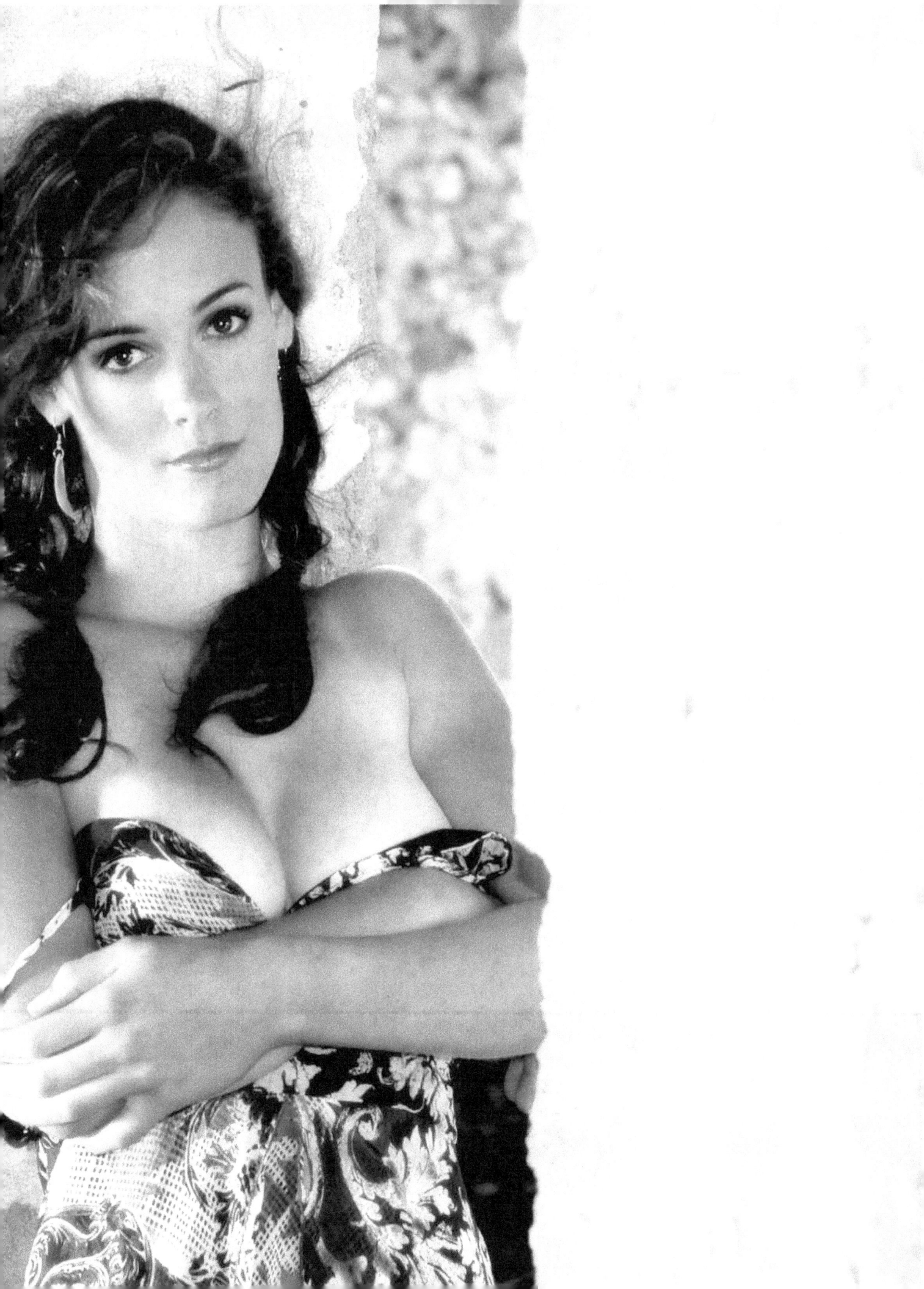

Even when doing a portrait, why not try something a little different?

Try lots of different lenses and looks for your models.

Talk to them and you will get ideas for who they are and what will suit them.

Their level of comfort will make your life easier and your pictures better

Sometimes they will surprise you with what they would like to shoot!

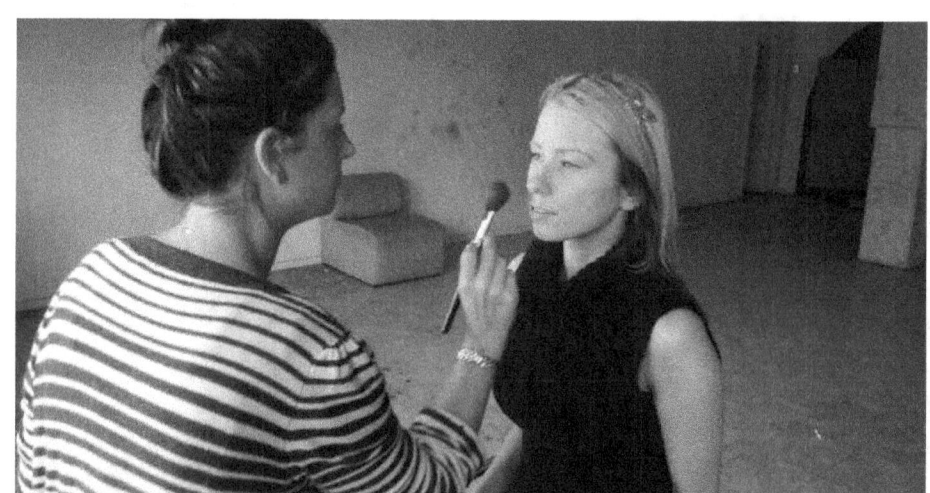

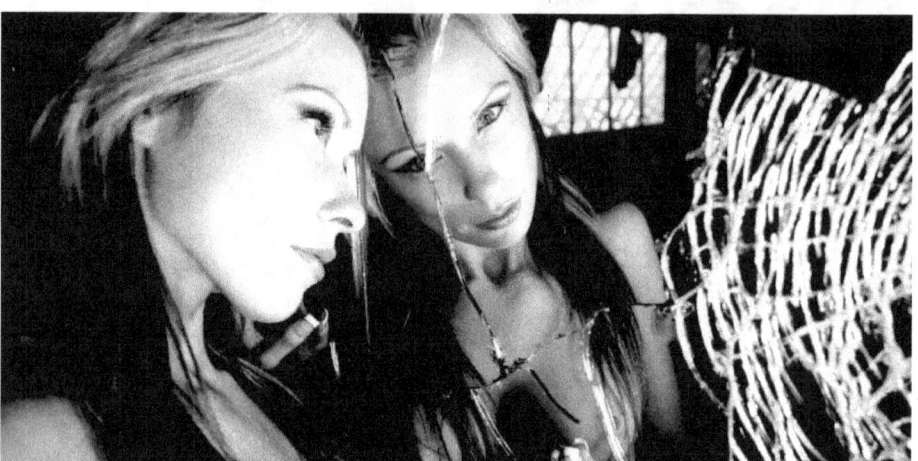

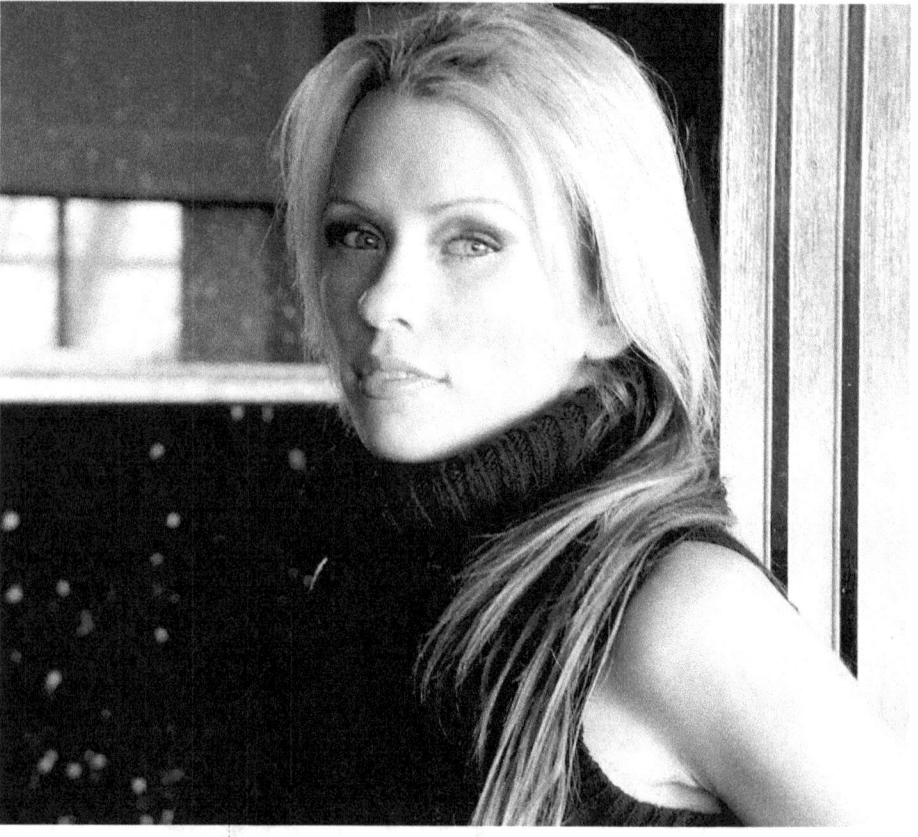

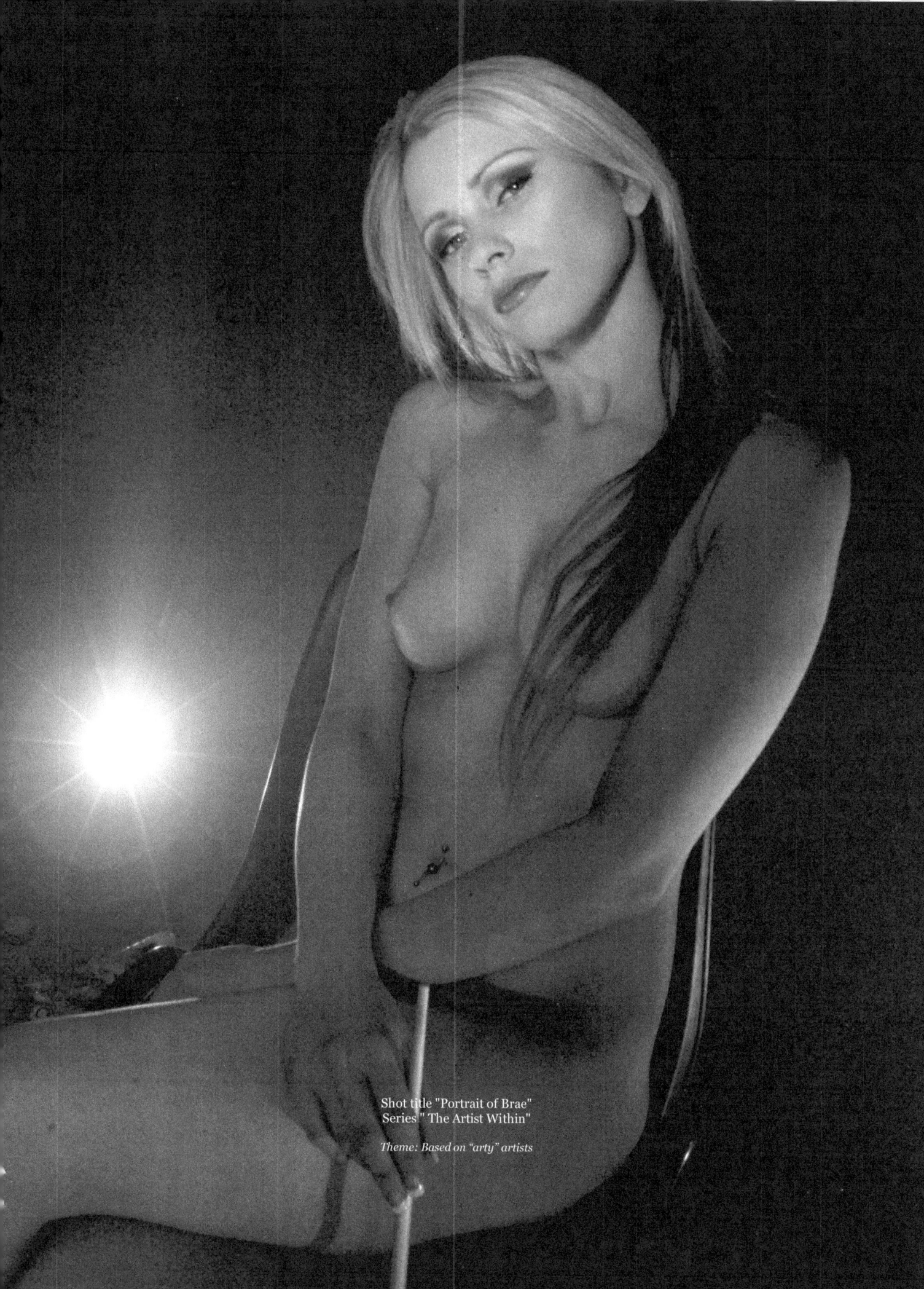

Shot title "Portrait of Brae"
Series " The Artist Within"

Theme: Based on "arty" artists

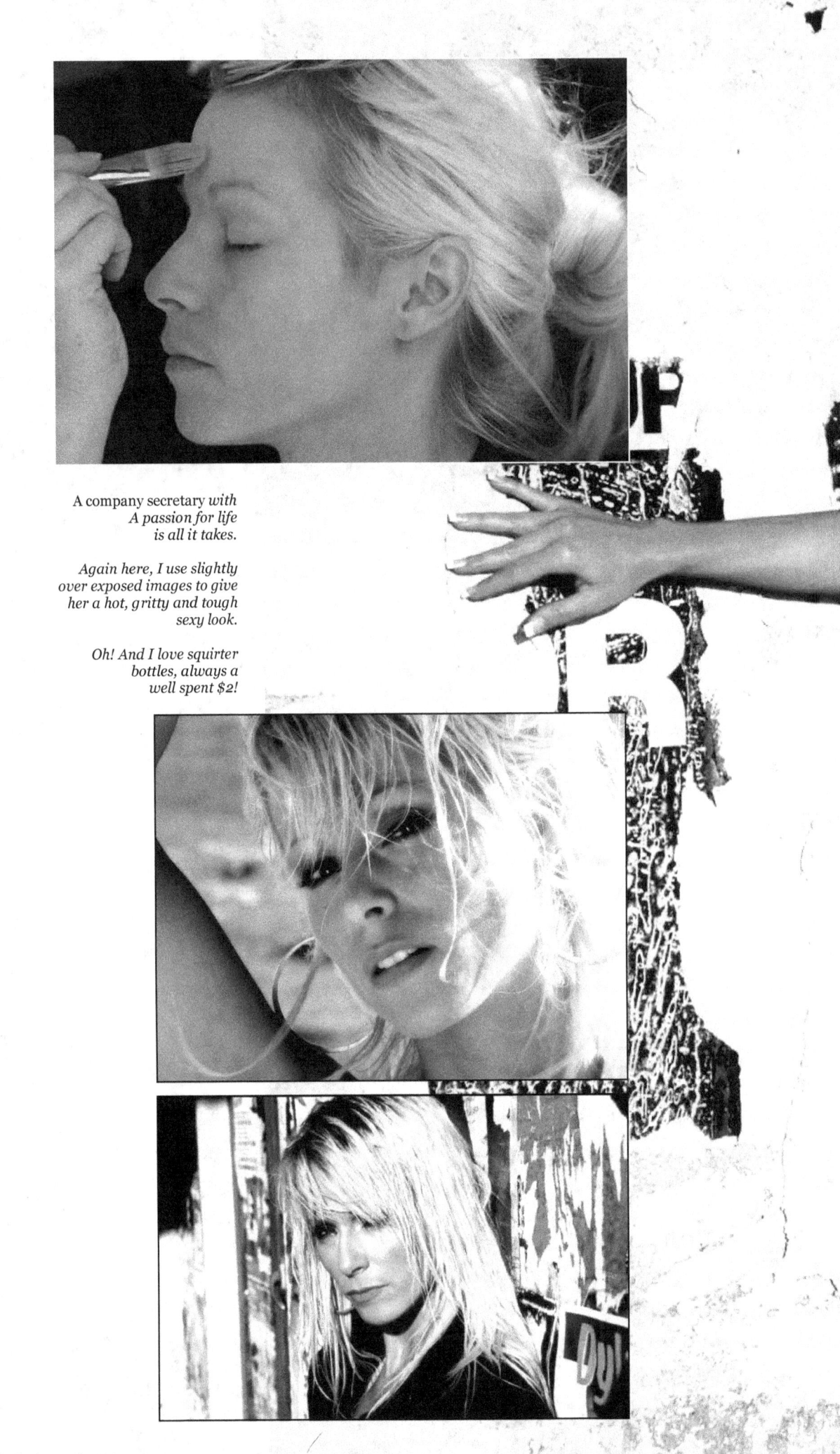

A company secretary *with
A passion for life
is all it takes.*

*Again here, I use slightly
over exposed images to give
her a hot, gritty and tough
sexy look.*

*Oh! And I love squirter
bottles, always a
well spent $2!*

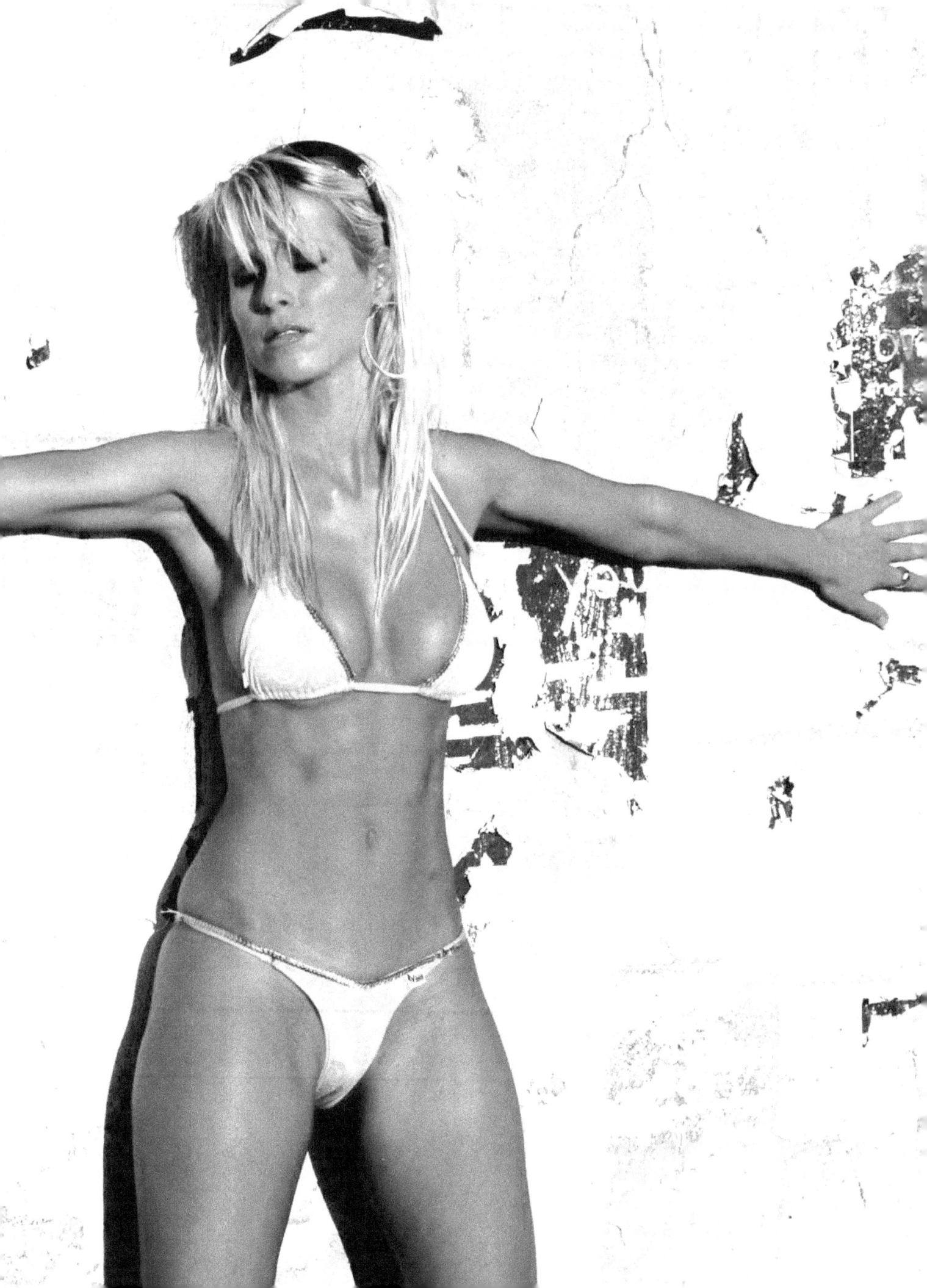

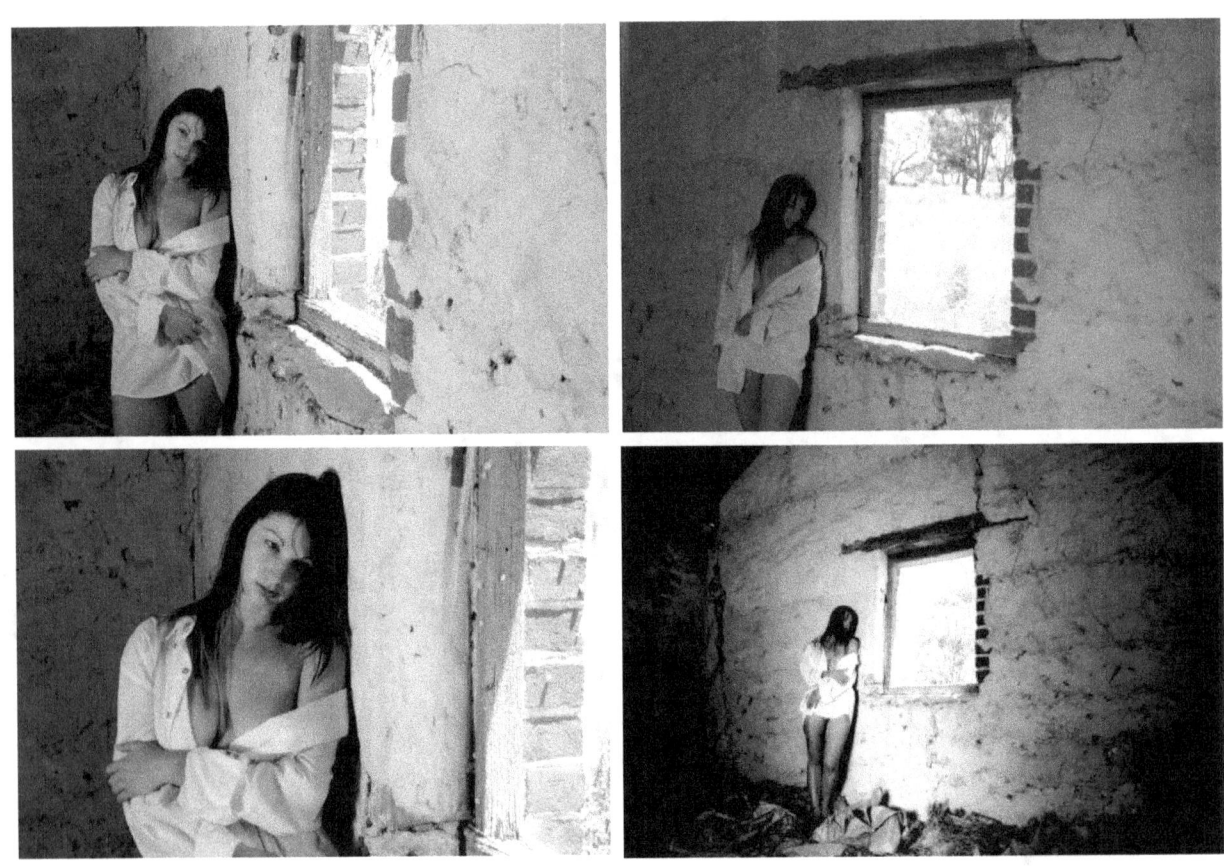

Take lots of angles of the same shot until you find the one that works best for you.
You can spend ages and ages, but it's just not working!

Sometimes, you need to stop and a have a think, move away from the action and think it through.
Get a coffee and go back to your notes.

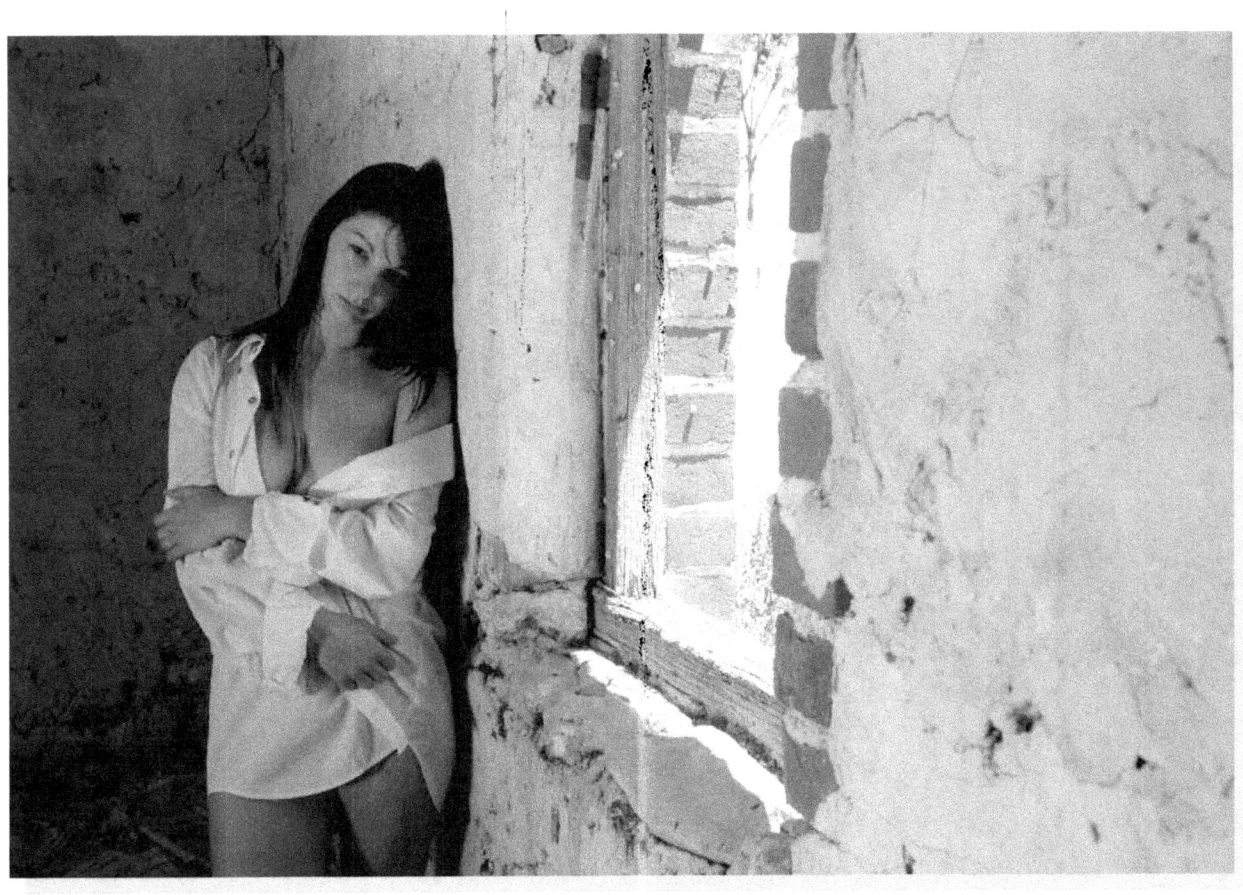

Shot title "Hiding"
Series " Ruined"
Location: Old Ruins, Adelaide, Country Area

As I nearly always work with untrained models, I was unsure of this girls look and experimented with B&W
We tried a number of looks, but sad and sultry seemed a comfortable place to be

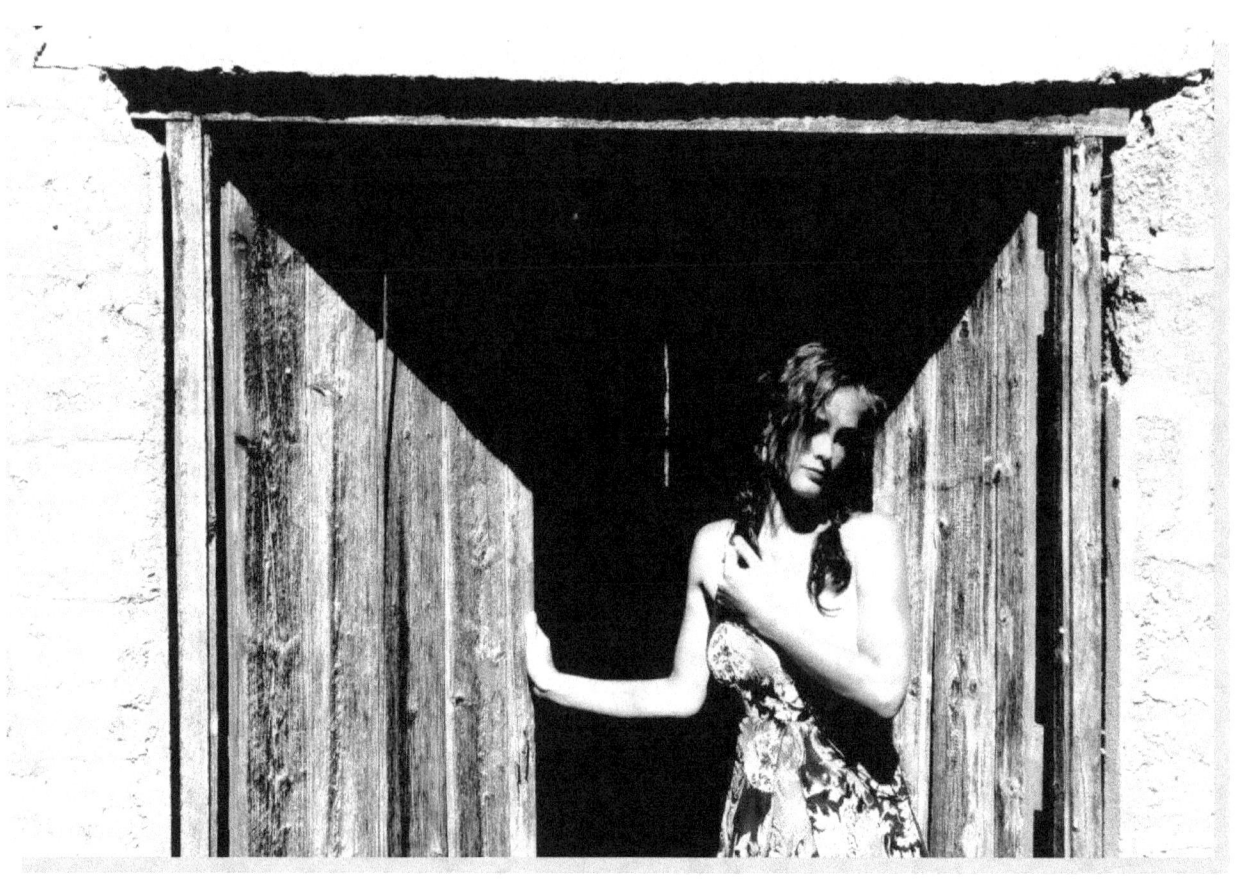

This models look was humble and peaceful, so a historic, humble home entrance suited.
The door texture works into her dress and the shadow of the doorway was used as a funnel to the focal point

This shot worked in black and white or colour,
but the textures of the door is accentuated in colour

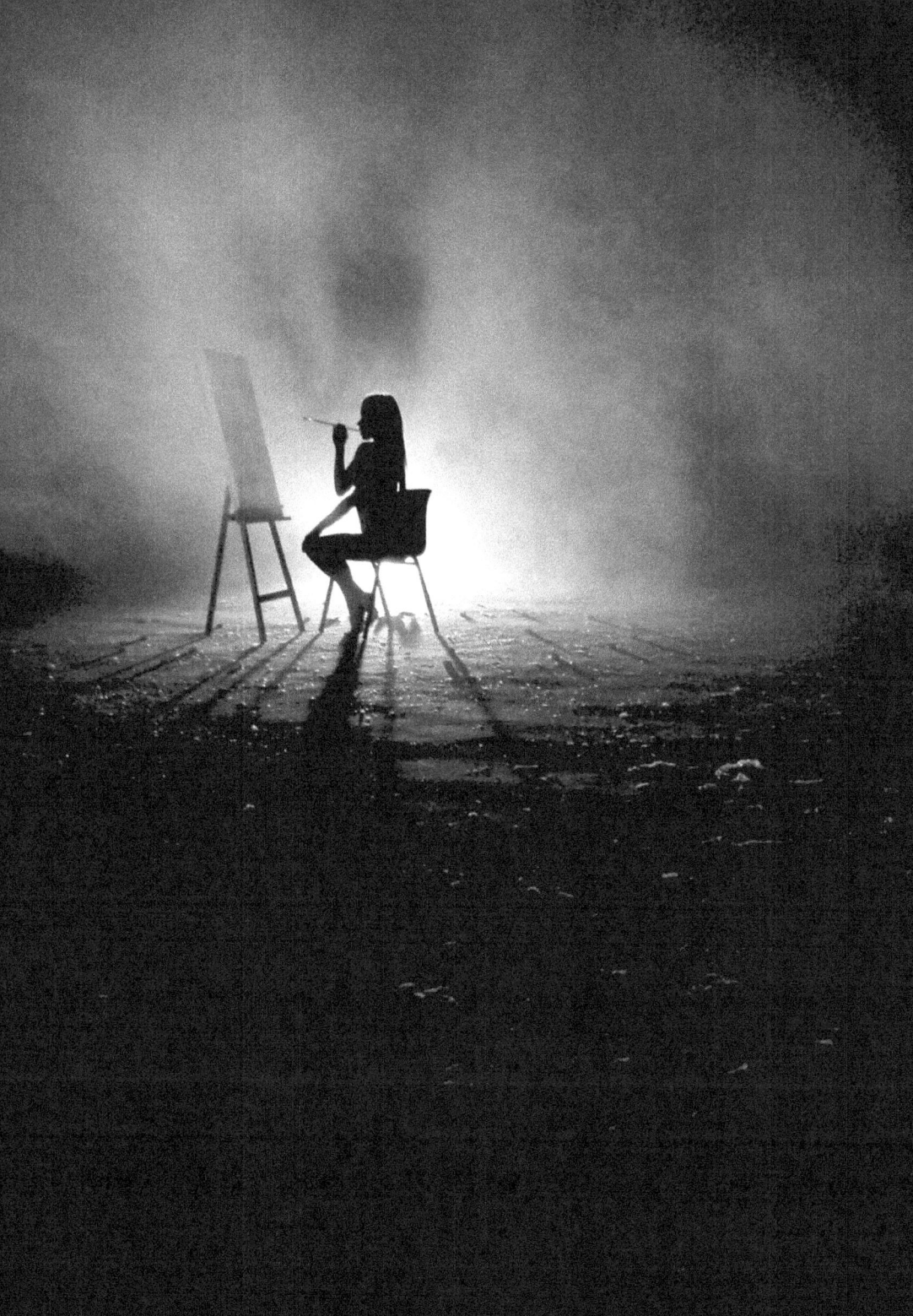

Shot title "Blank Canvas"
Series " The Artist Within"

Theme: Based on "arty" artists

"You are photographing real people,

so try and keep it real…"

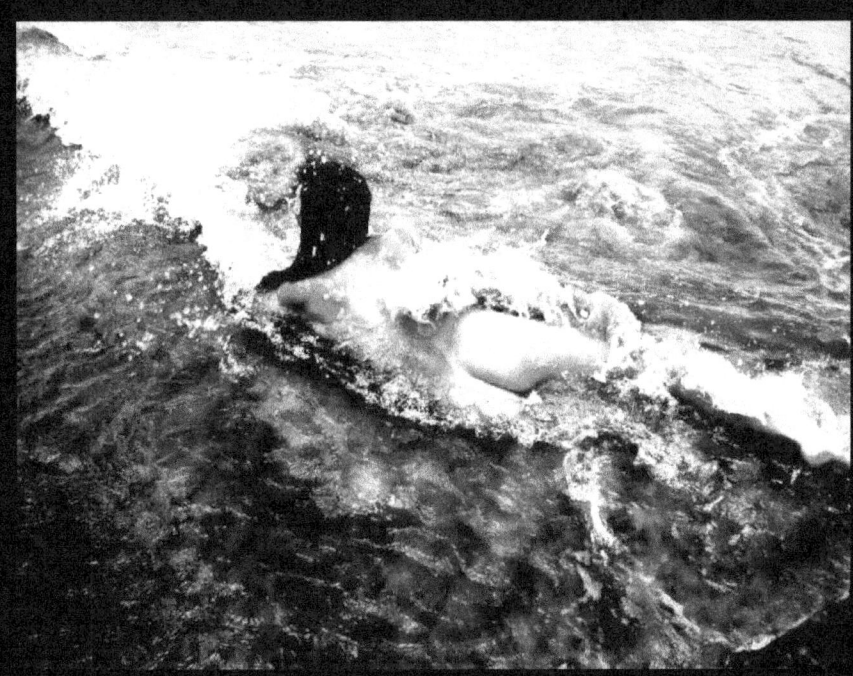

COMPOSITION & PROPS

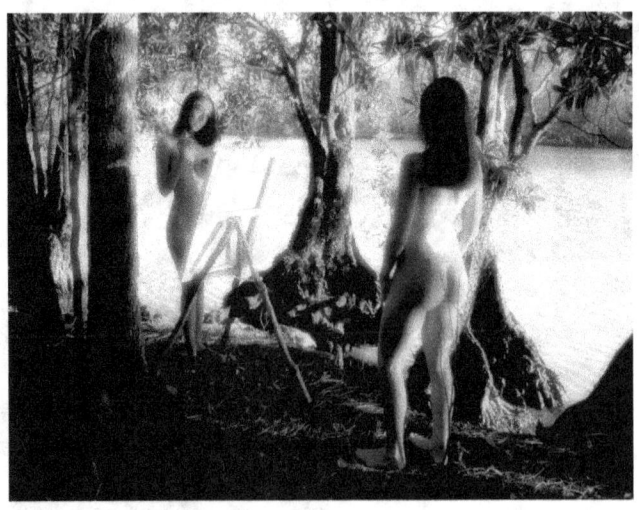

Well here it is, the big one!

Do you want people (your audience) to appreciate the subject, the model or your shot, the composition, the story?

When you show your print off for the first time, do you want people to say "wow, she looks great" or "what an awesome shot!"

You have total control over what is created!
Be clear about what it is you are creating!

So many photographers seem to get so wound up technically, they forget to actually take an interesting photo! It's like so many movies have become an animation fest' but the plots are awful!

OK, so its 20 megapixel, the lighting is spot on, the use of the flash adds some appropriate fill and the exposure choice accurate.

Who cares if it's 8 x 10 inches of boring!

If a book has a beautifully bound hard cover, but the story is crapola, its worthless.

Create and then capture an image that tells a story! Don't be too blatant, add some mystery, don't be afraid to offset your model. Spark a response from your viewer!

Even though you might have paid your model, it doesn't mean they have to centre stage all day. Know where they fit into your picture and your days work.

Is the picture about them or are they a part of the picture?

As discussed earlier, the composition is also completely different, knowing the end result. Is it going to end up 4 inches square, in a mag, a frame or on a web site?

The picture needs to be big, simple and uncluttered if is is to be viewed small, whereas a 1 metre print on a wall, is often more interesting if the image can be explored by the person standing in front of it.

Practice! Whatever you are about to do, practice it first!
I have a mannequin (Katie) that allows me to play with lighting techniques for many hours prior to trying anything with real people. If your talent get tired from your incompetence or too much experimentation, your shots will suffer.

Credibility! Keep your shots credible and give them a reason, a purpose. No point in grabbing a skimpy, fluro, bikini girl and sticking her in the middle of a national park! It looks out of place, token and ridiculous! Give your shot a reason to be!

If you can compose the vision in your mind and then can transfer this idea into your photograph, then you have achieved… it's often bard and looks better in your head!

On the following pages are some examples of compositional pieces and concept works. We hope you enjoy them and gain some ideas.

There is no right and no wrong when it comes to art.
You designed it and so that makes it right!

We always welcome feedback and will be happy to answer questions if we can.

Email us at images@hypervision.com .au

Katie, my closet practice model at home in the lounge room!

My kids think she's weird and they're probably right!

We put sunglasses on her when guests come over!

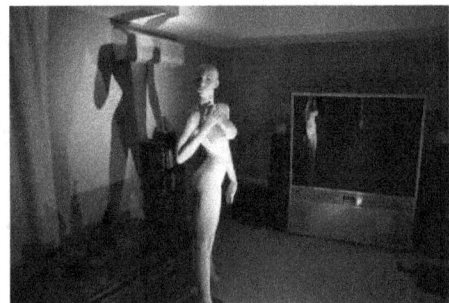

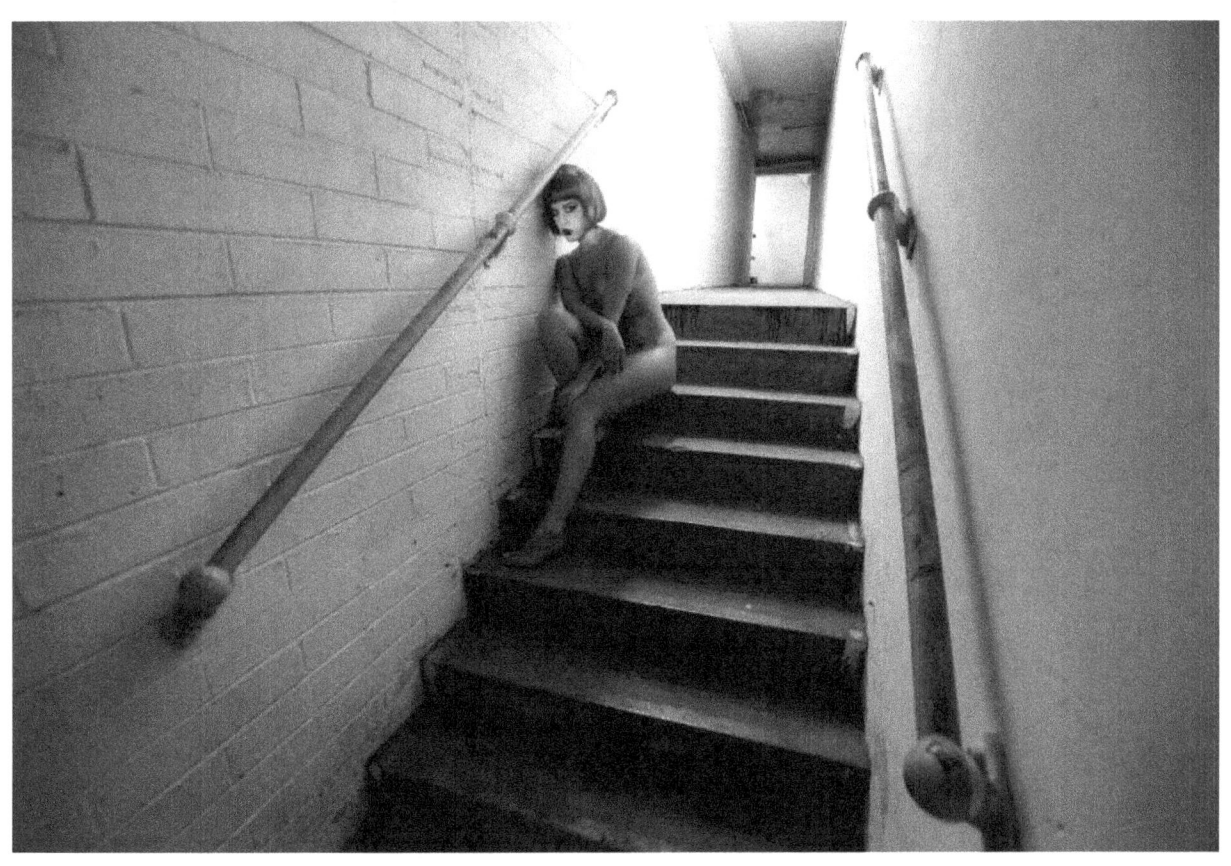

Shot title "Blank Stair"
Series "Art House"
Location: Melbourne

No colour treatment has been used in this image
I have used resident fluro's everywhere, except on her face where I used a 6500k daylight torch

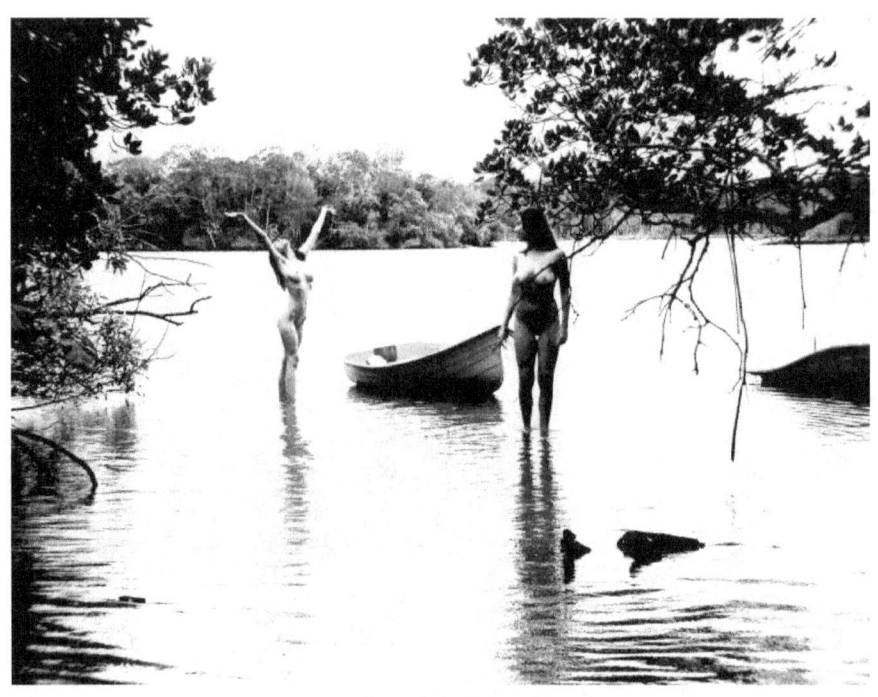

Shot title "Liberated"
Series " Everglades"
Location: Noosa, Australia

Over exposed and a raspberry filter, takes some of the realism away and simplifys this shot to arty expression

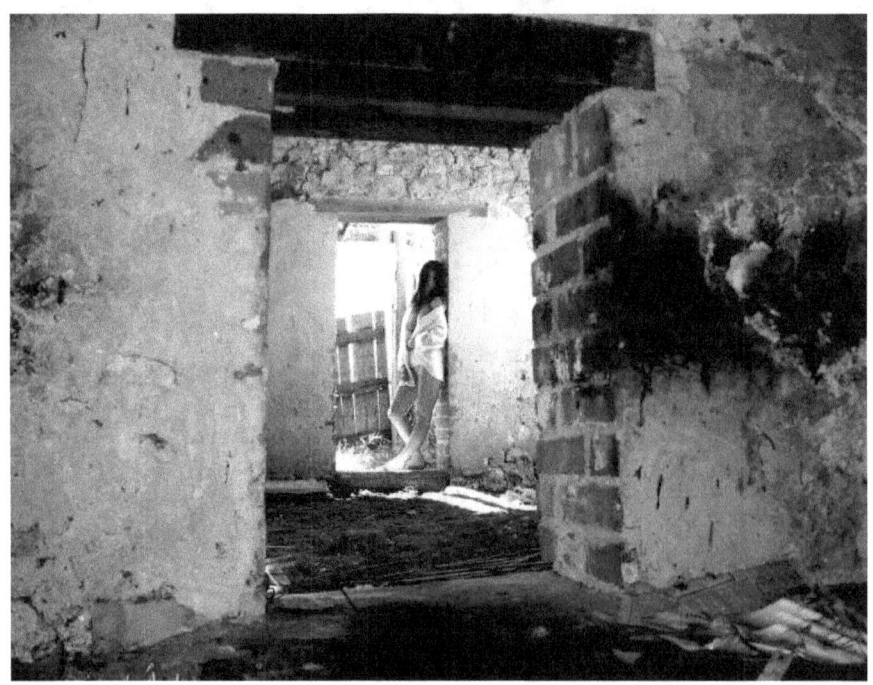

Shot title "Doorways"
Series " Ruined"
Location: Old ruin

Shooting through a doorway to a doorway adds a sense of dimension

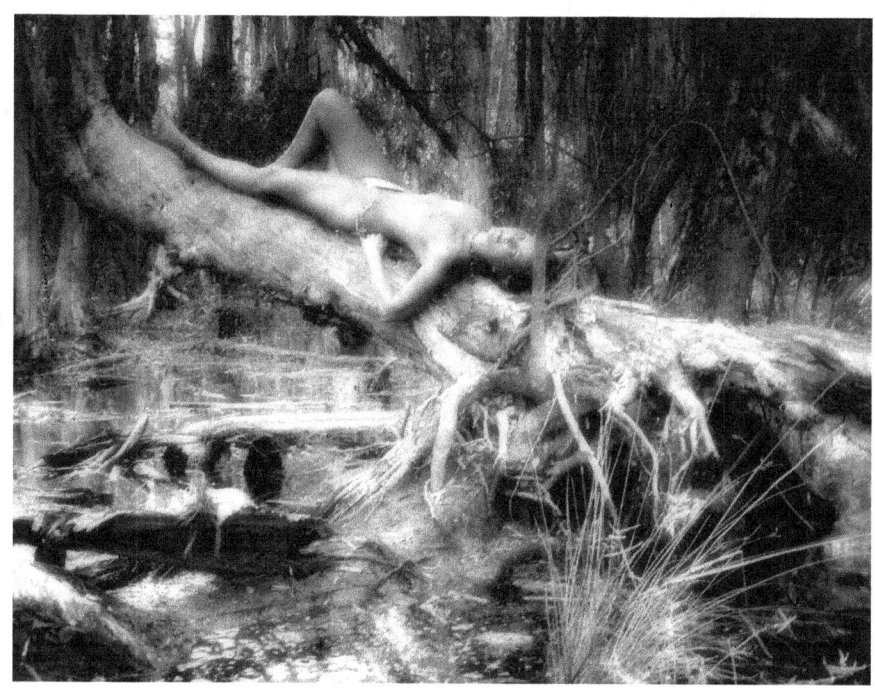

Shot title "Storm Damage"
Series " Paperbark"
Location: Elanda Point, Mangroves

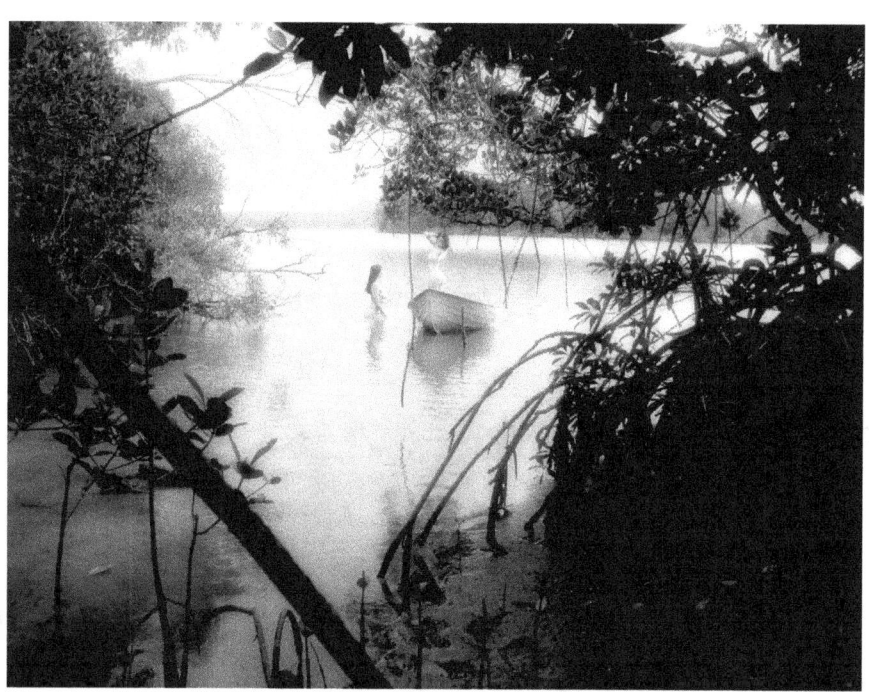

Shot title "Friends"
Series "Sunshine"
Location: Noosa River

The use of Black and White, brings soft calm

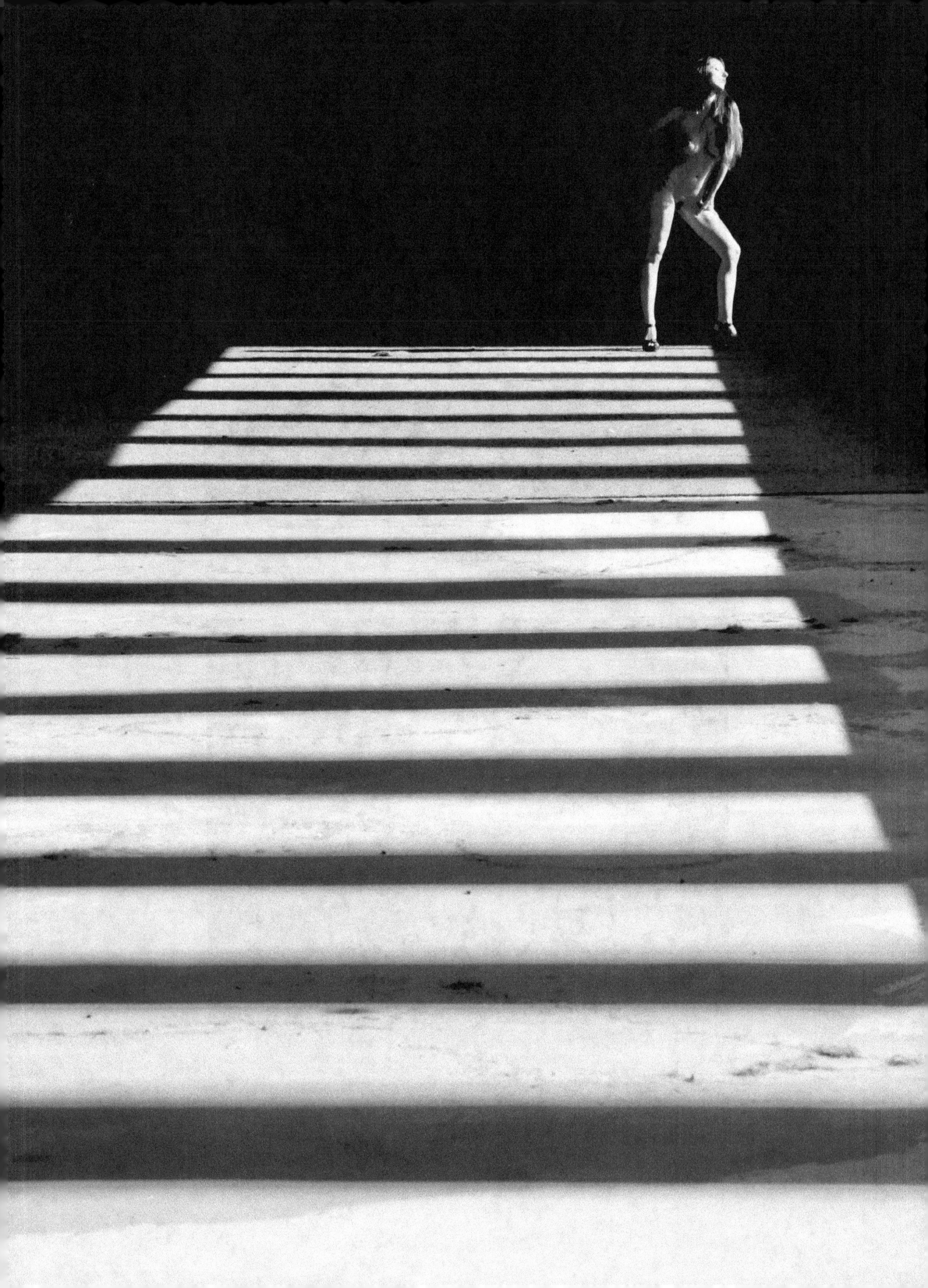

Shoot the scene many ways
before anyone arrives, do
your location work,
days before if you can

Use stand ins where
possible so that your
talent doesn't get tired
before you know what
you are even going to do

Top:
The chair and the wall
Ambient light source

Middle:
While my model is in
make up, my great
assistant Joe, steps
up to the chair while I
prepare exposures and
plan the angles

Bottom:
When satisfied that you
are ready to go, bring
in the model and
coach them as
Required

Over page:
The final Shot

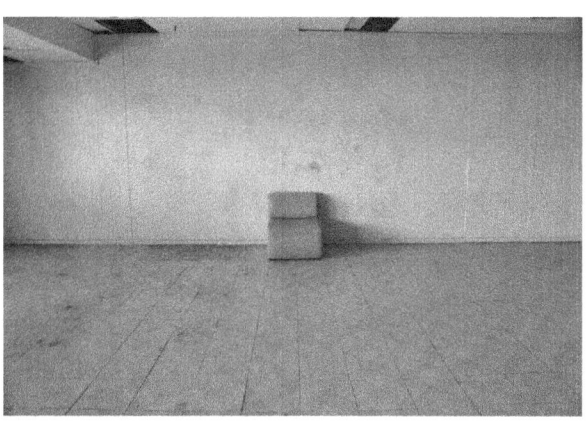

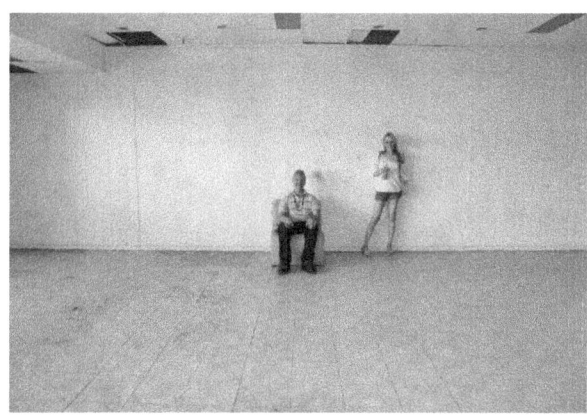

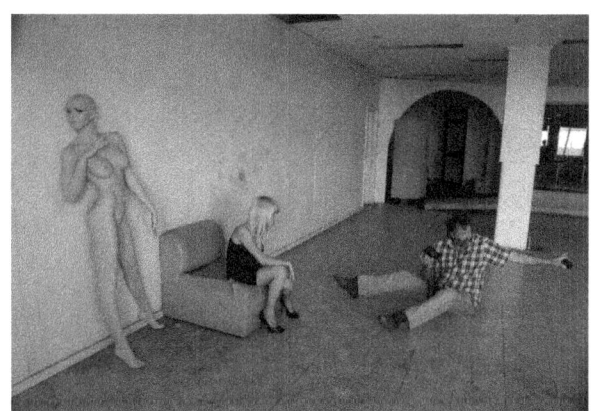

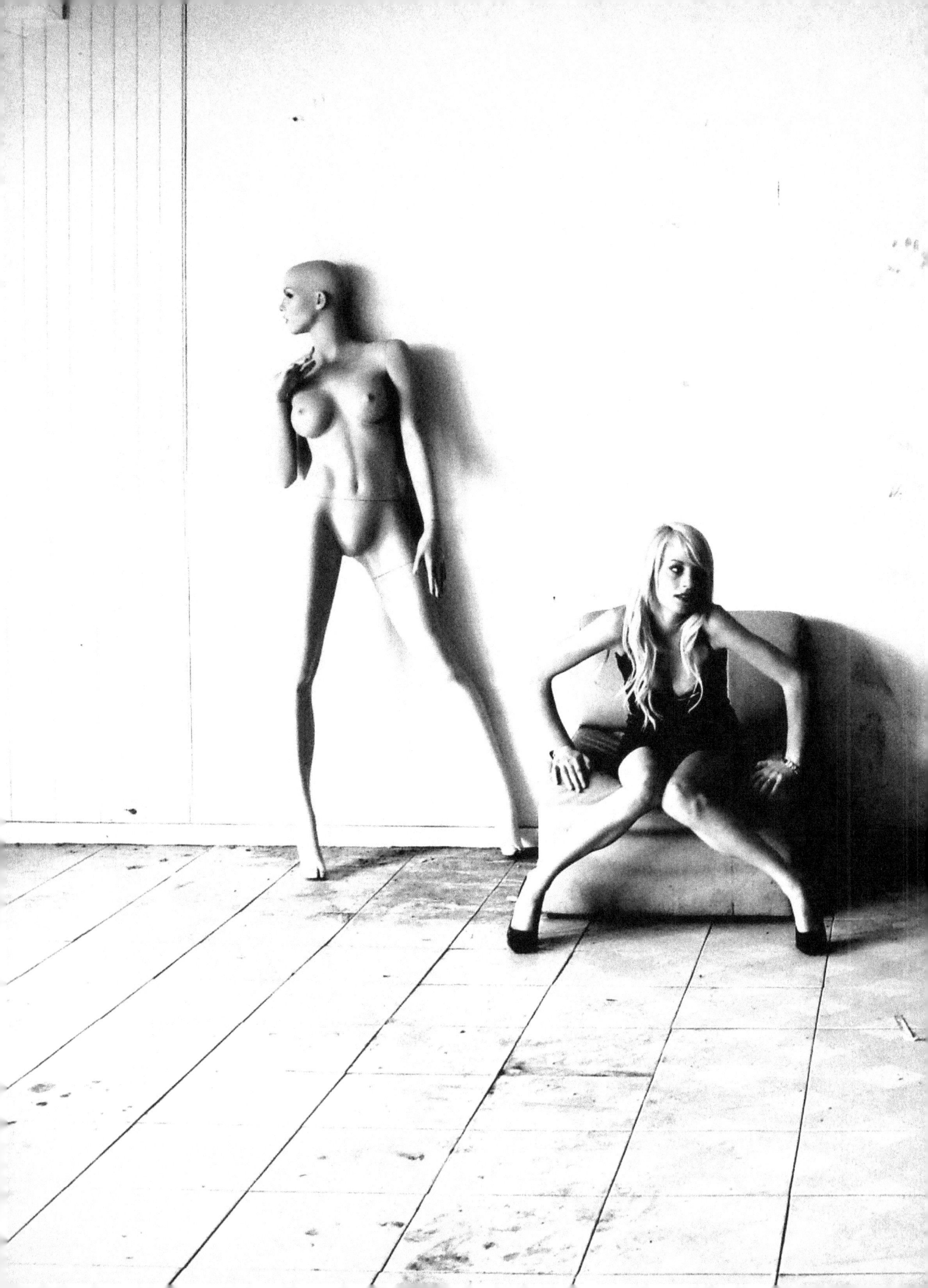

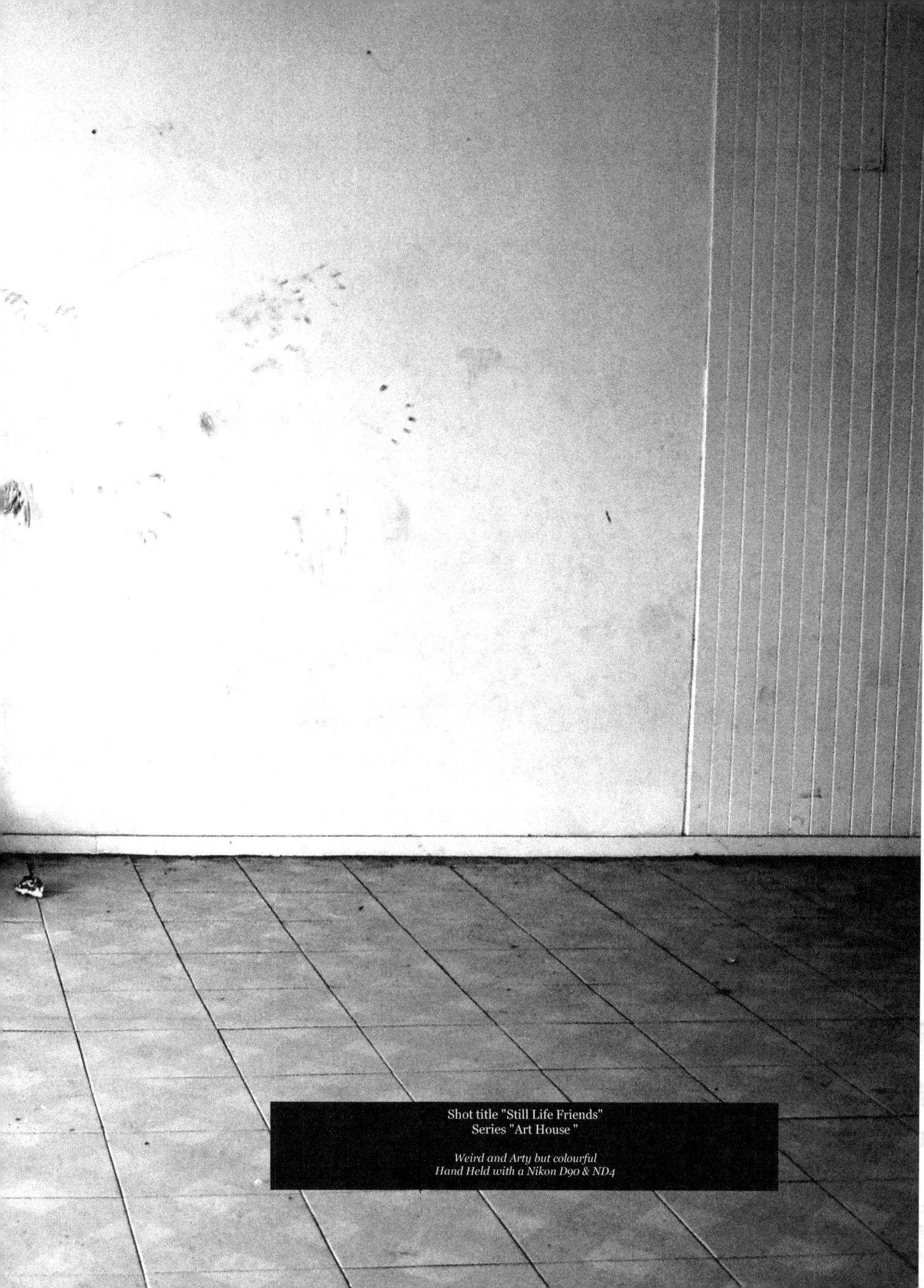

Shot title "Still Life Friends"
Series "Art House "

Weird and Arty but colourful
Hand Held with a Nikon D90 & ND4

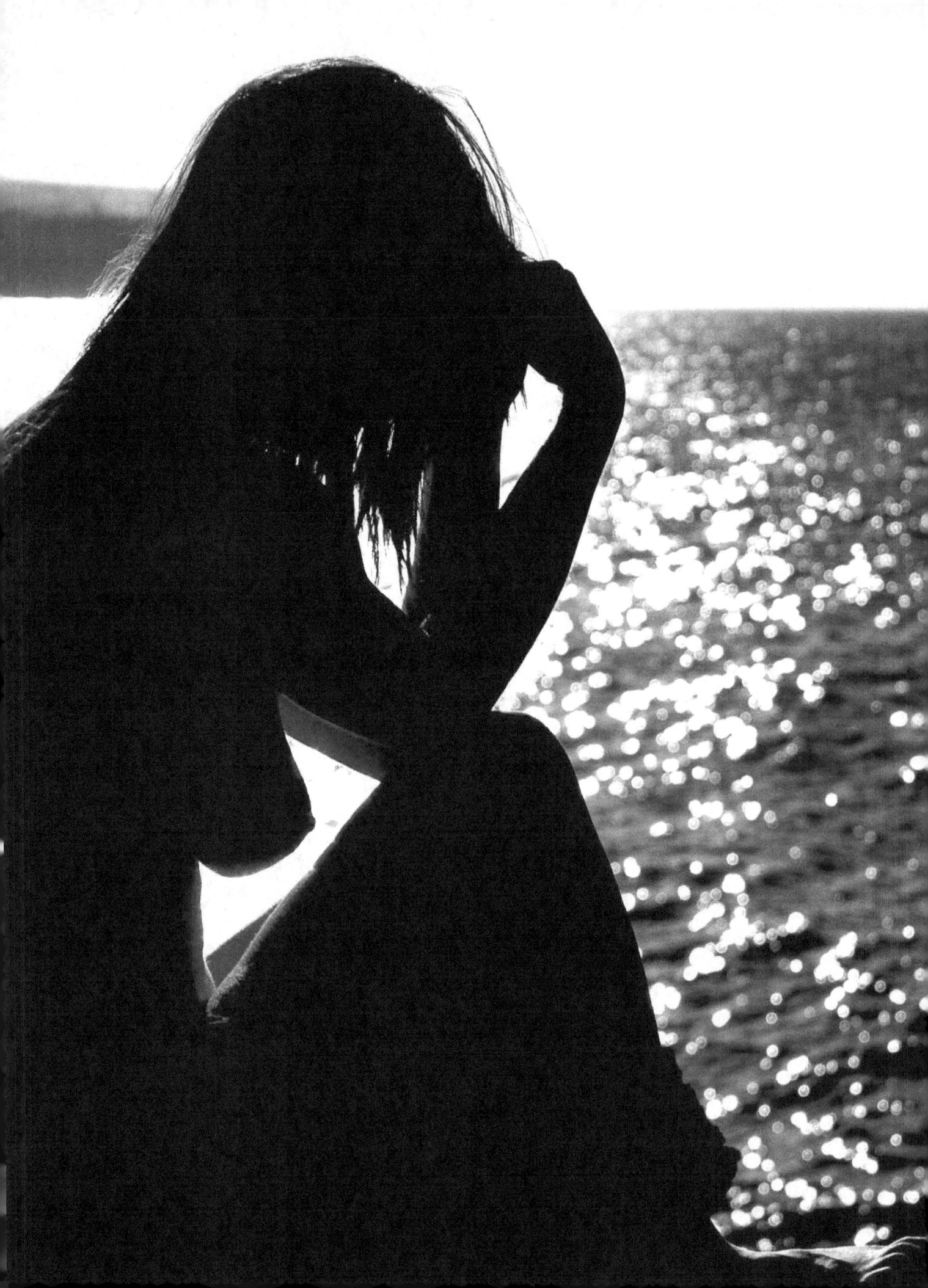

Sometimes when you walk
into an area it doesn't
seem very interesting.

But take your time,
sit down and let you
mind run free.

Top:
An old dance room

Bottom:
Keep your models
warm while planning

Over page:
The final Shot

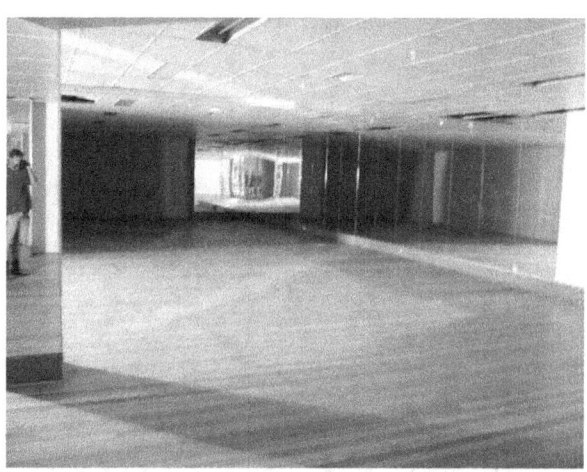

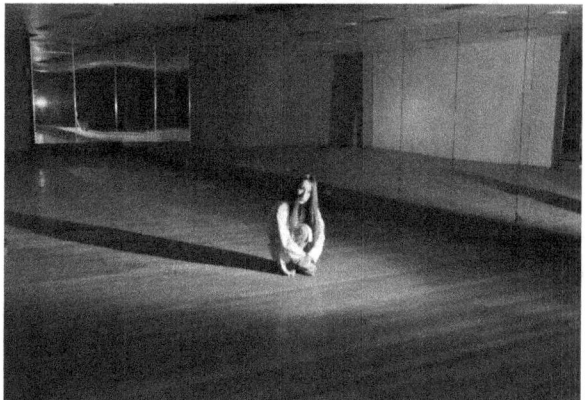

Series "Art House"

Light source is a single
2000w blonde
Nikon D90 + ND4

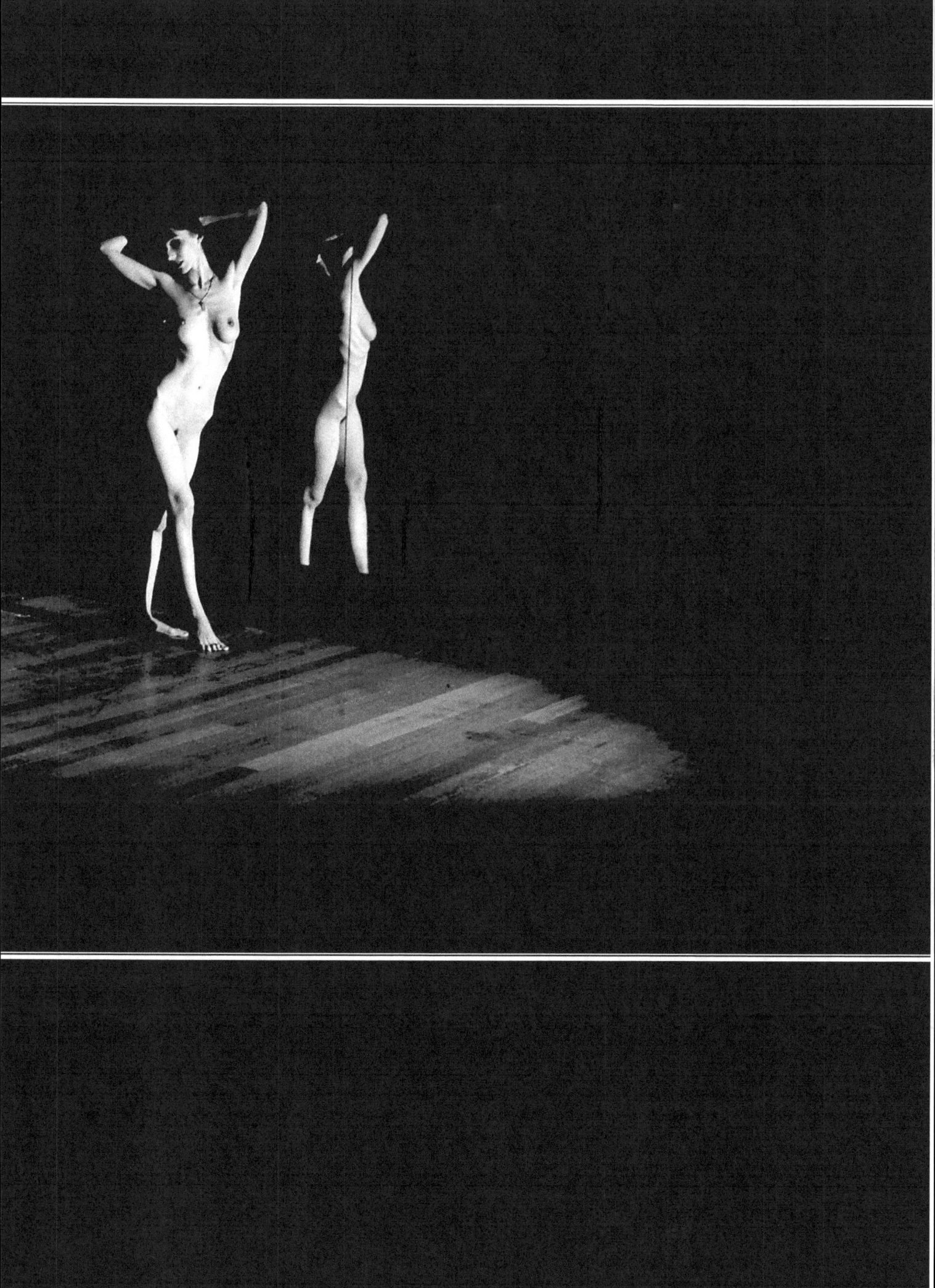

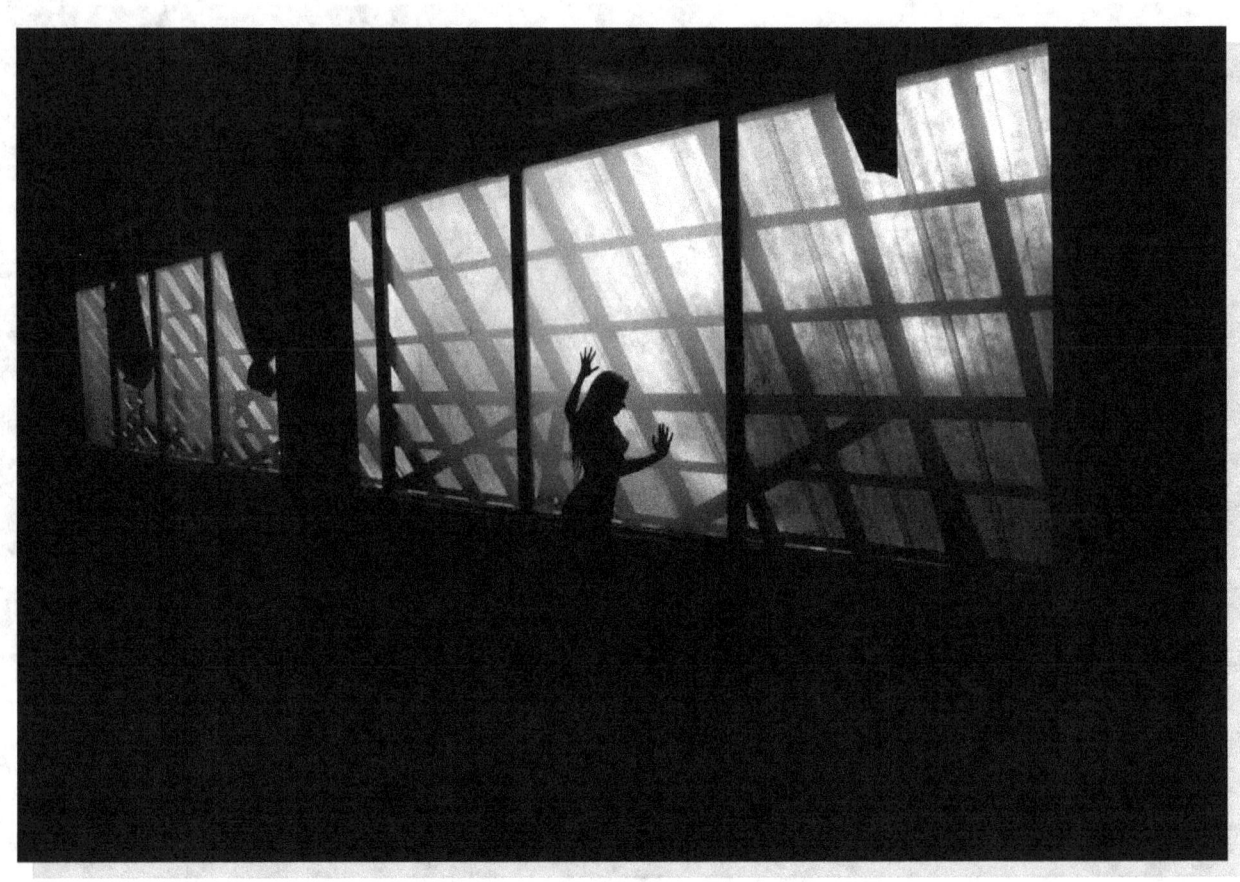

Shot title "Too Hard"
Series "Art House"

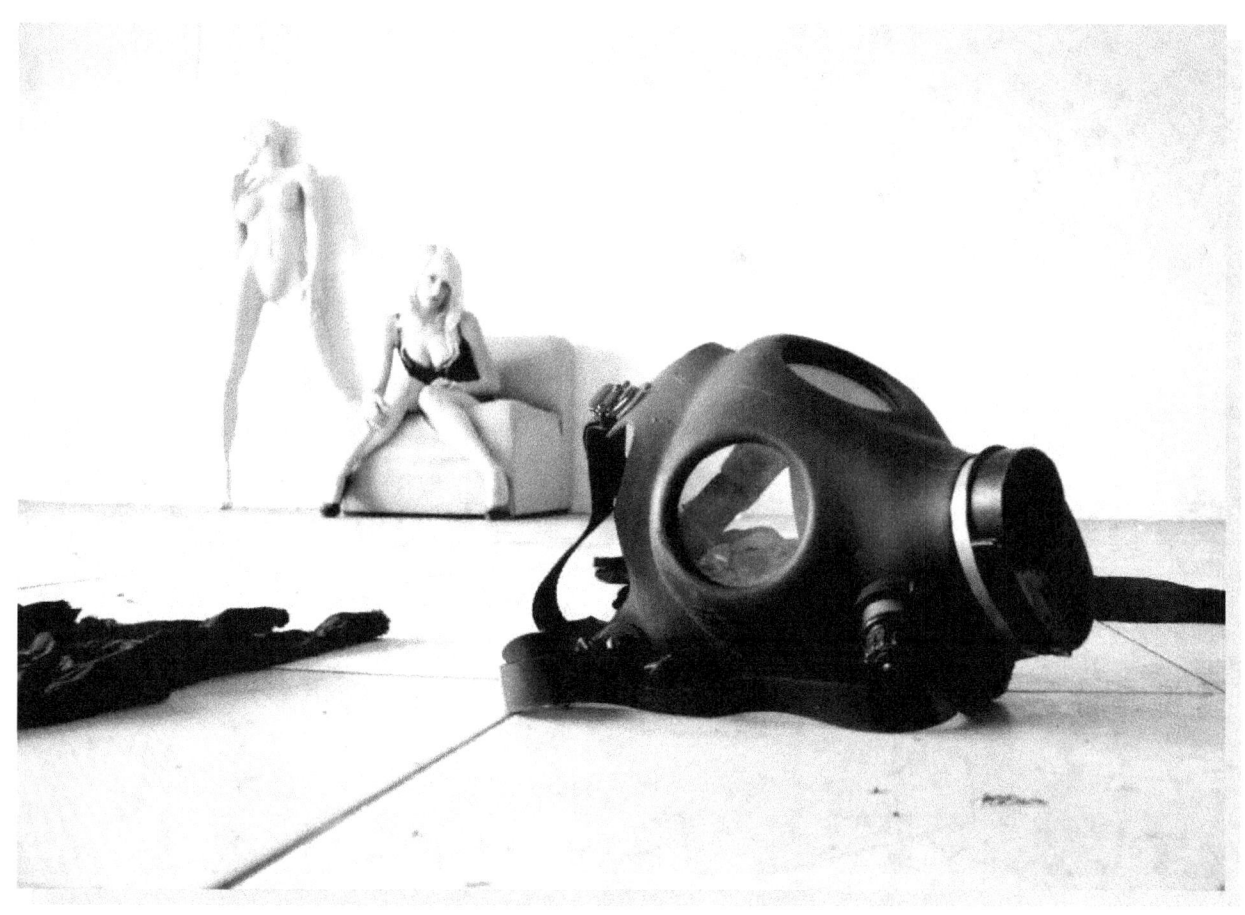

Shot title "Parties Over"
Series "Art House"

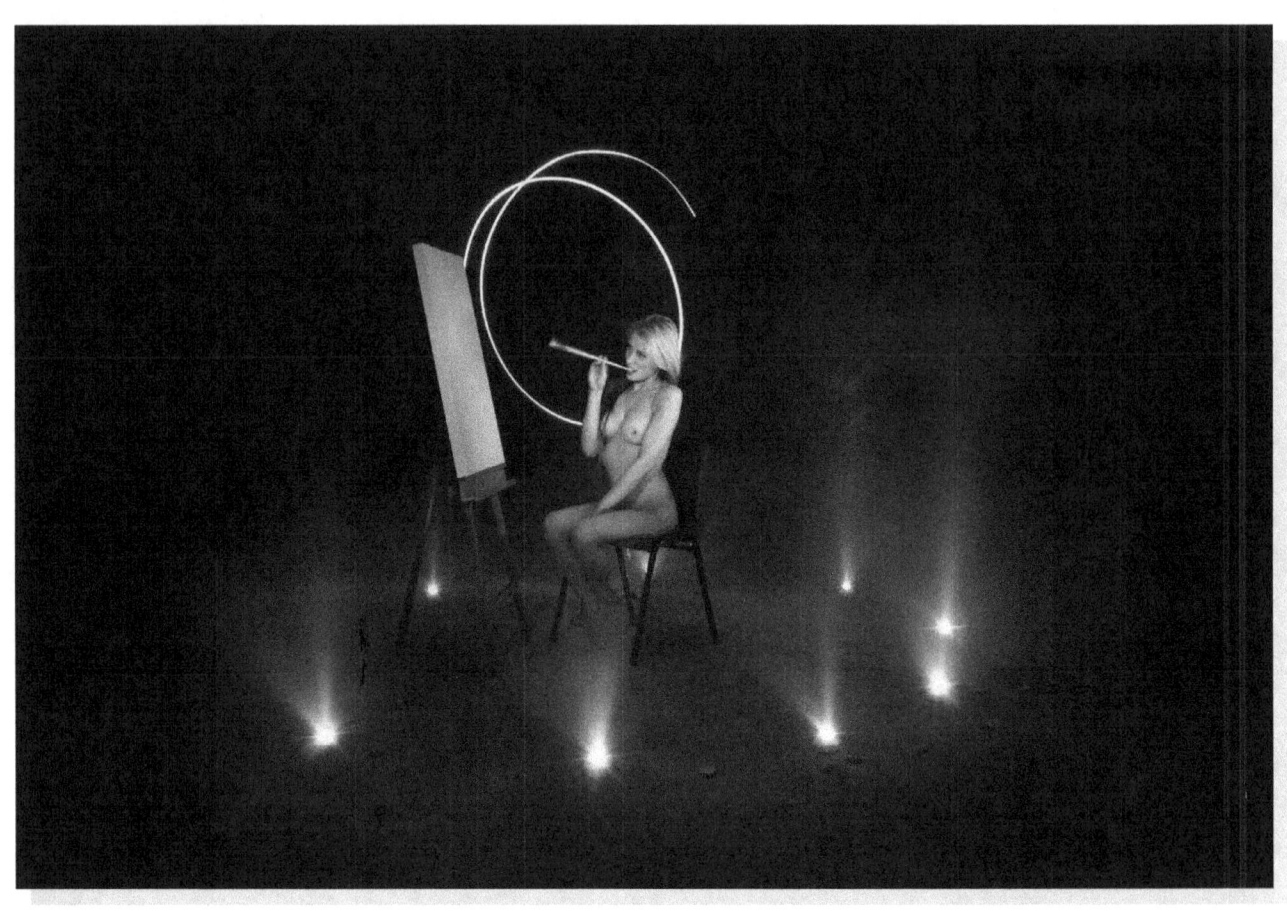

Shot title "Light Canvas"
Series "The Artist Within"

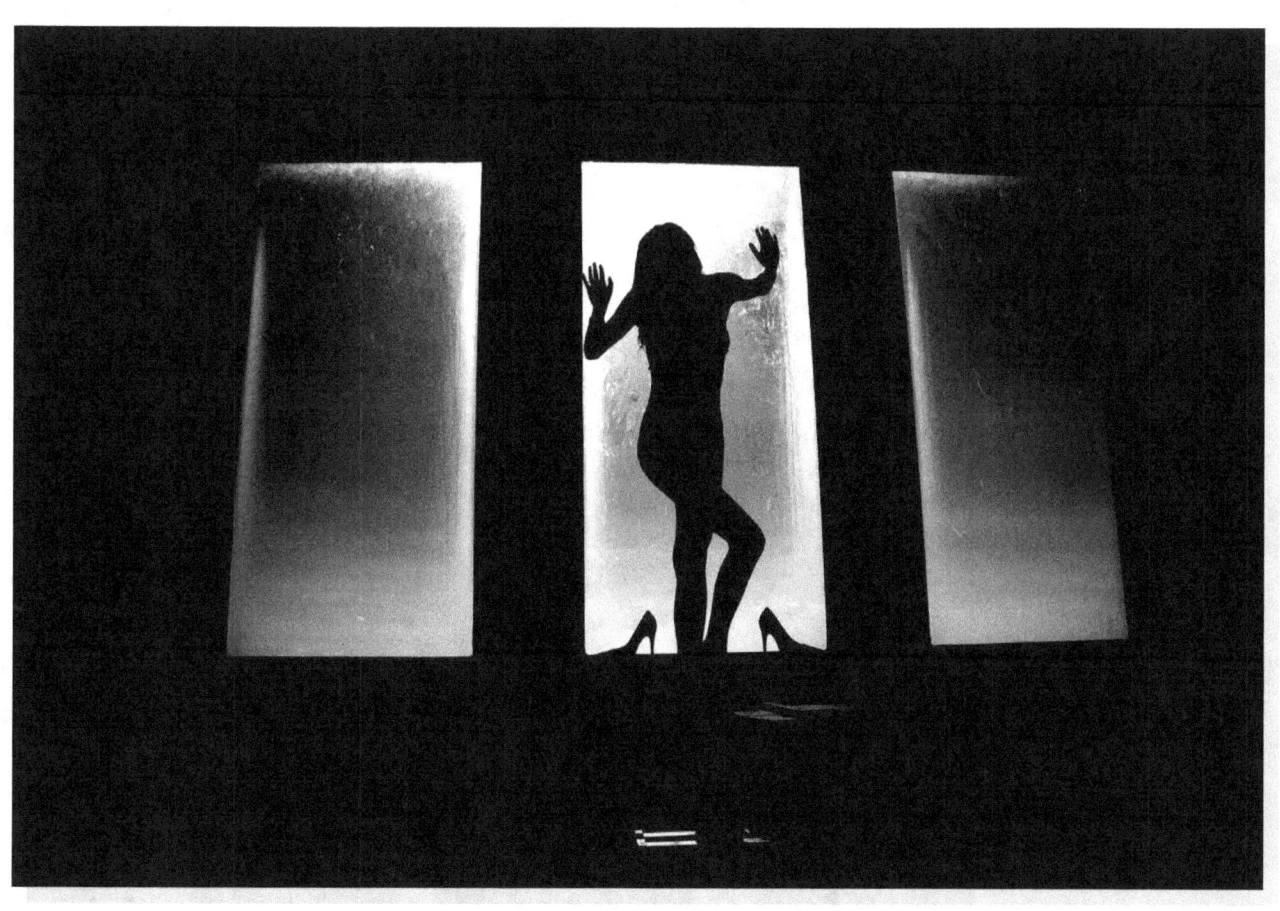

Shot title "The Jumper"
Series "Art House"

- *Black & White Spider Awards Nomination* -

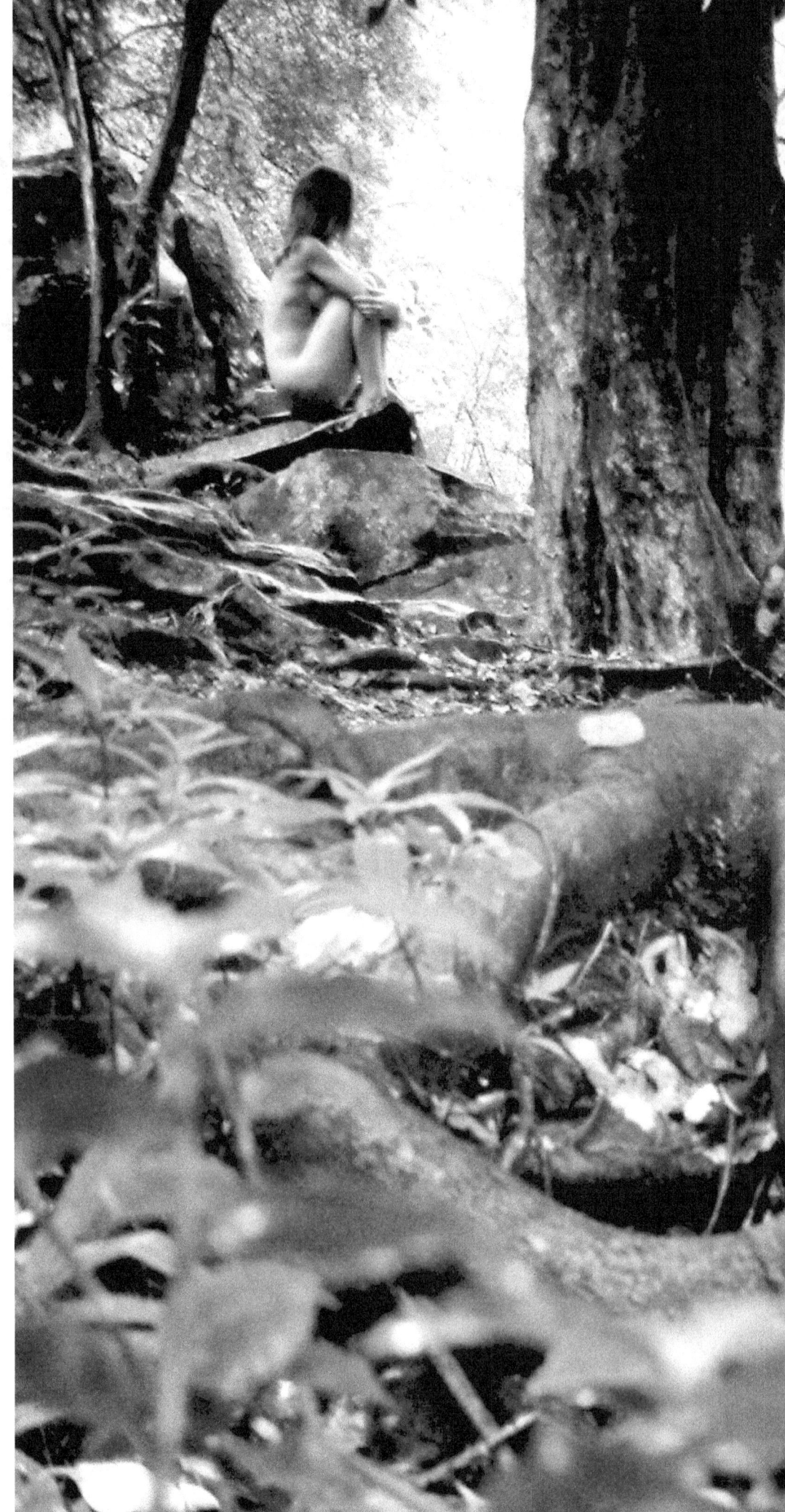

Shot title "Alone"
Series " Paperbarks"
Location:
Meleney, Queensland

*Use of foreground can
draw your attention
to the subject and
magnify the solitude*

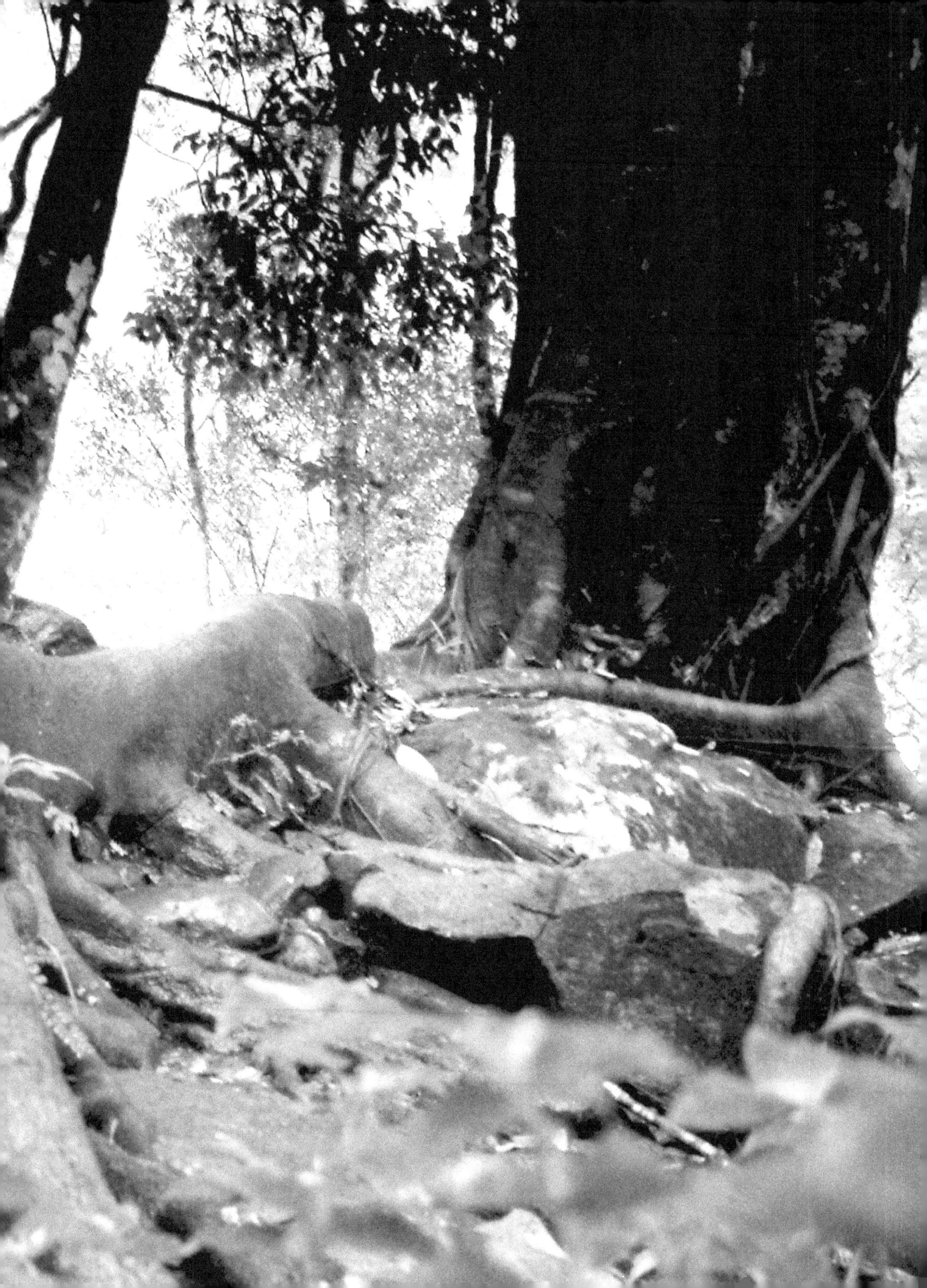

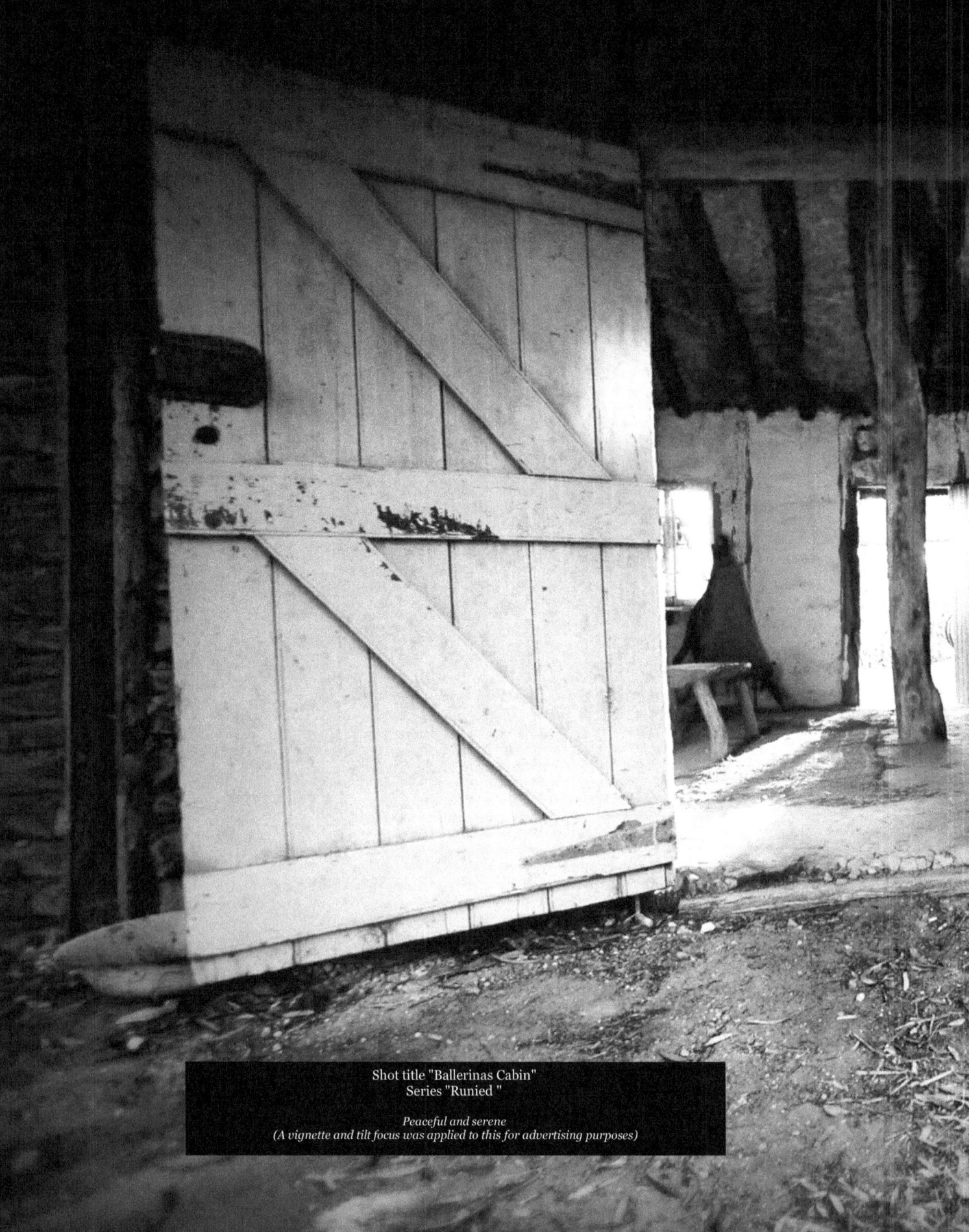

Shot title "Ballerinas Cabin"
Series "Runied "

Peaceful and serene
(A vignette and tilt focus was applied to this for advertising purposes)

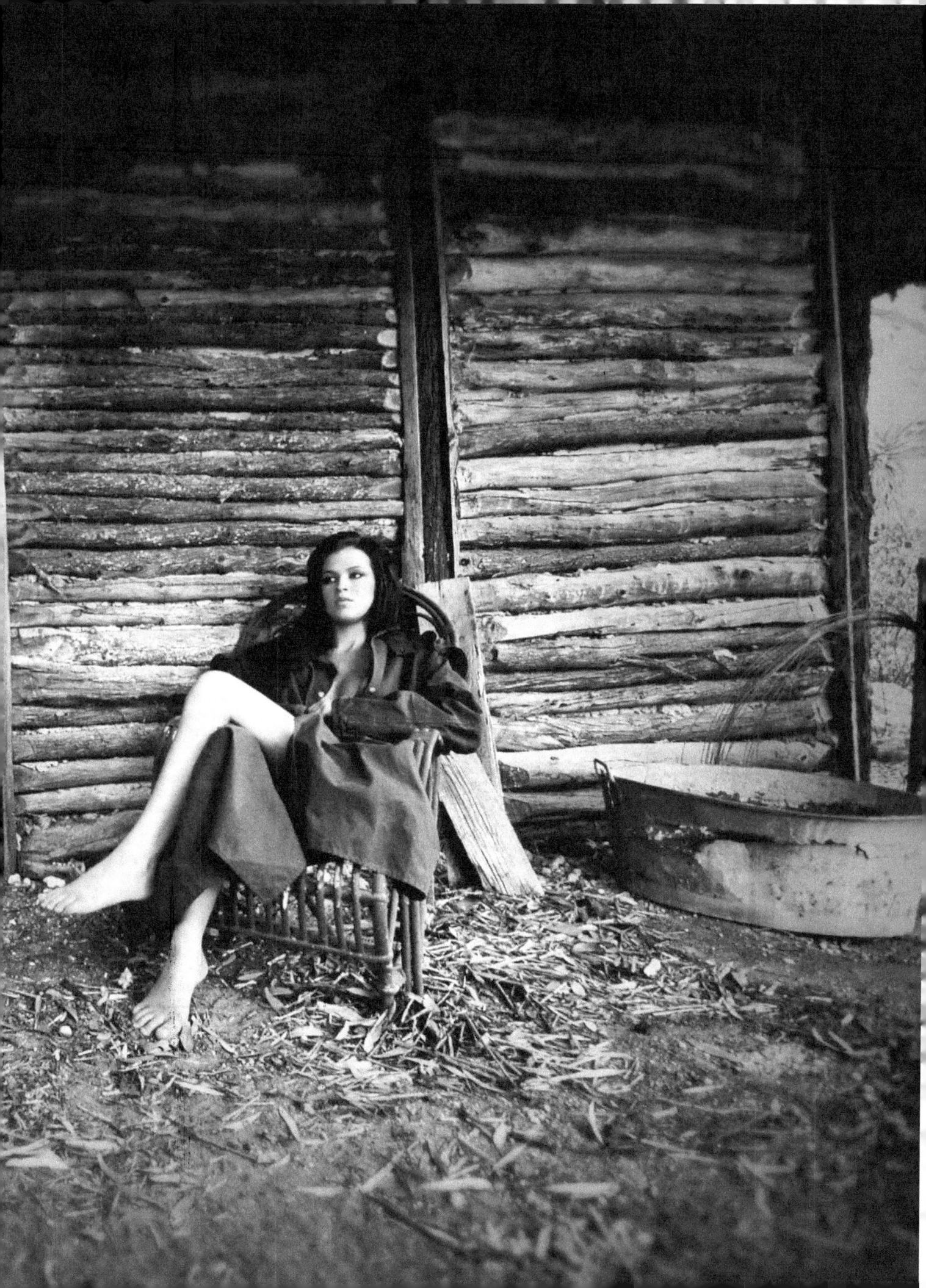

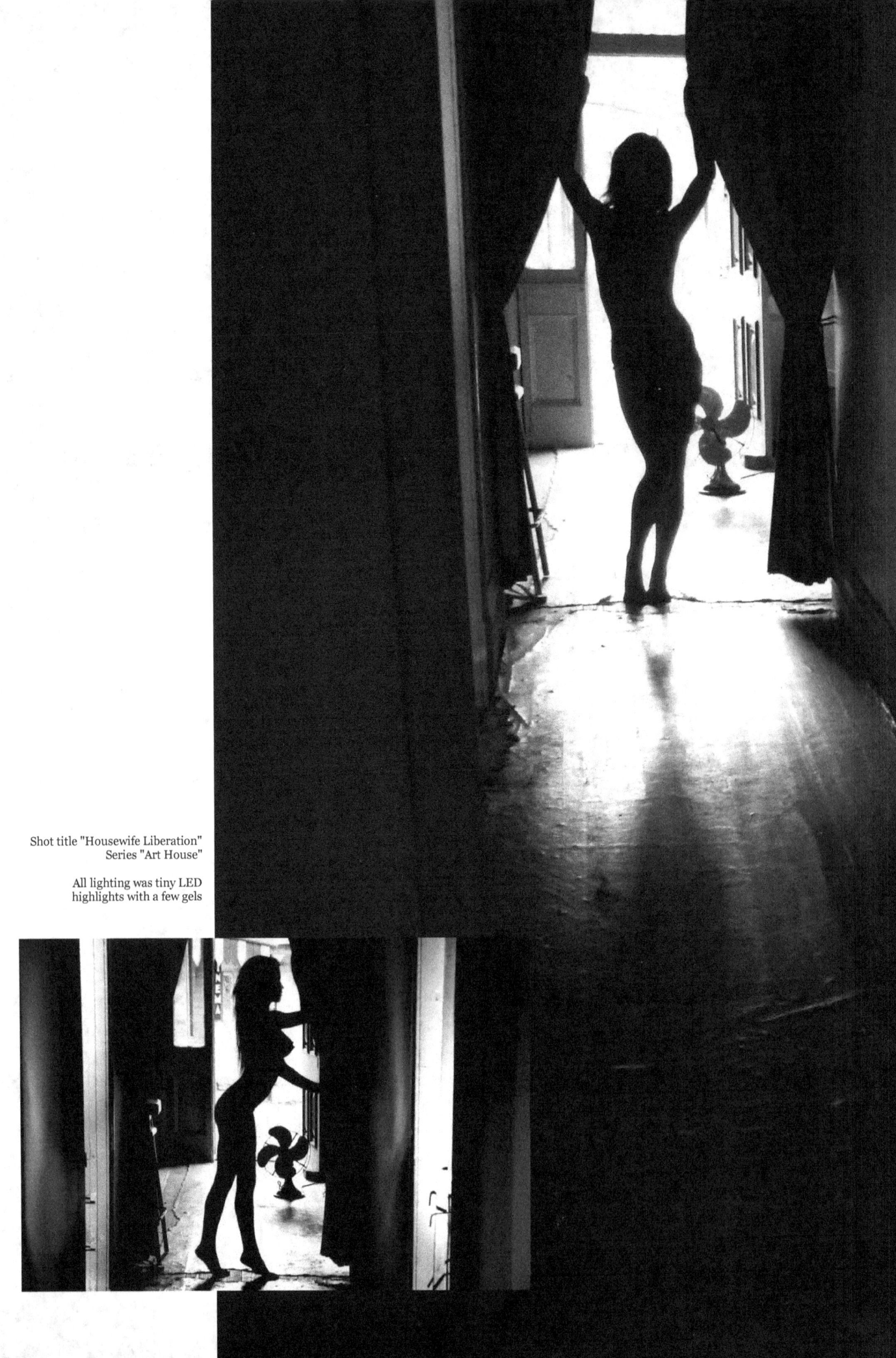

Shot title "Housewife Liberation"
Series "Art House"

All lighting was tiny LED
highlights with a few gels

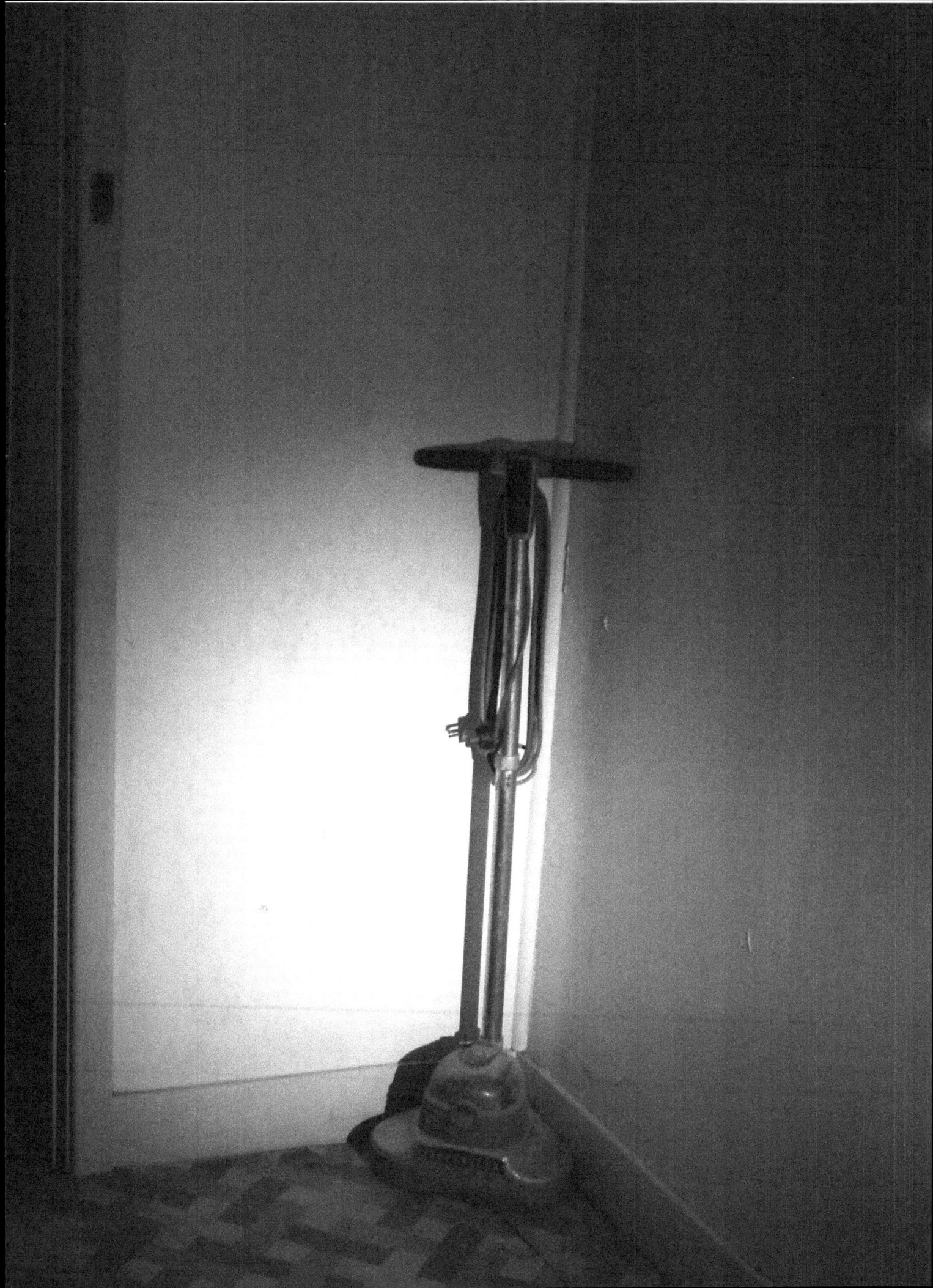

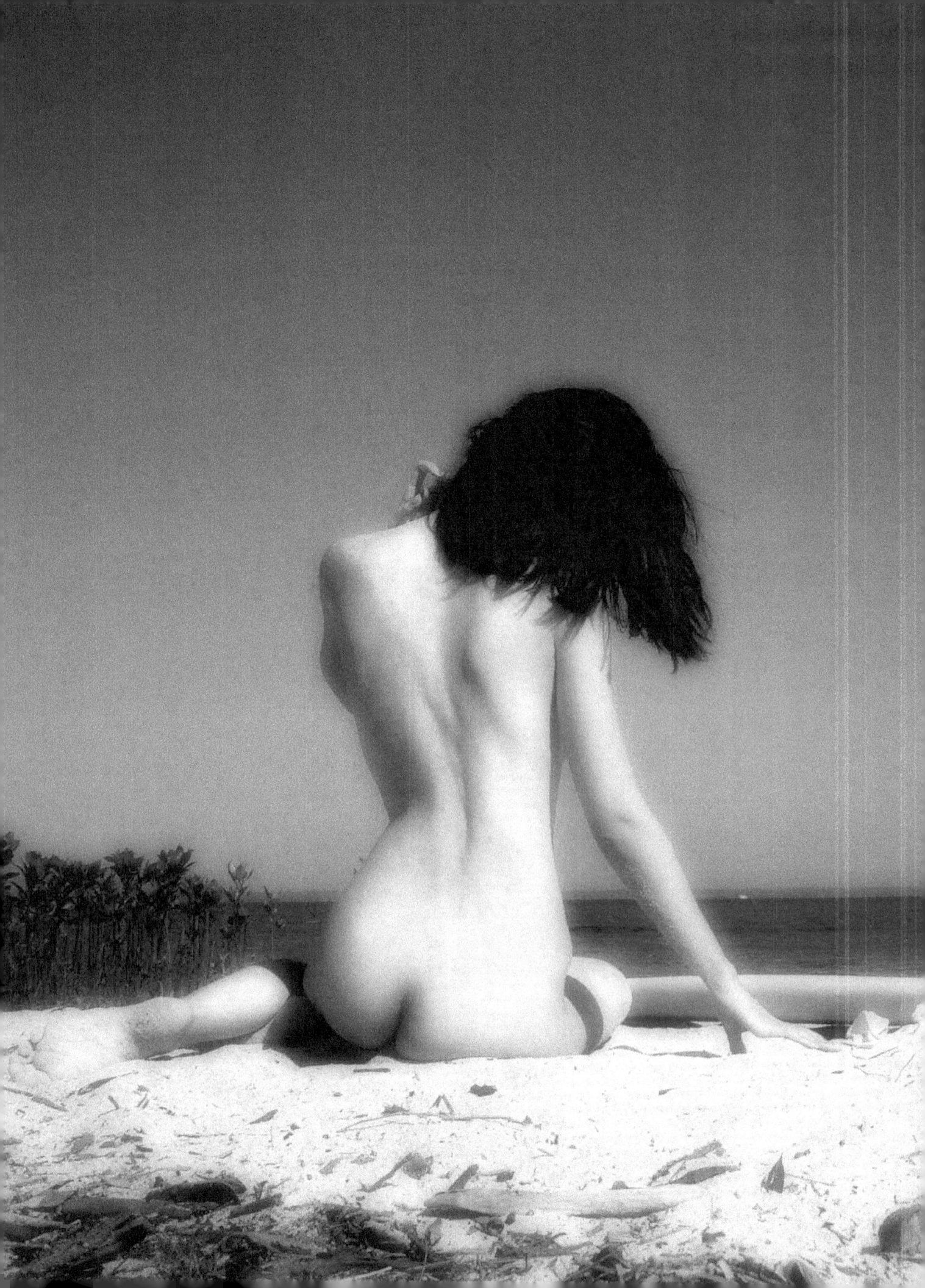

Shot title "Wiped out"
Series " Noosa Bue"
Location: Queensland

Simple often says it

FUJI 7000 Camera
ND16 Grad + copper filter

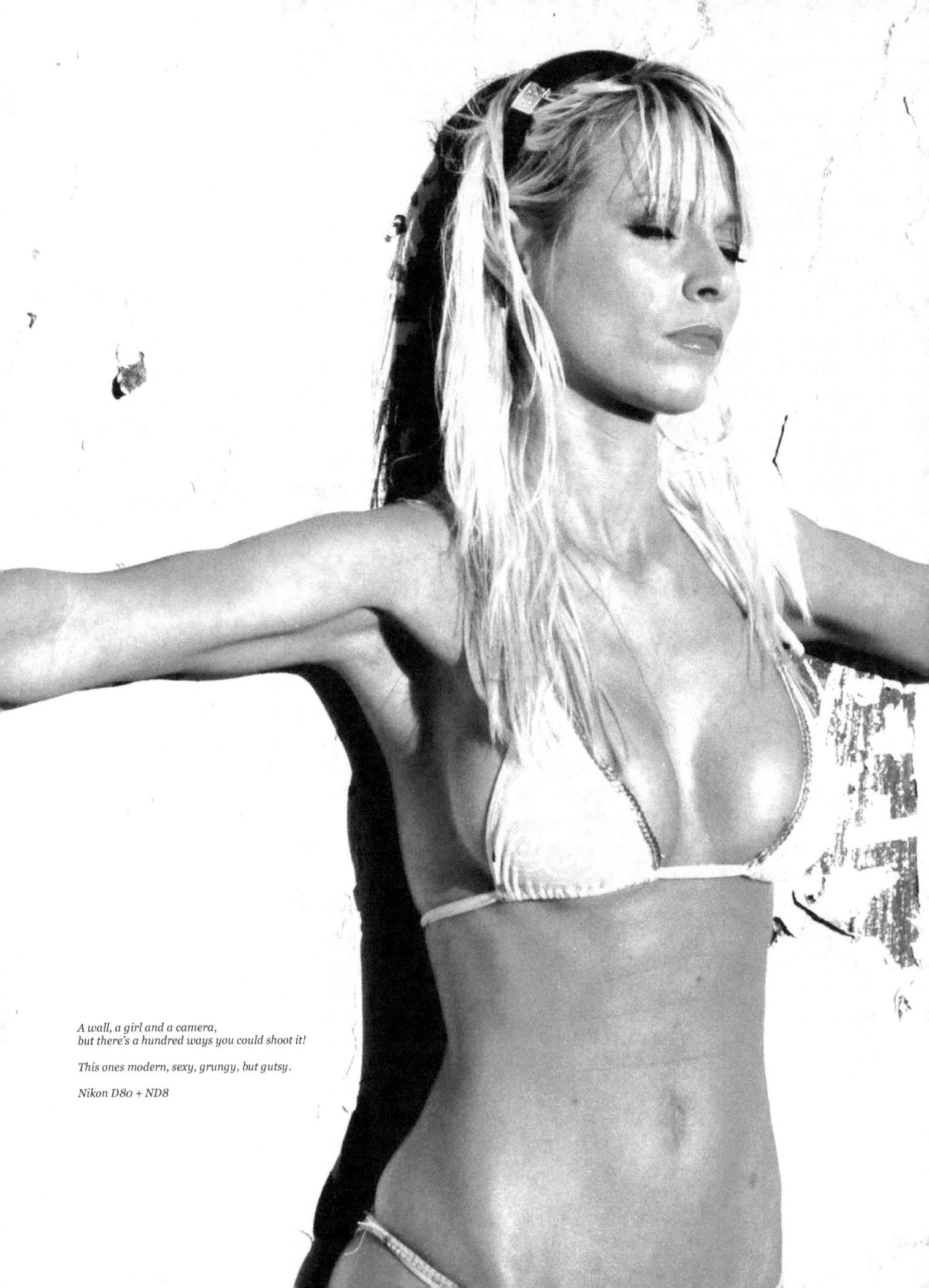

A wall, a girl and a camera,
but there's a hundred ways you could shoot it!

This ones modern, sexy, grungy, but gutsy.

Nikon D80 + ND8

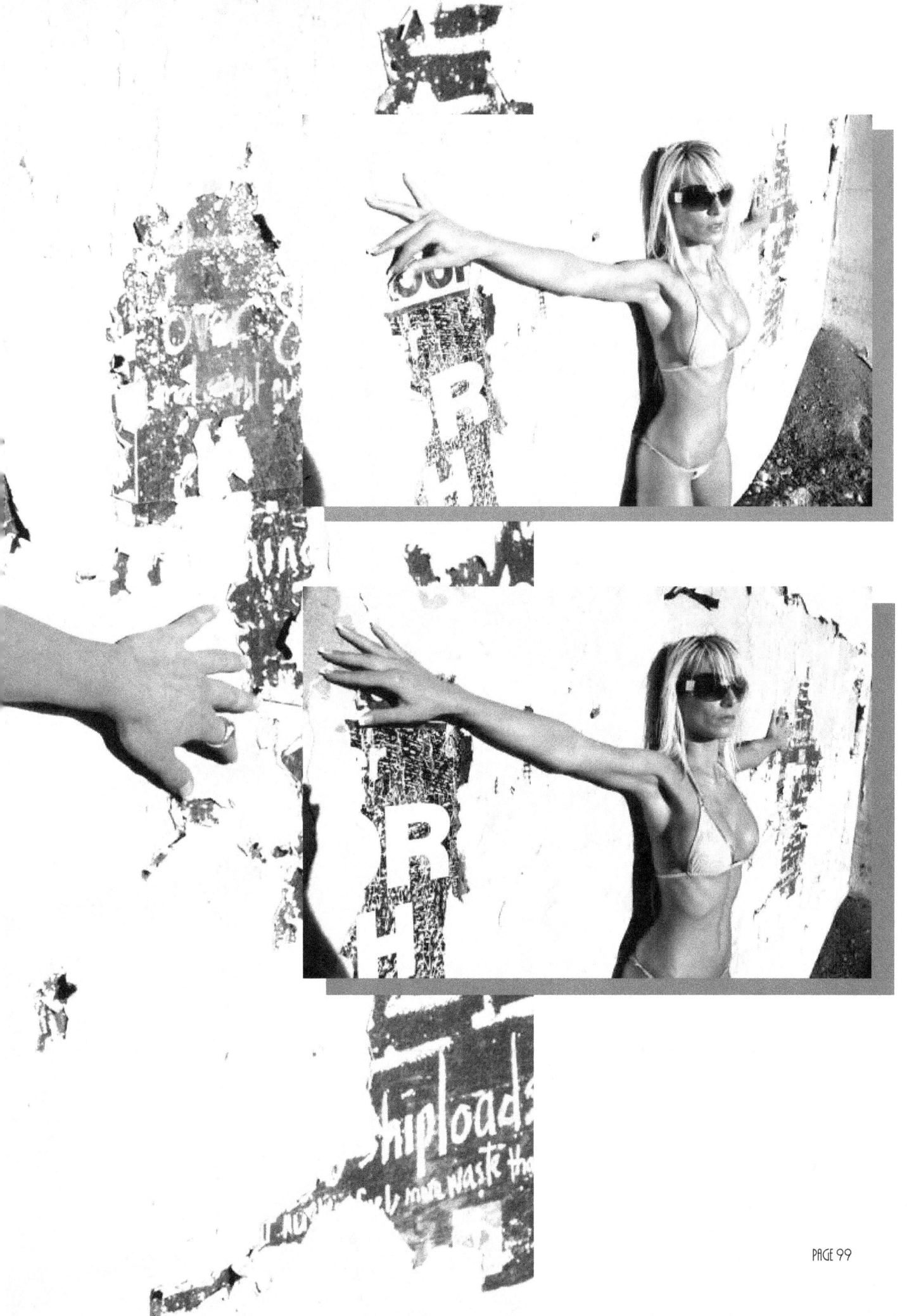

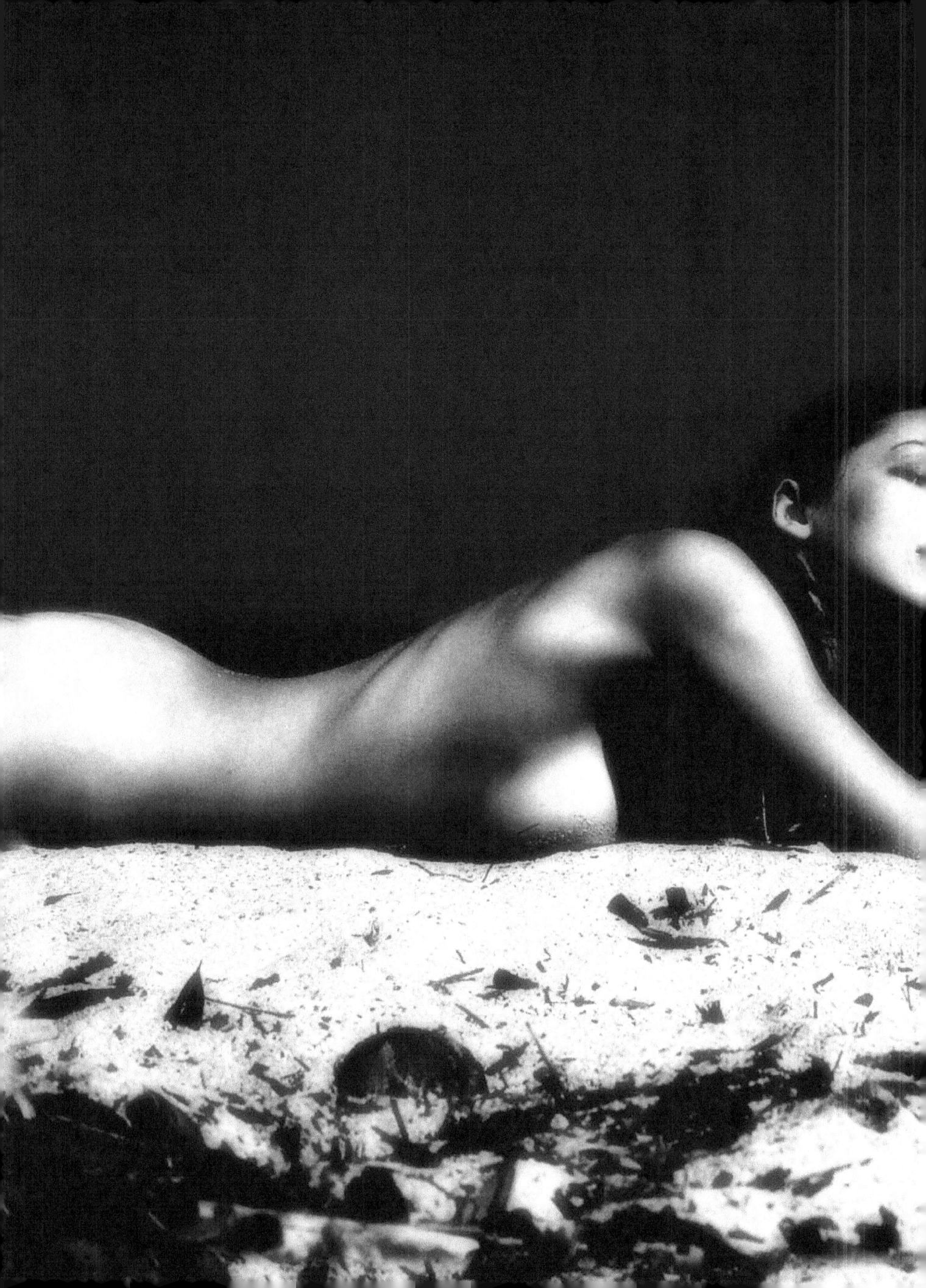

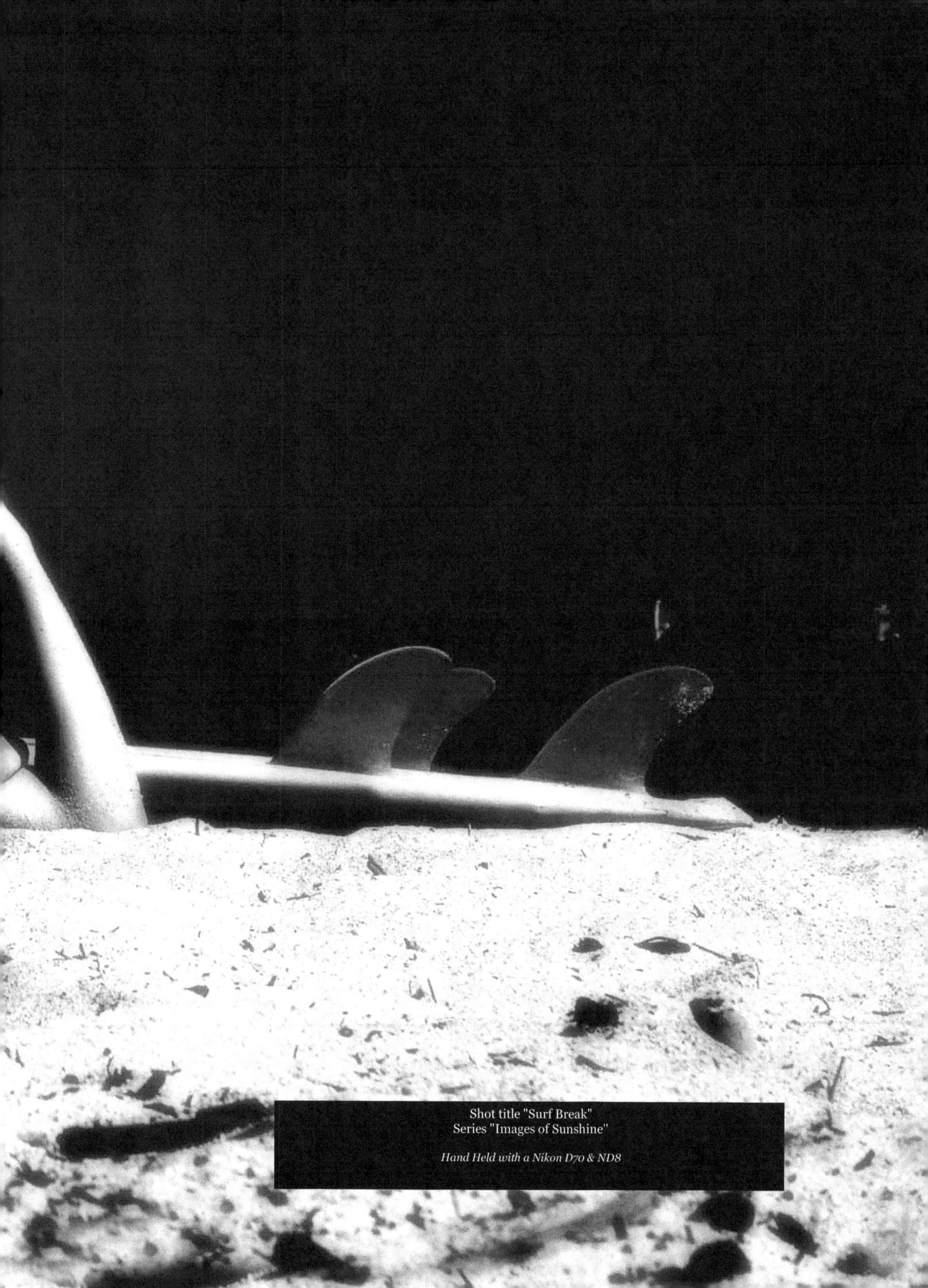

Shot title "Surf Break"
Series "Images of Sunshine"

Hand Held with a Nikon D70 & ND8

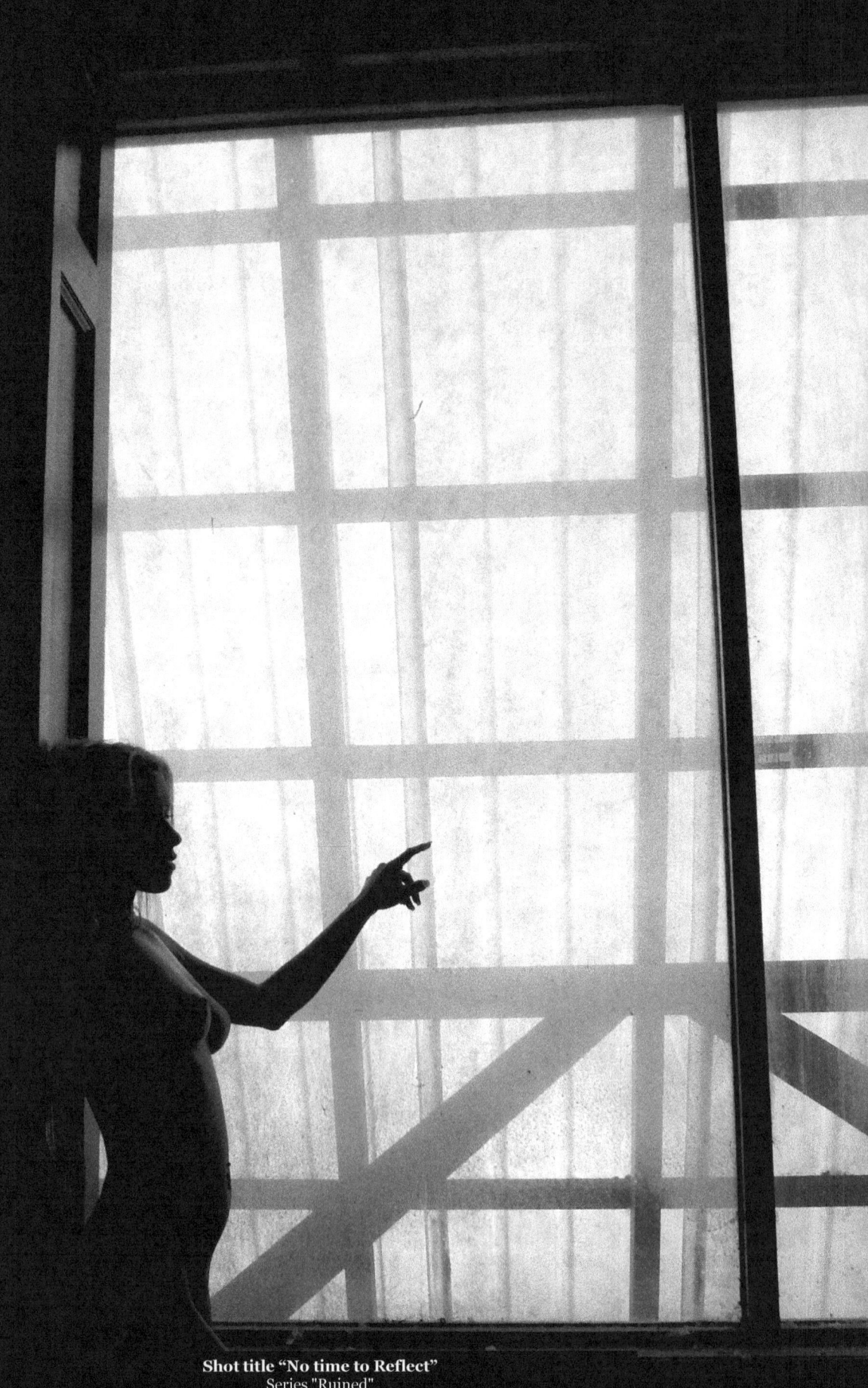

Shot title "No time to Reflect"
Series "Ruined"

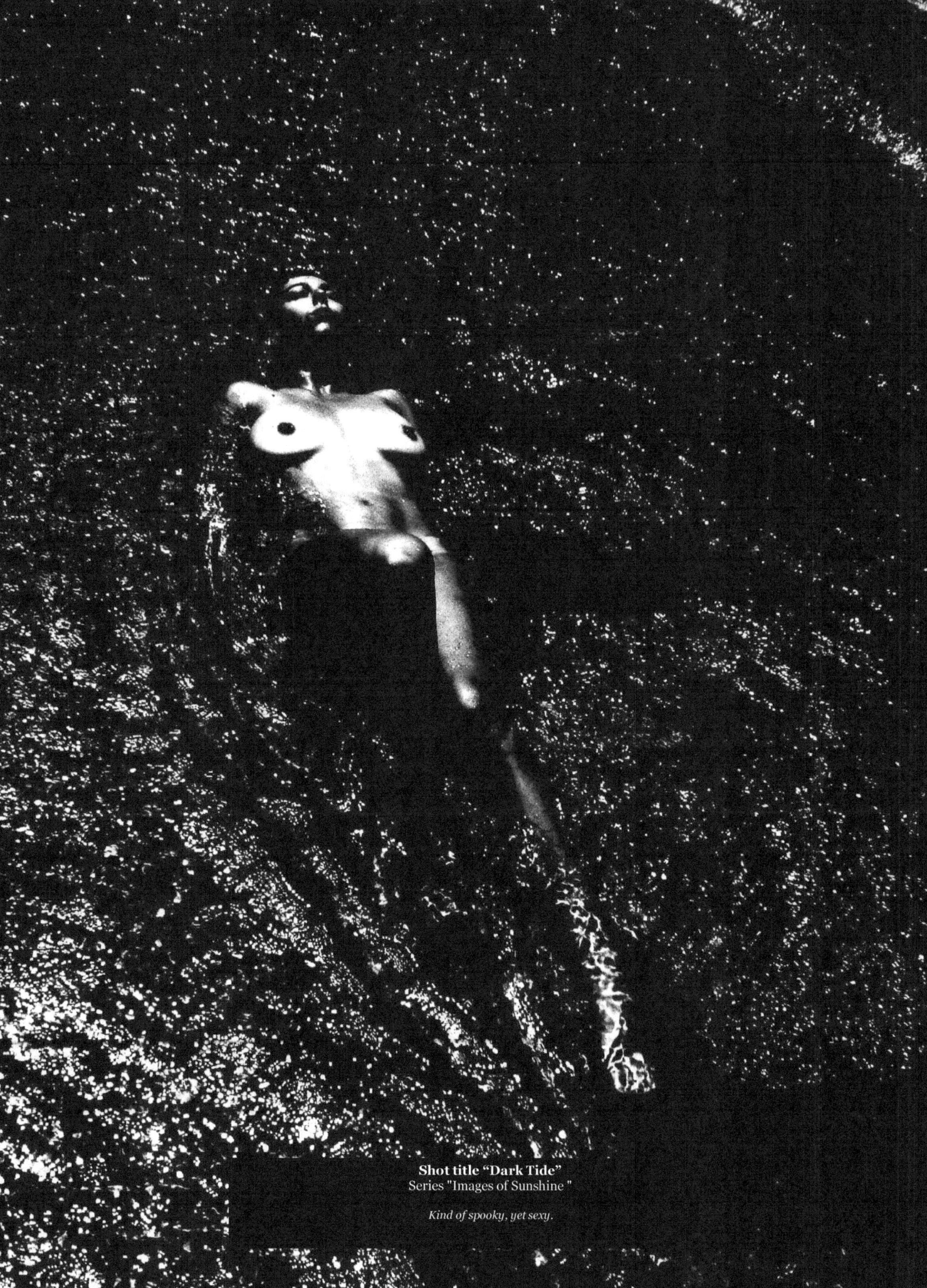

Shot title "Dark Tide"
Series "Images of Sunshine "

Kind of spooky, yet sexy.

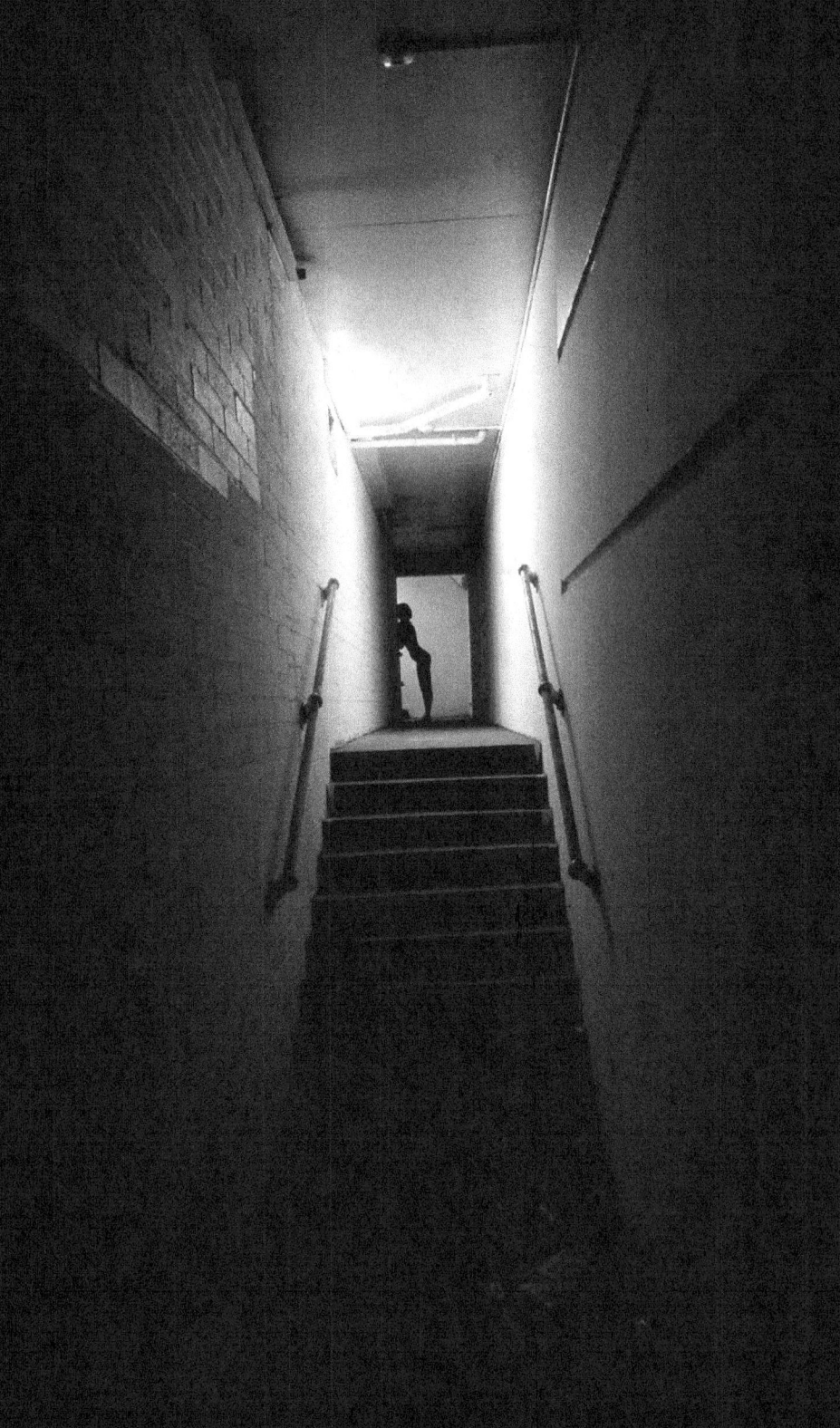

Shot title "Green Corridor"
Series "Art House"

All natural light, set off this stunning scene of intrigue

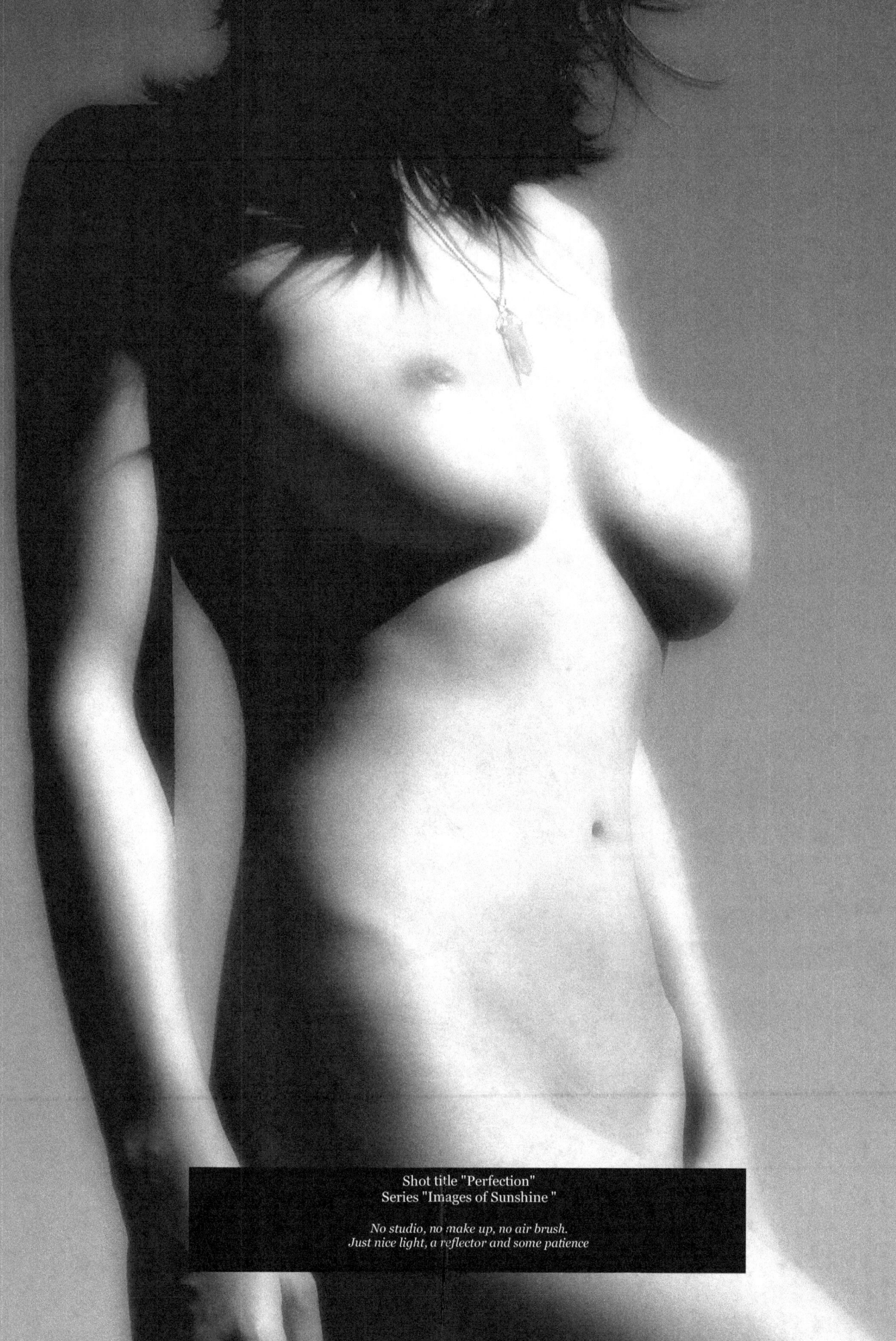

Shot title "Perfection"
Series "Images of Sunshine "

No studio, no make up, no air brush.
Just nice light, a reflector and some patience

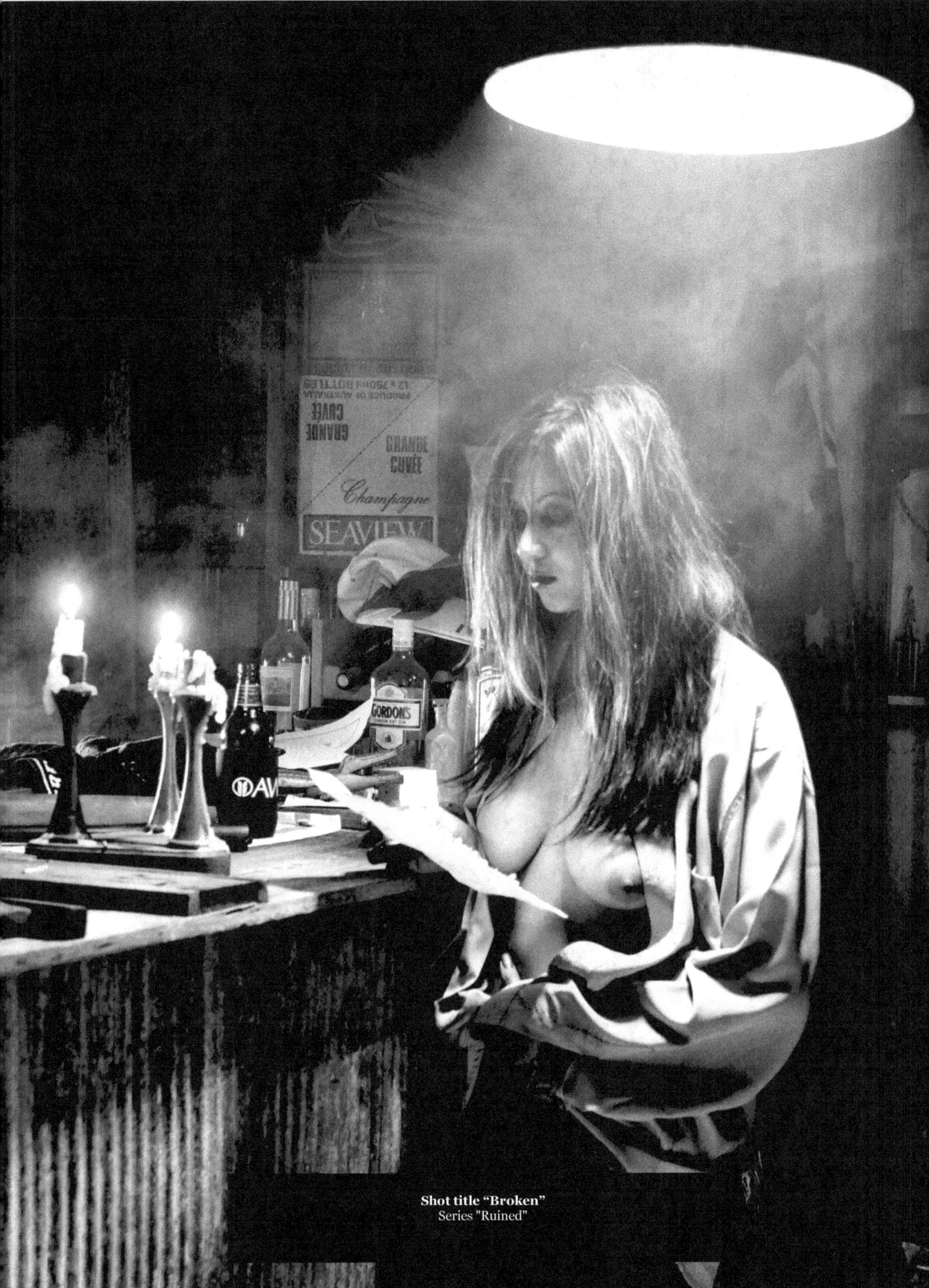

Shot title "Broken"
Series "Ruined"

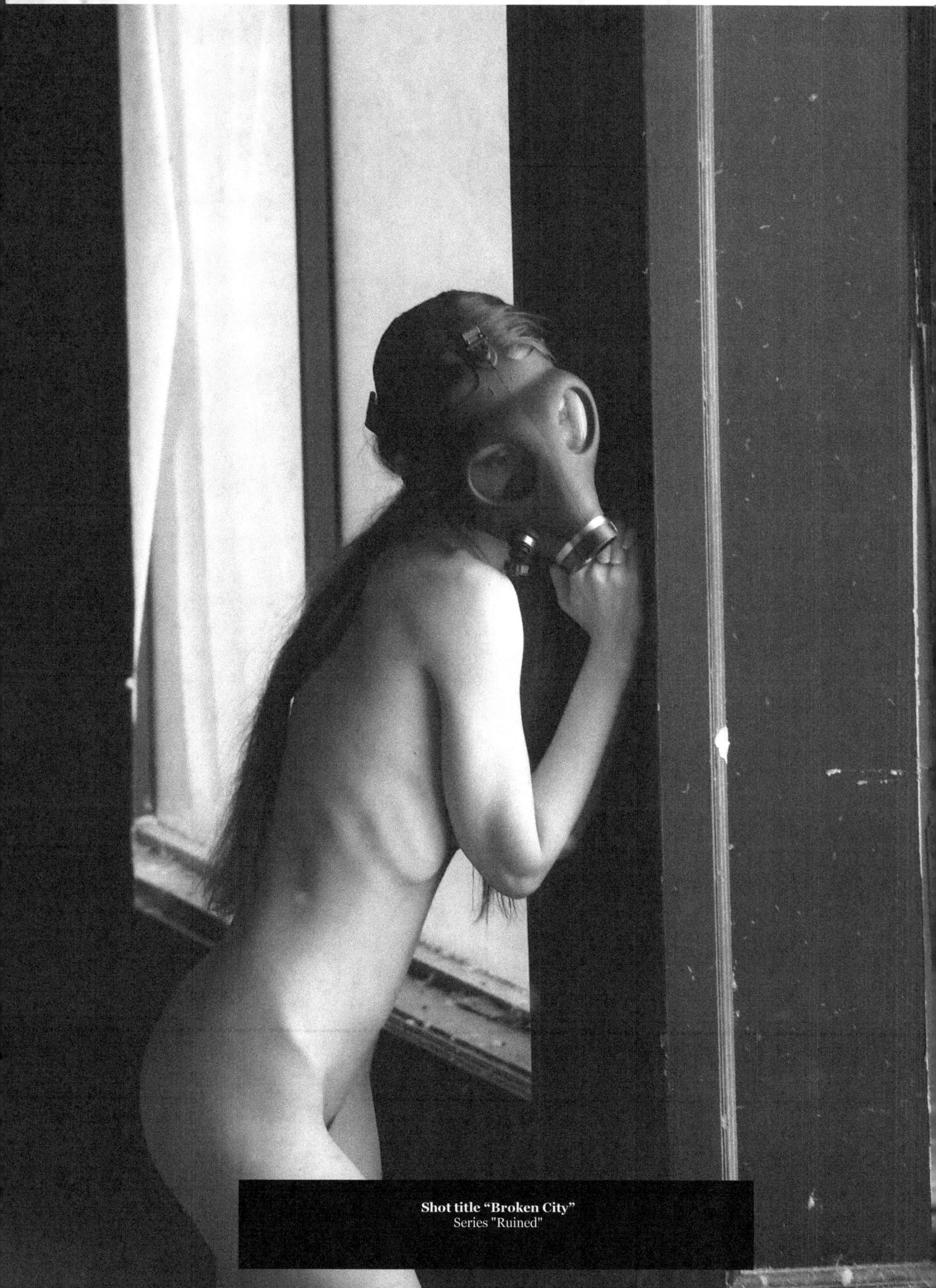

Shot title "Broken City"
Series "Ruined"

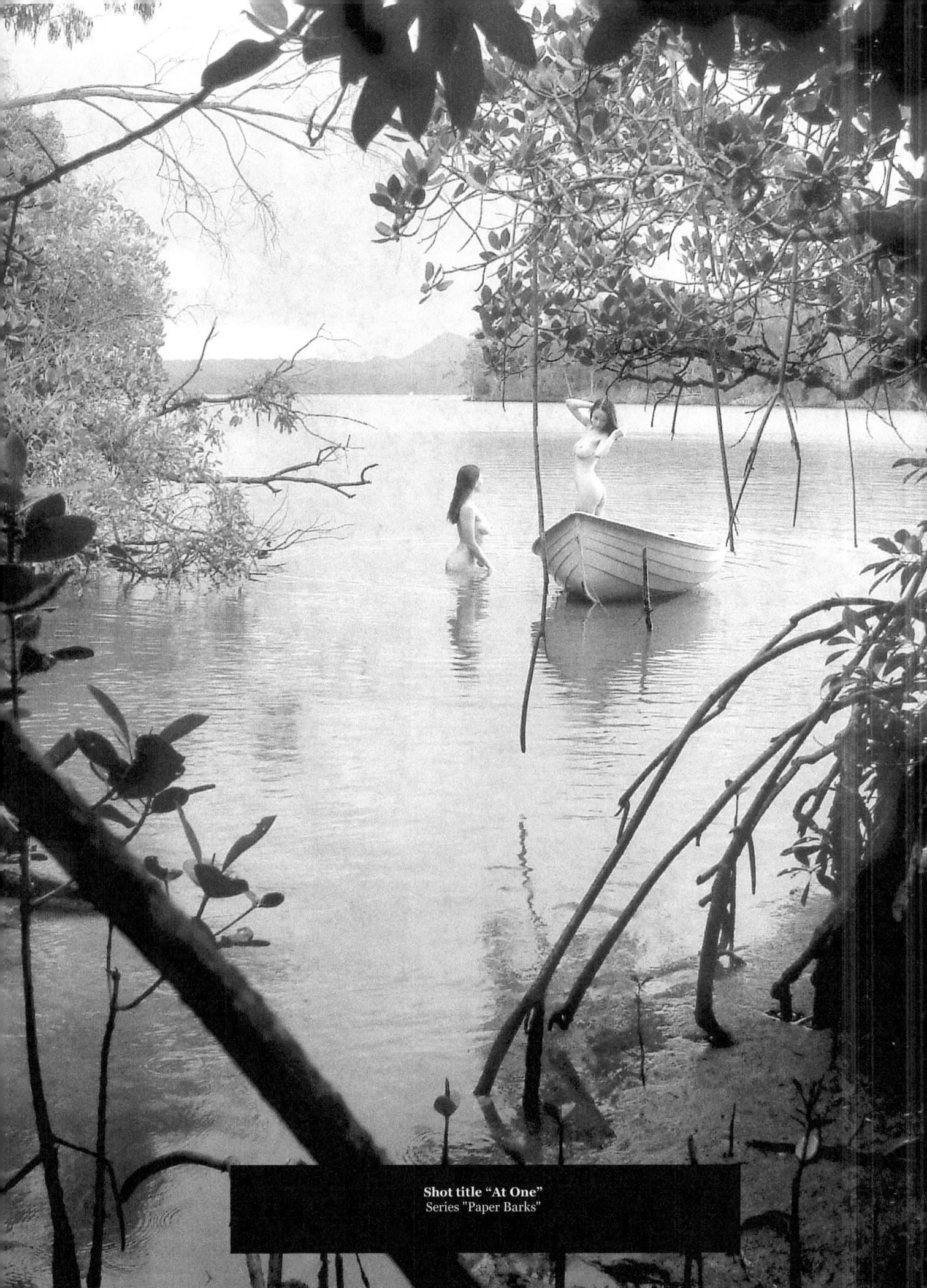

Shot title "At One"
Series "Paper Barks"

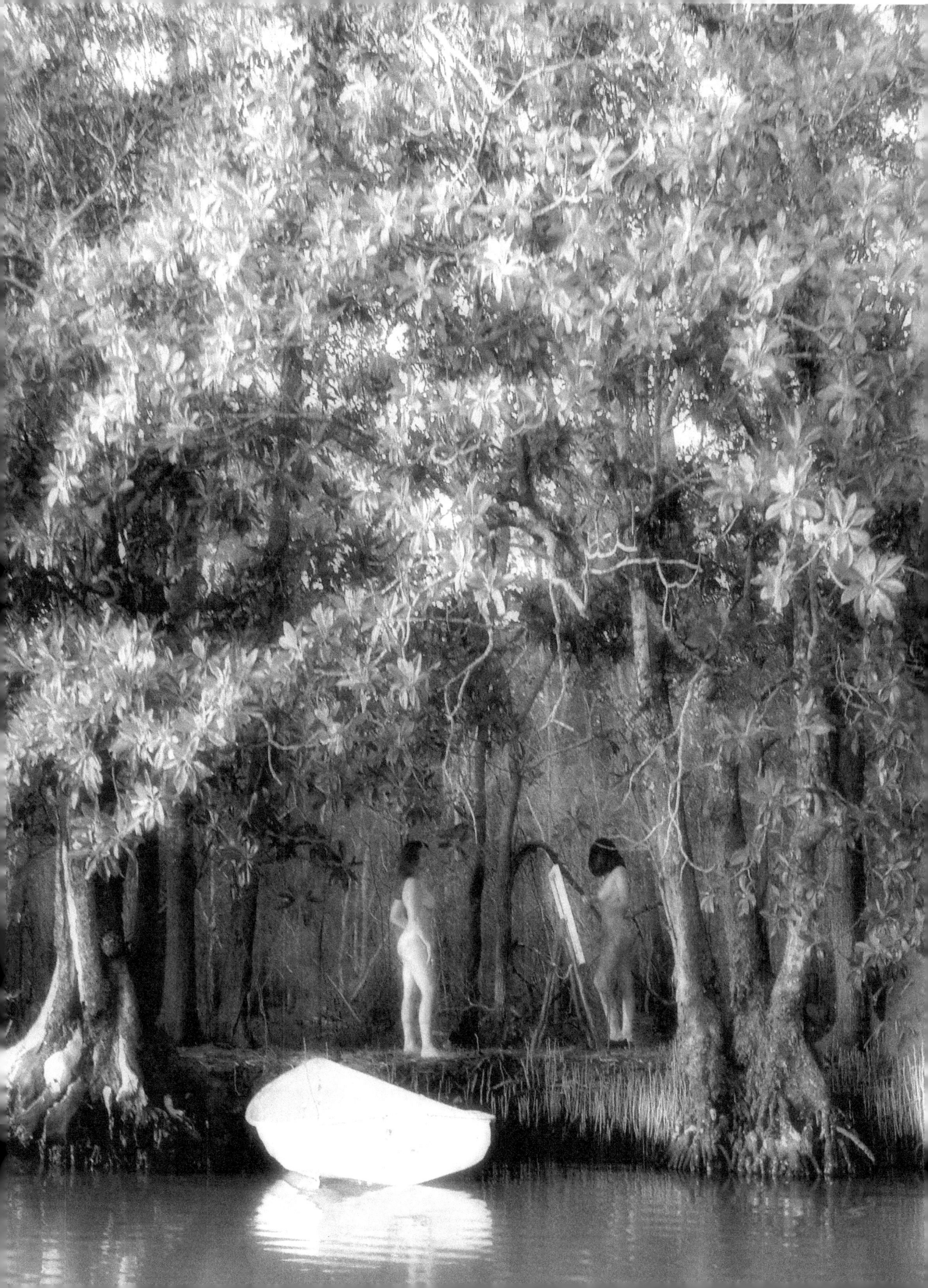

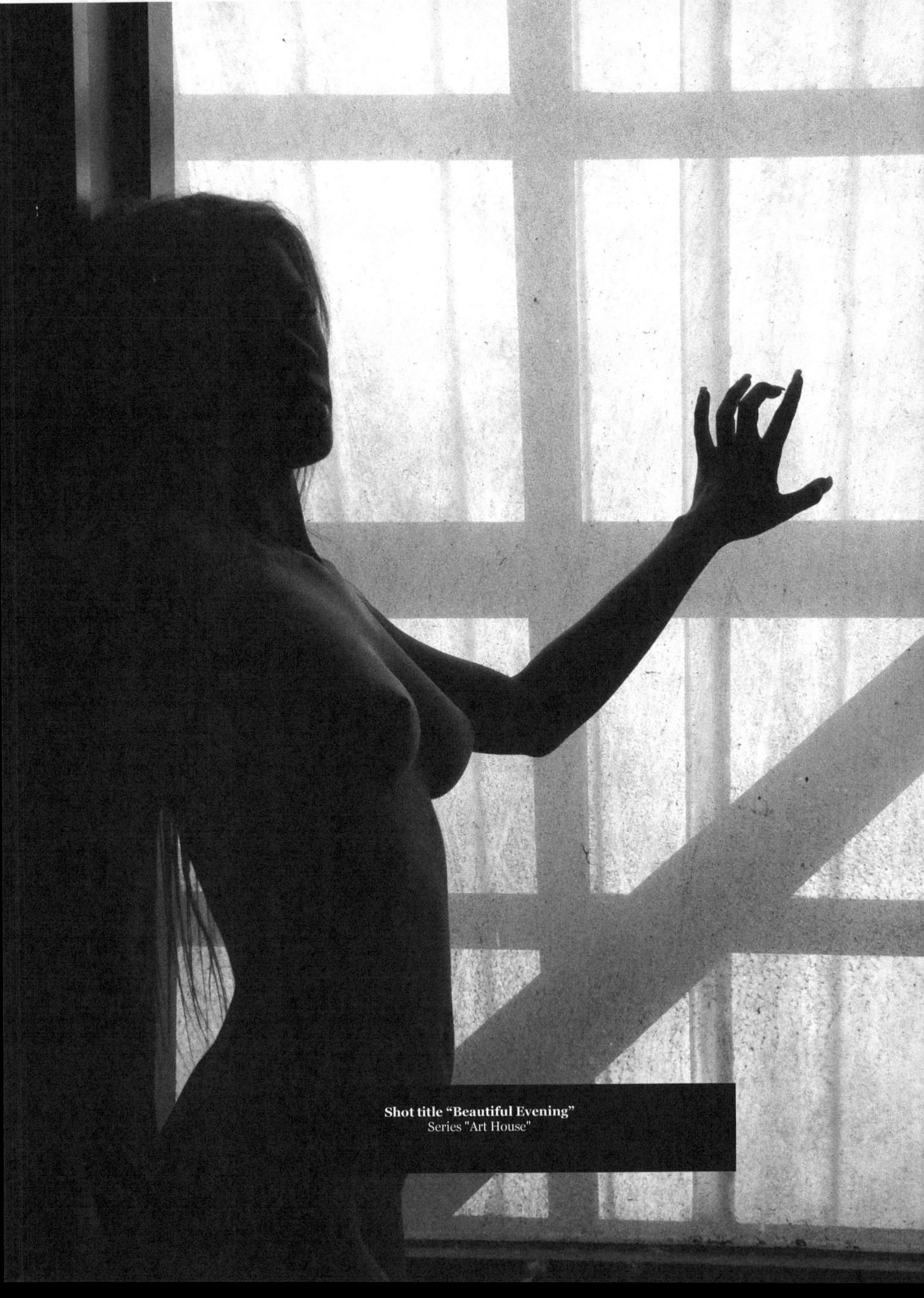

Shot title "Beautiful Evening"
Series "Art House"

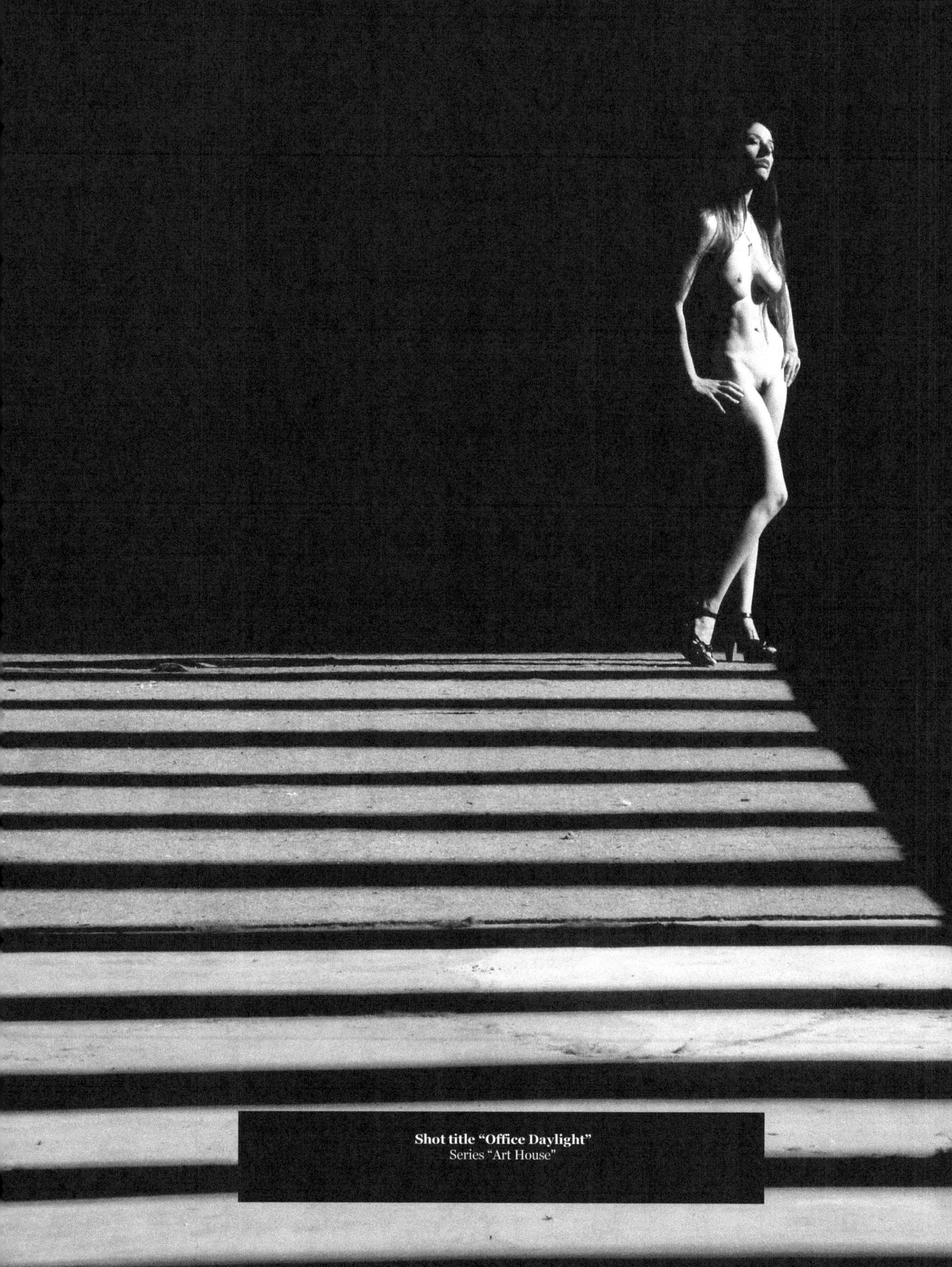

Shot title "Office Daylight"
Series "Art House"

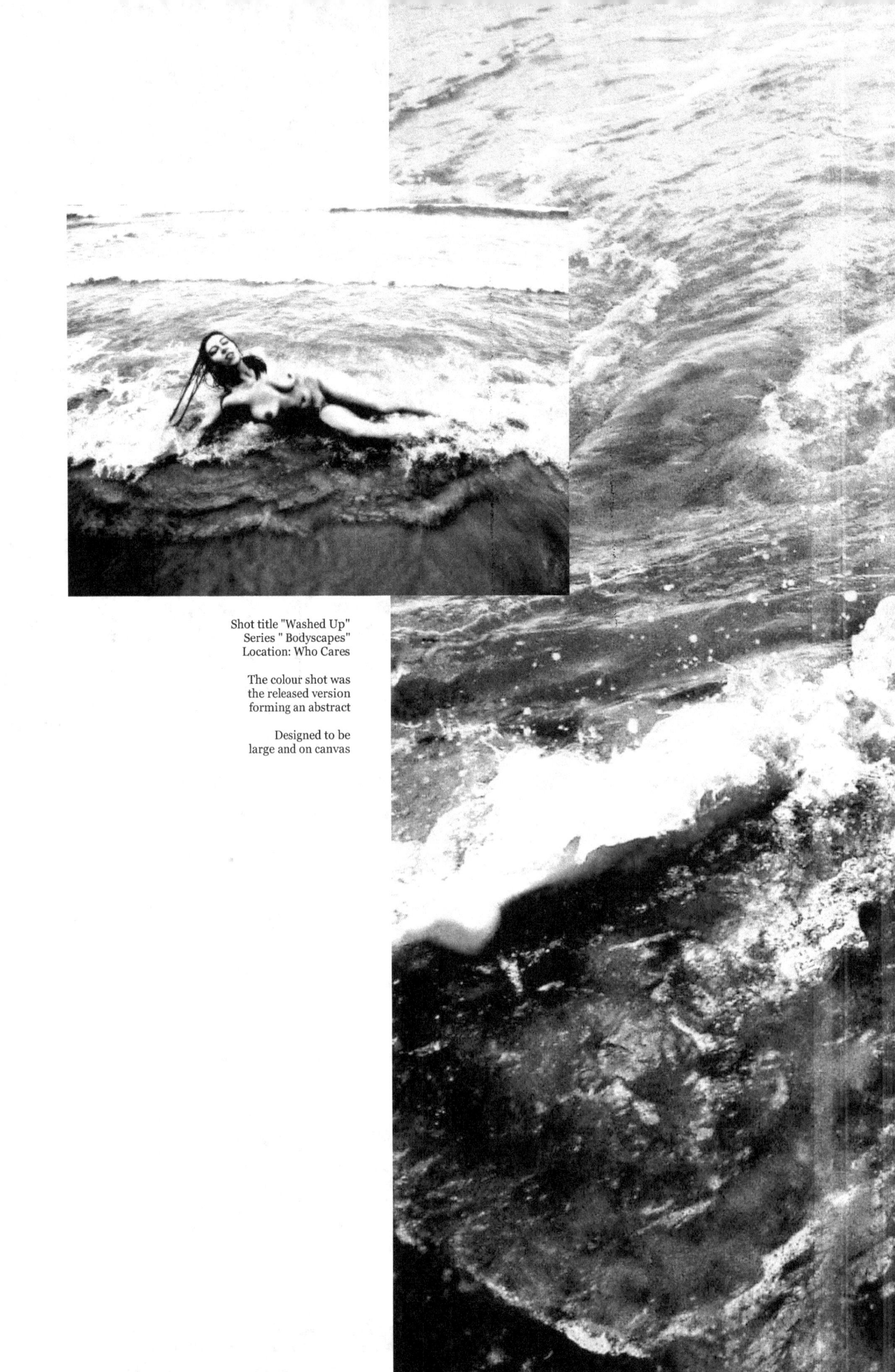

Shot title "Washed Up"
Series " Bodyscapes"
Location: Who Cares

The colour shot was
the released version
forming an abstract

Designed to be
large and on canvas

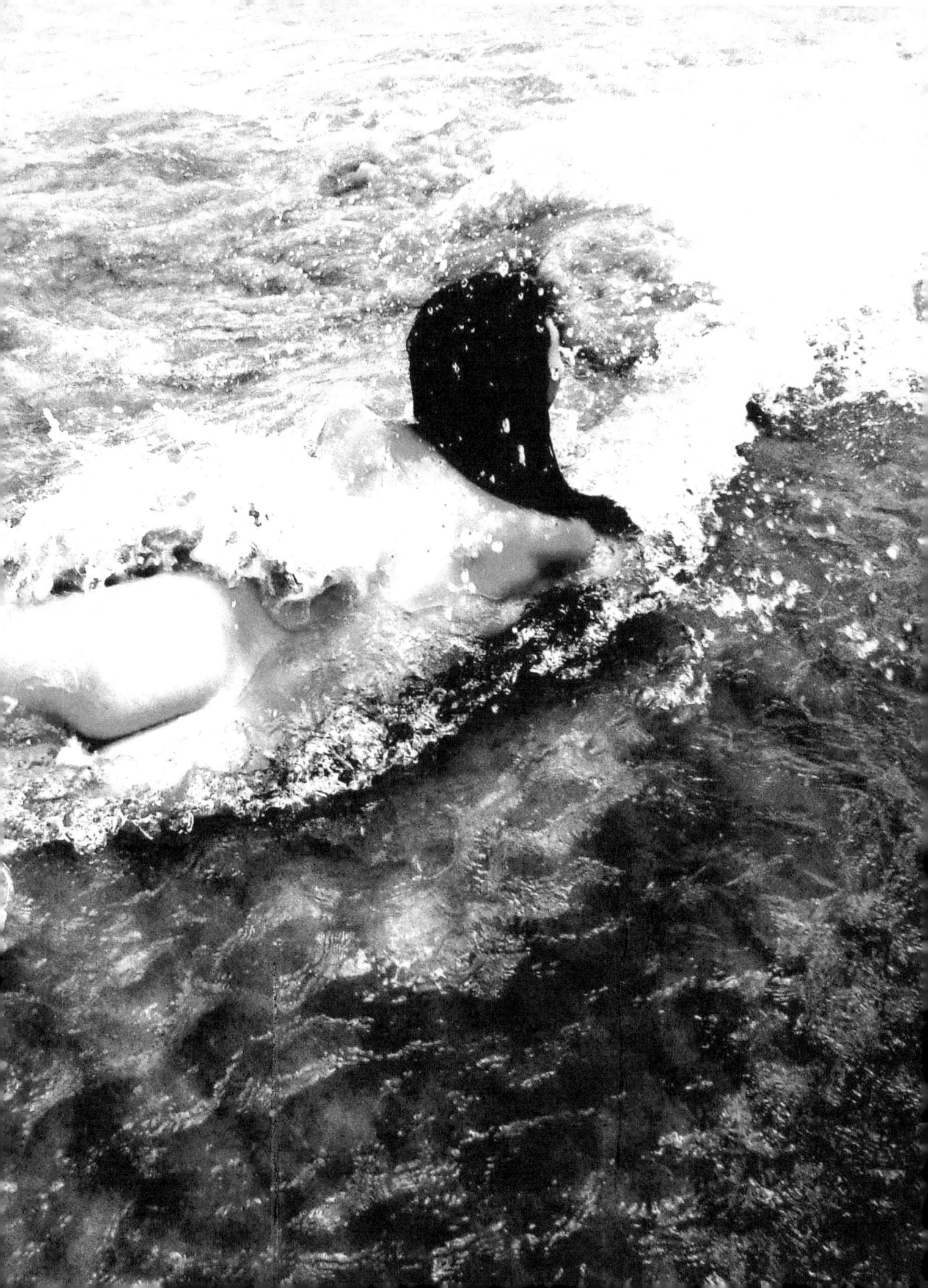

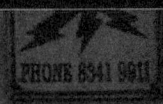

PHONE 8341 9911

314

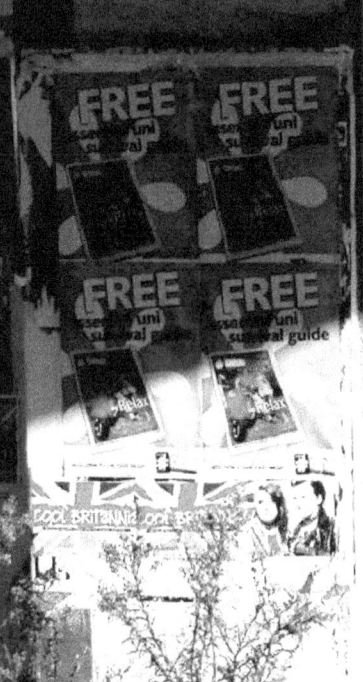

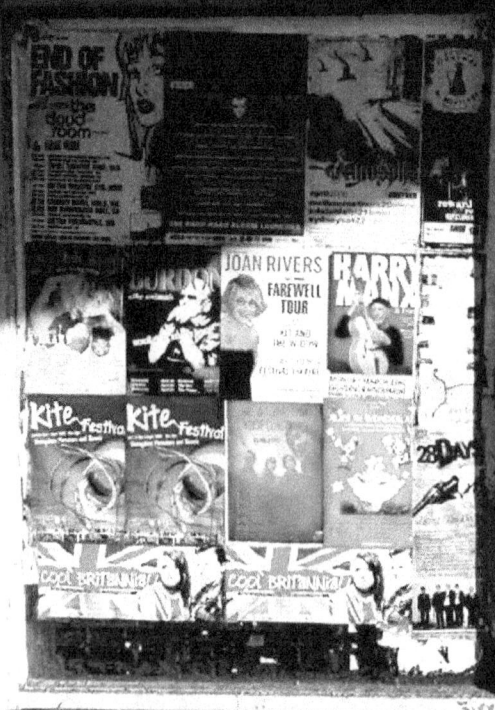

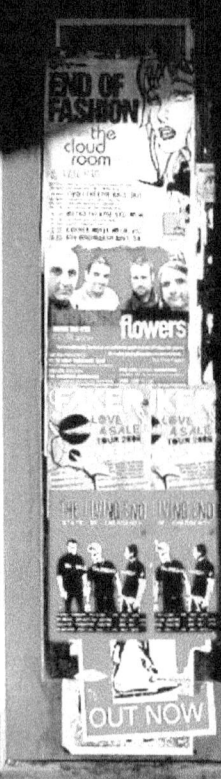

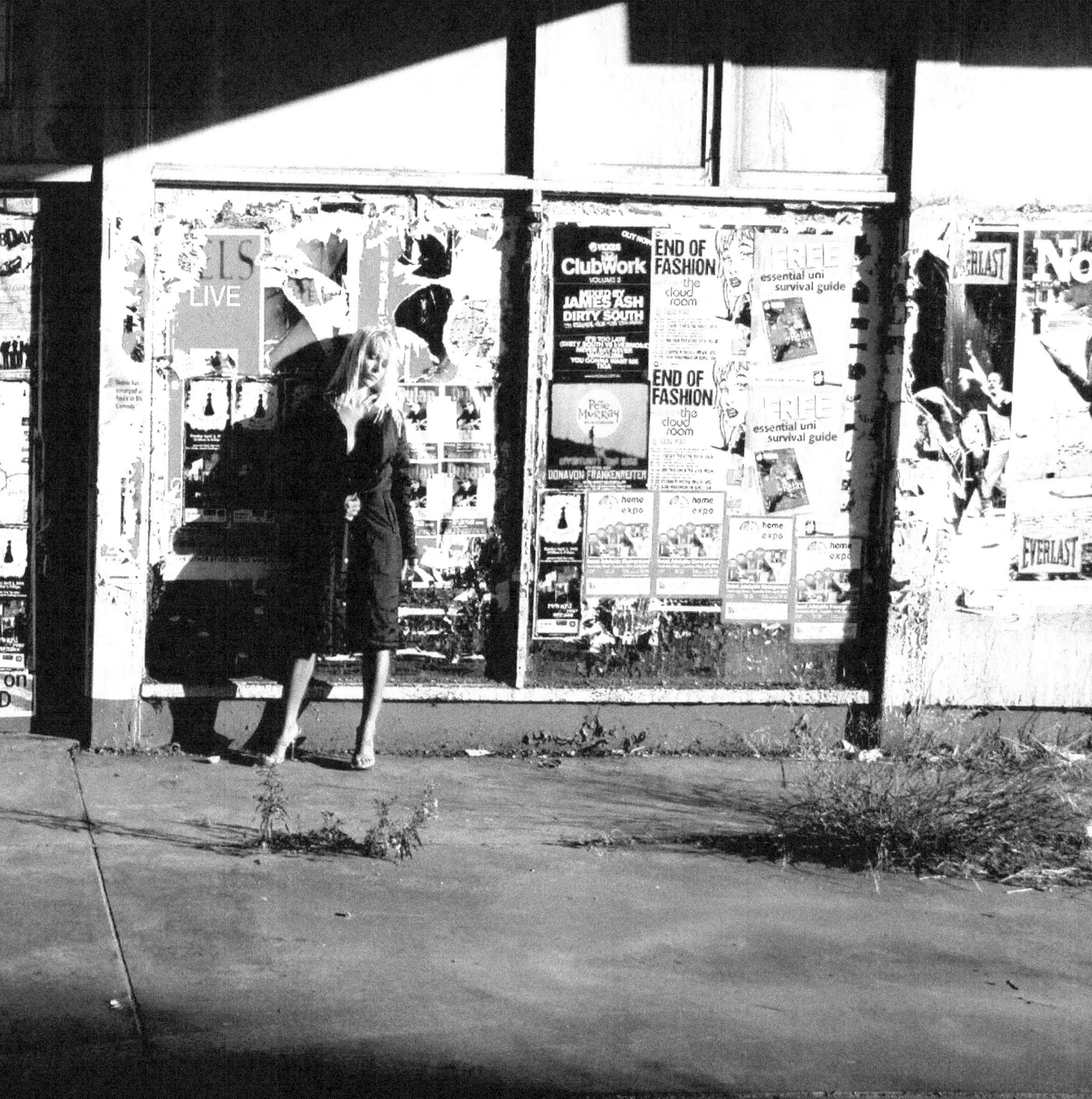

Particular recognition
for high standards

by Richard Lew

A special presentation was made to David Hancock of Hypervision in South Australia (profiled in *PAUSE* May) in recognition of outstanding work. David was recognised by the committee of the AVPA with a specially prepared plaque acknowledging his production for Faulding, *Delivering a World of Health.*

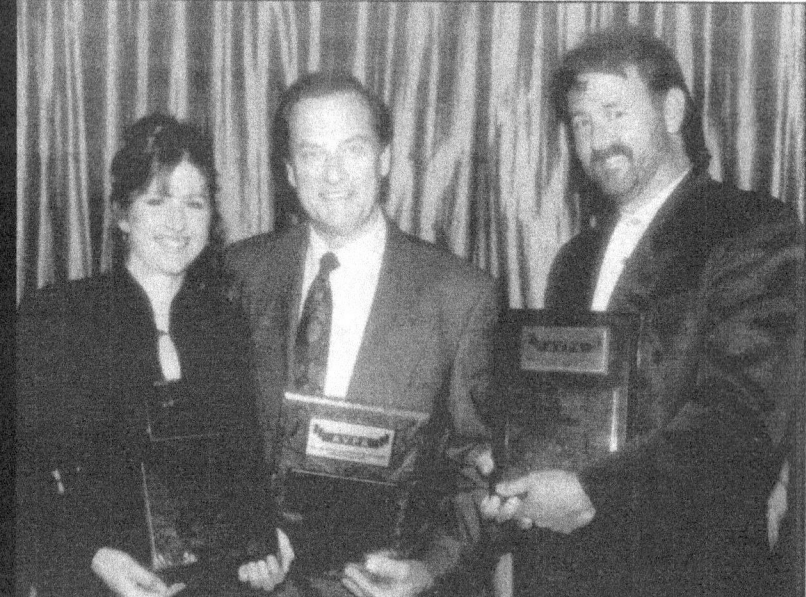

Michelle & David and Michelle Hancock (L & R) at the AVPA Awards with Presenter, Peter Smith (centre)

The program has been shown throughout Australia at AVPA general meetings during the year and has received unsolicited accolades from many members.

David was profiled in the previous edition of *PAUSE* and is an accredited corporate producer and member of the AVPA.

President of the AVPA, Bill Robertson, said, 'The AVPA assists producers to become ever more professional, whatever area of production they choose to specialise in. David's work inspires other corporate producers to excellence and the showing of his program reinforces the perception of quality that comes from using accredited AVPA members.'

With the Annual AVPA Awards coming up in September, we await with anticipation the prized works of the many high quality producers who value and use their membership with the AVPA.

The AVPA strives to promote professional conduct and values within the industry and particularly with its members. It promotes continuous improvement and supports formal training, networking, and peer assessment. The attention on substandard work or conduct in many industries often attracts the most publicity and this ex-gratia presentation is intended to reinforce the value the AVPA places on excellence. ■

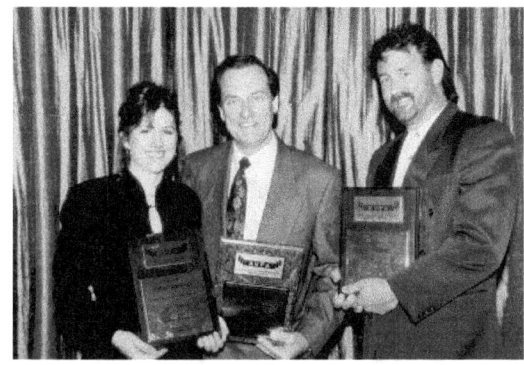

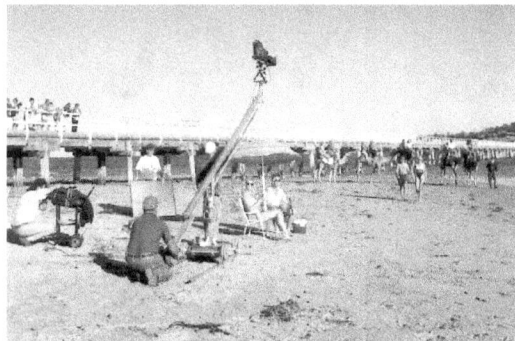

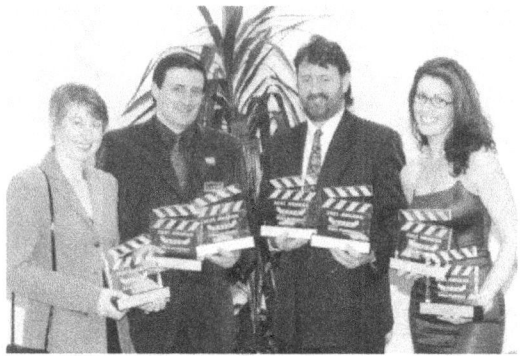

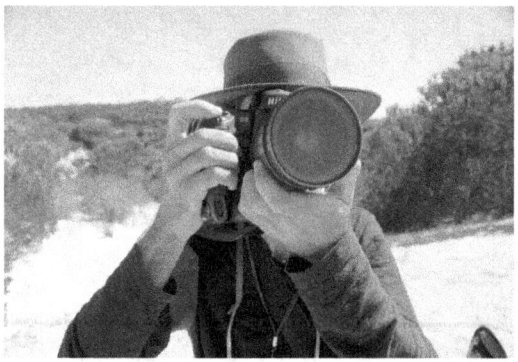

So there it is....Be free!

This is one of the few times in your life there are no rules
(creatively speaking) and you are in complete control.

There is no deadline, no timelines, no client and no boss.
You are the boss and head creative

Enjoy the experience each and every time you do it
Do it for you and you only and stay true to what you like.

If you have always had the ambition to start
and run a gallery.... Don't!
People don't pay for creative anymore.

I hope you have enjoyed browsing through this little book,
the first, in a series of "compose yourself" books
aimed at briefly exploring the lesser discussed
areas of the art.

Special thanks to all my models and the
constant stream of enquiries that come through
on a daily basis, thank you for your interest.

Good luck and happy shooting!
David

Top: Michelle (Wife), Pete Smith & David at the awards
A film shoot on location at Victor Harbour for SA Tourism
The awards again, most outstanding producer of the year
On location Australia, Flinders Ranges

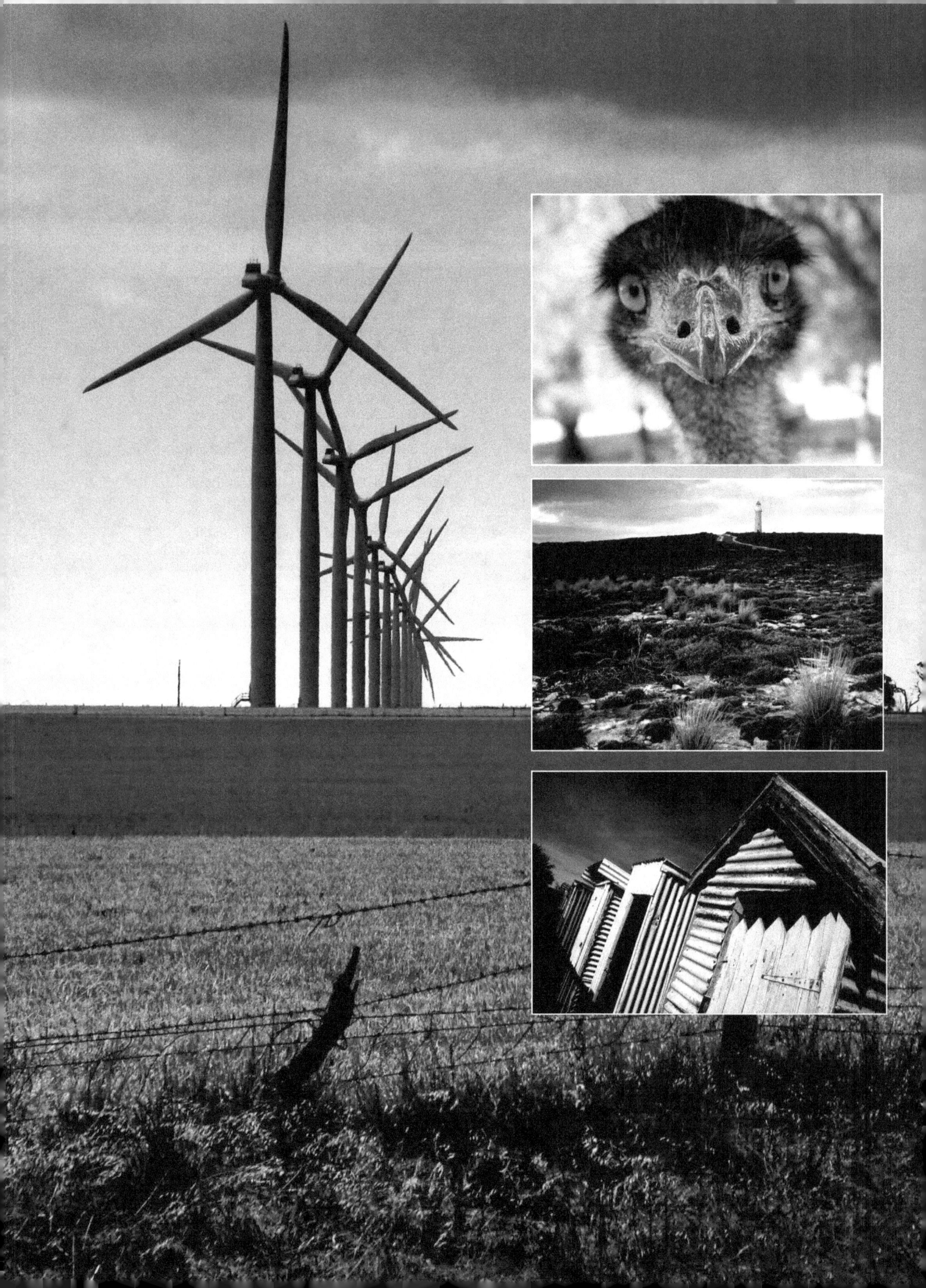

THE ESSENTIAL
"PHOTOGRAPHERS SHOOT NOTEBOOK"
AVAILABLE FROM

WWW.PRONOTES.COM.AU
NO SHOOT IS COMPLETE WITHOUT ONE!

A MUST HAVE FOR ALL PHOTOGRAPHERS

*"To say a photo is real or your own,
it has to be real or your own!*

*The moment you manipulate any part of the composition
(after the shot), it is no longer the photo you took"*

In a world of software manipulation programs, technical perfection
and megapixel madness, have we forgotten the fun of shooting?
Surely, story telling is the key and composition should reign supreme.

"Throw away the rule book, your expensive lights and the computer for a
while, stop being the same as everyone else and get back to basics." We
are all being trained the same way and chasing a perfection that is laced
with software manufacturers ideals and protocols.

New or old to photography, this is the perfect book to get you motivated
and started in artistic nude photography with some great image
examples and hints of what to think through and watch out for.

Written by award winning and twice Black & White Spider Award
nominee, David Hancock, this book features some
of his stunning artistic work from the Bodyscape Series,
the book shows off a number of images synonymous with his fresh
and at times refreshingly raw style.

A refreshing and informative viewpoint on figure work photography.

Being a cameraman, editor and then producer, David's skills in
organising, location planning, talent and composition makes for a very
interesting read and David believes being a good photographer is
about creative vision, not just technical know how.

Above all else...
"Compose yourself, before you compose the shot!"
Real world, Real art, Real life, Real people.